17.72

Tuning and Temperament

Da Capo Press Music Reprint Series

GENERAL EDITOR

FREDERICK FREEDMAN

VASSAR COLLEGE

Tuning and Temperament

A Historical Survey

By J. Murray Barbour

781.8
B2396
25069

DA CAPO PRESS • NEW YORK • 1972

Library of Congress Cataloging in Publication Data

Barbour, James Murray, 1897-
   Tuning and Temperament.

   (Da Capo Press music reprint series)
   Bibliography: p.
   1. Tuning. 2. Musical temperament. I. Title.
ML3809.B234   1972   781'.91   74-37288
ISBN 0-306-70422-6

This Da Capo Press edition of *Tuning and Temperament* is an
unabridged republication of the first edition published in
East Lansing, Michigan, in 1951. It is reprinted by special
arrangement with Michigan State University Press.

Published by Da Capo Press, Inc.
A Subsidiary of Plenum Publishing Corporation
227 W. 17th St., New York, N.Y. 10011

Manufactured in the United States of America

Tuning and Temperament

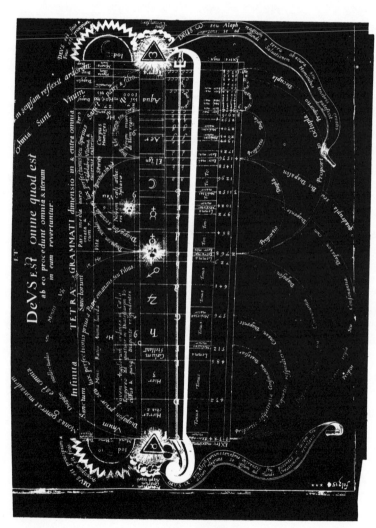

Fludd's Monochord, with Pythagorean Tuning and Associated Symbolism
Reproduced by courtesy of the Library of Cornell
University

Tuning and

Temperament

ℬ

A

Historical

Survey

J. Murray Barbour

East Lansing

Michigan State College Press

1951

PREFACE

This book is based upon my unpublished Cornell dissertation, Equal Temperament: Its History from Ramis (1482) to Rameau (1737), Ithaca, 1932. As the title indicates, the emphasis in the dissertation was upon individual writers. In the present work the emphasis is on the theories rather than on their promulgators. Since a great many tuning systems are discussed, a separate chapter is devoted to each of the principal varieties of tuning, with subsidiary divisions wherever necessary. Even so, the whole subject is so complex that it seemed best that these chapters be preceded by a running account (with a minimum of mathematics) of the entire history of tuning and temperament. Chapter I also contains the principal account of the Pythagorean tuning, for it is unnecessary to spend a chapter upon a tuning system that exists in one form only.

Most technical terms will be defined when they first occur, as well as in the Glossary, but a few of these terms should be defined immediately. Of small intervals arising from tuning, the comma is the most familiar. The ordinary (syntonic or Ptolemaic) comma is the interval between a just major third, with ratio 5:4, and a Pythagorean ditone or major third, with ratio 81:64. The ratio of the comma (the ratio of an interval is obtained by dividing the ratio of the higher pitch by that of the lower) is 81:80.

The Pythagorean (ditonic) comma is the interval between six tones, with ratio 531441:262144, and the pure octave, with ratio 2:1. Thus its ratio is 531441:524288, which is approximately 74:73. The ditonic comma is about 12/11 as large as the syntonic comma. In general, when the word comma is used without qualification, the syntonic comma is meant.

There is necessarily some elasticity in the manner in which the different tuning systems are presented in the following chapters. Sometimes a writer has described the construction of a monochord, a note at a time. That can be set down easily in the form of ratios. More often he has expressed his monochord as a series of string-lengths, with a convenient length for the fundamental. (Except in the immediate past, the use of vibration numbers, inversely proportional to the string-lengths, has been so rare that it can be ignored.) Or he may speak of there being so many pure fifths, and other fifths flattened by a fractional

v

part of the comma. Such systems could be transformed into equivalent string-lengths, but this has not been done in this book when the original writer had not done so.

Systems with intervals altered by parts of a comma can be shown without difficulty in terms of Ellis' logarithmic unit called the cent, the hundredth part of an equally tempered semitone, or 1/1200 part of an octave.[*] Since the ratio of the octave is 2:1, the cent is $2^{1/1200}$. As a matter of fact, such eighteenth century writers on temperament as Neidhardt and Marpurg had a tuning unit very similar to the cent: the twelfth part of the ditonic comma, which they used, is 2 cents, thus making the octave contain 600 parts instead of 1200.

The systems originally expressed in string-lengths or ratios may be translated into cents also, although with greater difficulty. They have been so expressed in the tables of this book, in the belief that the cents representation is the most convenient way of affording comparisons between systems. In systems where it was thought they would help to clarify the picture, exponents have been attached to the names of the notes. With this method, devised by Eitz, all notes joined by pure fifths have the same exponent. Since the fundamental has a zero exponent, all the notes of the Pythagorean tuning have zero exponents. The exponent -1 is attached to notes a comma lower than those with zero exponents, i.e., to those forming pure thirds above those in the zero series. Thus in just intonation the notes forming a major third would be $C^0 - E^{-1}$, etc. Similarly, notes that are pure thirds lower than notes already in the system have exponents which are greater by one than those of the higher notes. This use of exponents is especially advantageous in comparing various systems of just intonation (see Chapter V). It may be used also, with fractional exponents, for the different varieties of the meantone temperament. If the fifth C-G, for example, is tempered by 1/4 comma, these notes would be labeled C^0 and $G^{-1/4}$.

A device related to the use of integral exponents for the notes in just intonation is the arrangement of such notes to show their

---

[*]For a discussion of methods of logarithmic representation of intervals see J. Murray Barbour, "Musical Logarithms," Scripta Mathematica, VII (1940), 21-31.

harmonic relationships. Here, all notes that are related by fifths, i.e., that have the same exponent, lie on the same horizontal line, while their pure major thirds lie in a parallel line above them, each forming a 45^0 angle with the related note below. Since the pure minor thirds below the original notes are lower by a fifth than the major thirds above them, they will lie in the same higher line, but will form 135^0 angles with the original notes. For example:

$$A^{-1} \quad C^0 E^{-1} \quad G^0 B^{-1}.$$

This arrangement is especially good for showing extensions of just intonation with more than twelve notes in the octave, and it is used for that purpose only in this book (see Chapter VI).

It is desirable to have some method of evaluating the various tuning systems. Since equal temperament is the ideal system of twelve notes if modulations are to be made freely to every key, the semitone of equal temperament, 100 cents, is taken as the ideal, from which the deviation of each semitone, as $C-C^{\#}$, $C^{\#}-D$, $D-E^b$, etc., is calculated in cents. These deviations are then added and the sum divided by twelve to find the mean deviation (M.D.) in cents. The standard deviation (S.D.) is found in the usual manner, by taking the root-mean-square.

It should be added that there may be criteria for excellence in a tuning system other than its closeness to equal temperament. For example, if no notes beyond E^b or $G^{\#}$ are used in the music to be performed and if the greatest consonance is desired for the notes that are used, then probably the 1/5 comma variety of mean-tone temperament would be the ideal, since its fifths and thirds are altered equally, the fifths being 1/5 comma flat and its thirds 1/5 comma sharp. If keys beyond two flats or three sharps are to be touched upon occasionally, but if it is considered desirable to have the greatest consonance in the key of C and the least in the key of G^b, then our Temperament by Regularly Varied Fifths would be the best. This is a matter that is discussed in detail at the end of Chapter VII, but it should be mentioned now.

My interest in temperament dates from the time in Berlin when Professor Curt Sachs showed me his copy of Mersenne's

Harmonie universelle. I am indebted to Professor Otto Kinkeldey, my major professor at Cornell, and to the Misses Barbara Duncan and Elizabeth Schmitter of the Sibley Musical Library of the Eastman School of Music, for assistance rendered during my work on the dissertation. Most of my more recent research has been at the Library of Congress. Dr. Harold Spivacke and Mr. Edward N. Waters of the Music Division there deserve especial thanks for encouraging me to write this book. I want also to thank the following men for performing so well the task of reading the manuscript: Professor Charles Warren Fox, Eastman School of Music; Professor Bonnie M. Stewart, Michigan State College; Dr. Arnold Small, San Diego Navy Electronics Laboratory; and Professor Glen Haydon, University of North Carolina.

J. Murray Barbour

East Lansing, Michigan
November, 1950

GLOSSARY

Arithmetical Division — The equal division of the difference between two quantities, so that the resultant forms an arithmetical progression, as 9:8:7:6.

Bonded Clavichord — A clavichord upon which two or more consecutive semitones were produced upon a single string.

Cent — The unit of interval measure. The hundredth part of an
equal semitone, with ratio $\sqrt[1200]{2}$.

Circle of Fifths — The arrangement of the notes of a closed system by fifths, as C, G, D, A, E, etc.

Circulating Temperaments — Temperaments in which all keys
are playable, but in which keys with few sharps or flats are
favored.

Closed System — A regular temperament in which the initial note
is eventually reached again.

Column of Differences — See Tabular Differences.

Comma — A tuning error, such as the interval $B^{\#}$–C in the Pythagorean tuning. See Ditonic Comma and Syntonic Comma.

Ditone — A major third, especially one formed by two equal tones,
as in the Pythagorean tuning (81:64).

Ditonic Comma — The interval between two enharmonically
equivalent notes, as $B^{\#}$ and C, in the Pythagorean tuning. Its
ratio is 531441:524288 or approximately 74:73, and it is conventionally taken as 24 cents.

Duplication of the Cube — A problem of antiquity, equivalent to
finding two geometrical means between two quantities one of
which is twice as large as the other, or to finding the cube root
of 2.

Exponents — In tuning theory exponents are used to indicate deviations from the Pythagorean tuning, the unit being the syntonic comma. Plus values are sharper and minus values flatter
than the corresponding Pythagorean notes. Fractional exponents indicate subdivisions of the comma, as in the meantone
and many irregular temperaments.

Equal Temperament — The division of the octave into an equal number of parts, specifically into 12 semitones, each of which has the ratio of $\sqrt[12]{2}$.

Euclidean Construction — Euclid's method for finding a mean proportional between two lines, by describing a semicircle upon the sum of the lines taken as a diameter and then erecting a perpendicular at the juncture of the two lines.

Fretted Clavichord — See Bonded Clavichord.

Fretted Instruments — Such modern instruments as the guitar and banjo, or the earlier lute and viol.

Generalized Keyboard — A keyboard arranged conveniently for the performance of multiple divisions.

Geometrical Division — The proportional division of two quantities, so that the resultant forms a geometrical progression, as 27:18:12:8.

Golden System — A system of tuning based on the ratio of the golden section ($\sqrt{5}-1$):2.

Good Temperaments — See Circulating Temperaments.

Irregular System — Any tuning system with more than one odd-sized fifth, with the exception of just intonation.

Just—Pure: A term applied to intervals, as the just major third.

Just Intonation — A system of tuning based on the octave (2:1), the pure fifth (3:2), and the pure major third (5:4).

Linear Correction — The arithmetical division of the error in a string-length.

Mean-Semitone Temperament — A temperament in which the diatonic notes are in meantone temperament, and the chromatic notes are taken as halves of meantones.

Meantone Temperament — Strictly, a system of tuning with flattened fifths ($\sqrt[4]{5:1}$) and pure major thirds (5:4). See Varieties of Meantone Temperament.

Meride — Sauveur's tuning unit, 1/43 octave, that is, $\sqrt[43]{2}$. Each meride was divisible into 7 eptamerides, and each of the eptamerides into 10 decamerides.

Mesolabium — An instrument of the ancients for finding mechanically 2 mean proportionals between 2 given lines. See illustration, p. 51.

Monochord — A string stretched over a wooden base upon which are indicated the string-lengths for some tuning system; a diagram containing these lengths; directions for constructing such a diagram.

Monopipe — A variable open pipe, with indicated lengths for a scale in a particular tuning system, thus fulfilling a function similar to that of a monochord.

Multiple Division — The division of the octave into more than 12 parts, equal or unequal.

Negative System — A regular system whose fifth has a ratio smaller than 3:2.

Positive System — A regular system whose fifth has a ratio larger than 3:2.

Ptolemaic Comma — See Syntonic Comma.

Pythagorean Comma — See Ditonic Comma.

Pythagorean Tuning — A system of tuning based on the octave (2:1) and the pure fifth (3:2).

Regular Temperament — A temperament in which all the fifths save one are of the same size, such as the Pythagorean tuning or the meantone temperament. (Equal temperament, with all fifths equal, is also a regular temperament, and so are the closed systems of multiple division.)

Schisma — The difference between the syntonic and ditonic commas, with ratio 32805:32768, or approximately 2 cents.

Semi-Meantone Temperament — See Mean-Semitone Temperament.

Sesqui- — The prefix used to designate a superparticular ratio, as sesquitertia (4:3).

Sexagesimal Notation — The use of 60 rather than 10 as a base of numeration, as in the measurement of angles.

Split Keys — Separate keys on a keyboard instrument for such a pair of notes as $G^\#$ and A^b.

String-Length — The portion of a string on the monochord that will produce a desired pitch.

Subsemitonia — See Split Keys.

Superparticular Ratio — A ratio in which the antecedent exceeds the consequent by 1, as 5:4. See Sesqui-.

Syntonic Comma — The interval between a just major third (5:4) and a Pythagorean third (81:64). Its ratio is 81:80 and it is conventionally taken as 22 cents.

Tabular Differences — The differences between the successive terms in a sequence of numbers, such as a geometrical progression.

Temper — To vary the pitch slightly. A tempered fifth is specifically a flattened fifth.

Temperament — A system, some or all of whose intervals cannot be expressed in rational numbers.

A Tuning — A system all of whose intervals can be expressed in rational numbers.

Tuning Pipe — See Monopipe.

Unequal Temperament — Any temperament other than equal temperament, particularly the meantone temperament or some variety thereof.

Varieties of Meantone Temperament — Regular temperaments formed on the same principle as the meantone temperament, with flattened fifths and (usually) sharp thirds.

Wolf Fifth — The dissonant fifth, usually $G^\#-E^b$ (notated as a diminished sixth), in any unequal temperament, such as the meantone wolf fifth of 737 cents.

CONTENTS

LIST OF ILLUSTRATIONS

            Tuning and Associated Symbolism

Fig. A. Schneegass' Division of the Monochord.   38

     B. The Mesolabium   51

     C. Roberval's Method for Finding Two Geo-
            metric Mean Proportionals   52

     D. Nicomedes' Method for Finding Two
            Geometric Mean Proportionals   53

     E. Strähle's Geometrical Approximation for
            Equal Temperament   66

     F. Gibelius' Tuning Pipe   86

     G. Mersenne's Keyboard with Thirty-One
            Notes in the Octave   109

     H. Ganassi's Method for Placing Frets on
            the Lute and Viol   142

     I. Bermudo's Method for Placing Frets on
            the Vihuela   165

The tuning of musical instruments is as ancient as the musical scale. In fact, it is much older than the scale as we ordinarily understand it. If primitive man played upon an equally primitive instrument only two different pitches, these would represent an interval of some sort — a major, minor, or neutral third; some variety of fourth or fifth; a pure or impure octave. Perhaps his concern was not with interval as such, but with the spacing of soundholes on a flute or oboe, the varied lengths of the strings on a lyre or harp. Sufficient studies have been made of extant specimens of the wind instruments of the ancients, and of all types of instruments used by primitive peoples of today, for scholars to come forward with interesting hypotheses regarding scale systems anterior to our own. So far there has been no general agreement as to whether primitive man arrived at an instrumental scale by following one or another principle, several principles simultaneously, or no principle at all. Since this is the case, there is little to be gained by starting our study prior to the time of Pythagoras, whose system of tuning has had so profound an influence upon both the ancient and the modern world.

The Pythagorean system is based upon the octave and the fifth, the first two intervals of the harmonic series. Using the ratios of 2:1 for the octave and 3:2 for the fifth, it is possible to tune all the notes of the diatonic scale in a succession of fifths and octaves, or, for that matter, all the notes of the chromatic scale. Thus a simple, but rigid, mathematical principle under-lies the Pythagorean tuning. As we shall see in the more detailed account of Greek tunings, the Pythagorean tuning per se was used only for the diatonic genus, and was modified in the chromatic and enharmonic genera. In this tuning the major thirds are a ditonic comma (about 1/9 tone) sharper than the pure thirds of the harmonic series. When the Pythagorean tuning is extended to more than twelve notes in the octave, a sharped note, as $G^{\#}$, is higher than the synonymous flatted note, as A^{b}.

The next great figure in tuning history was Aristoxenus, whose dispute with the disciples of Pythagoras raised a question that is eternally new: are the cogitations of theorists as important as

the observations of musicians themselves? His specific contention was that the judgment of the ear with regard to intervals
was superior to mathematical ratios. And so we find him talking
about "parts" of an octave rather than about string-lengths. One
of Aristoxenus' scales was composed of equal tones and equal
halves of tones. Therefore Aristoxenus was hailed by sixteenth
century theorists as the inventor of equal temperament. However, he may have intended this for the Pythagorean tuning, for
most of the other scales he has expressed in this unusual way
correspond closely to the tunings of his contemporaries. From
this we gather that his protest was not against current practice,
but rather against the rigidity of the mathematical theories.

Claudius Ptolemy, the geographer, is the third great figure in
early tuning history. To him we are in debt for an excellent
principle in tuning lore: that tuning is best for which ear and
ratio are in agreement. He has made the assumption here that
it is possible to reach an agreement. The many bitter arguments
between the mathematicians and the plain musicians, even to our
own day, are evidence that this agreement is not easily obtained,
but may actually be the result of compromise on both sides. To
Ptolemy the matter was much simpler. For him a tuning was
correct if it used superparticular ratios, such as 5:4, 11:10, etc.
All of the tuning varieties which he advocated himself are constructed exclusively with such ratios. To us, nearly 2000 years
later, his tunings seem as arbitrary as was that of Pythagoras.

Ptolemy's syntonic diatonic has especial importance to the
modern world because it coincides with just intonation, a tuning
system founded on the first five intervals of the harmonic series
— octave, fifth, fourth, major third, minor third. Didymus' diatonic used the same intervals, but in slightly different order. If
it could be shown that Ptolemy favored his syntonic tuning above
any of the others which he has presented, the adherents of just
intonation from the sixteenth century to the twentieth century
would be on more solid ground in hailing him as their patron
saint. Actually he approved the syntonic tuning because its ratios
are superparticular; but so are the ratios of three of the four
other diatonic scales he has given.

Just intonation, in either the Ptolemy or the Didymus ver-

2

sion, was unknown throughout the Middle Ages. Boethius discussed all three of the above-mentioned authorities on tuning,
but gave in mathematical detail only the system of Pythagoras.
It was satisfactory for the unisonal Gregorian chant, for its small
semitones are excellent for melody and its sharp major thirds
are no drawback. Even when the first crude attempt at harmony
resulted in the parallel fourths and fifths of organum, the Pythagorean tuning easily held its own.

But, later, thirds and sixths were freely used and were considered imperfect consonances rather than dissonances. It has
been questioned whether these thirds and sixths were as rough as
they would have been in the strict Pythagorean tuning, or whether
a process of softening (tempering) had not already begun. At
least one man, the Englishman Walter Odington, had stated that
consonant thirds had ratios of 5:4 and 6:5, and that singers intui-
tively used these ratios instead of those given by the Pythagorean
monochord. In reply one might note that some theorists continued
to advocate the Pythagorean tuning for centuries after the common practice had become something quite different. If it was
good enough for them, surrounded as they were by other, less
harsh, tuning methods, it must have sufficed for most of those
who lived in an age when no other definite system of tuning was
known.

The later history of the Pythagorean tuning makes interesting
reading.[1] It was still strongly advocated in the early sixteenth
century by such men as Gafurius and Ornithoparchus, and formed
the basis for the excellent modification made by Grammateus
and Bermudo. At the end of the century Papius spoke in its favor,
and so, forty years later, did Robert Fludd. In the second half
of the seventeenth century Bishop Caramuel, who has the invention of "musical logarithms" to his credit, said that "very many"
(plurimi) of his contemporaries still followed in the footsteps of
Pythagoras. Like testimony was given half a century later from
England, where Malcolm wrote that "some and even the Generality
... tune not only their Octaves, but also their 5ths as perfectly ...
Concordant as their Ear can judge, and consequently make their

---

[1]See J. Murray Barbour, "The Persistence of the Pythagorean Tuning System," Scripta Mathematica, I (1933), 286–304.

4ths perfect, which indeed makes a great many Errors in the other Intervals of 3rd and 6th." After another half century we find Abbé Roussier extolling "triple progression," as he called the Pythagorean tuning, and praising the Chinese for continuing to tune by perfect fifths.

Like the systems of Agricola in the sixteenth century and of Dowland in the early seventeenth century, many of the numerous irregular systems of the eighteenth century contained more pure than impure fifths. The instruments of the violin family, tuned by fifths, have a strong tendency toward the Pythagorean tuning. And a succession of roots moving by fifths is the basis of our classic system of harmony from Rameau to Prout and Goetschius. Truly the Pythagorean tuning system has been long-lived, and is still hale and hearty!

To return to the fifteenth century and the dissatisfied performers: Almost certainly some men did dislike the too-sharp major thirds and the too-flat minor thirds so much that they attempted to improve them. But history has preserved no record of their experiments. And the vast majority must have still been using the Pythagorean system, with all its imperfections, when Ramis de Pareja presented his tuning system to the world.

To be sure, Ramis did not present himself as the champion of a tremendous innovation. He was not a Luther nailing his ninety-five theses to the church door. His tuning was offered as a method which would be easier to work out on the monochord, and thus would be of greater utilitarian value to the singer, than was the Pythagorean tuning, with its cumbersome ratios. Although Ramis' monochord contained four pure thirds, with ratio 5:4, it was not the usual form of just intonation applied to the chromatic octave, in which eight thirds will be pure. It is rather to be considered an irregular tuning, combining features of both the Pythagorean tuning and just intonation. Some of Ramis' contemporaries assailed his tuning method, but his pupil Spataro explained it as a sort of temperament of the Pythagorean tuning. From these polemics arose the entirely false notion that Ramis was an advocate of equal temperament.[2] But he is worthy of our

[2]It occurs, for example, in such a general work as Sir James Jeans' Science and Music (New York, 1937).

4

respect as the first of a long line of innovators and reformers in the field of tuning.

As the words "tuning" and "temperament" are used today, the former is applied to such systems as the Pythagorean and just, in which all intervals may be expressed as the ratio of two integers. Thus for any tuning it is possible to obtain a monochord in which every string-length is an integer. A temperament is a modification of a tuning, and needs radical numbers to express the ratios of some or all of its intervals. Therefore, in monochords for temperaments the numbers given for certain (or all) string-lengths are only approximations, carried out to a particular degree of accuracy. Actually it is difficult in extreme cases to distinguish between tunings and temperaments. For example, Bermudo constructed a monochord in which the tritone G–C# has the ratio 164025:115921. This differs by only 1/7 per cent from the tritone of equal temperament, and in practice could not have been differentiated from it. But his system, which consists solely of linear divisions, should be called a tuning rather than a temperament.

It is not definitely known when the practice of temperament first arose in connection with instruments of fixed pitch, such as organs and claviers. Even in tuning an organ by Pythagorean fifths and octaves, the result would not be wholly accurate if the tuner's method was to obtain unisons between pitches on a monochord and the organ pipes. This would be a sort of unconscious temperament. More consciously he may have tried to improve some of the harsh Pythagorean thirds by lopping a bit off one note or another. Undoubtedly this was being done during the fifteenth century, for we find Gafurius, at the end of that century, mentioning that organists assert that fifths undergo a small diminution called temperament (participata).[3]

We have no way of knowing what temperament was like in Gafurius' age; but it is my belief that this diminution which Gafurius characterized as "minimae ac latentis incertaeque quodemmodo quantitatis" was actually so small that organs so tuned came closer to being in equal temperament than in just intonation

---

[3]Franchinus Gafurius, Practica musica (Milan, 1496), Book 2, Chapter 3.

or the meantone temperament. This belief is substantiated by two German methods of organ temperament which appeared in print a score of years later than Gafurius' tome. The earlier of the two was Arnold Schlick's temperament, an irregular method for which his directions were somewhat vague, but in which there were ten flattened and two raised fifths, as well as twelve raised thirds. Shohé Tanaka's description of Schlick's method[4] as the meantone temperament is wholly false; for in the latter the eight usable thirds are pure. Actually, from Schlick's own account, the method lay somewhere between the meantone temperament and the equal temperament. More definite and certainly very near to equal temperament was Grammateus' method, in which the white keys were in the Pythagorean tuning and the black keys were precisely half way between the pairs of adjoining white keys.

Just what the players themselves at this time understood by equal semitones is not known. Perhaps they would have been satisfied with a tuning like that of Grammateus, with ten semitones equal and the other two smaller. The first precise mathematical definition of equal temperament was given by Salinas: "We judge this one thing must be observed by makers of viols, so that the placing of the frets may be made regular, namely that the octave must be divided into twelve parts equally proportional, which twelve will be the equal semitones."[5] To facilitate constructing this temperament on the monochord, Salinas advised the use of the mesolabium, a mechanical method for finding two mean proportionals between two given lines. Zarlino also gave mechanical and geometric methods for finding the mean proportionals, intended primarily for the lute. (Zarlino did include, however, Ruscelli's enthusiastic plea that all instruments, even organs, should be tuned equally.) The history of equal temperament, then, is chiefly the history of its adoption upon keyboard instruments.

[4]"Studien im Gebiete der reinen Stimmung," Vierteljahrsschrift für Musikwissenschaft, VI (1890), 62, 63.

[5]Francisco Salinas, De musica libri VII (Salamanca, 1577), p. 173.

Neither Salinas nor Zarlino gave monochord lengths for equal temperament, although the problem was not extremely difficult: to obtain the 12th root of 2, take the square root twice and then the cube root. The first known appearance in print of the correct figures for equal temperament was in China, where Prince Tsai-yü's brilliant solution remains an enigma, since the music of China had no need for any sort of temperament. More significant for European music, but buried in manuscript for nearly three centuries, was Stevin's solution. As important as this achievement was his contention that equal temperament was the only logical system for tuning instruments, including keyboard instruments. His contemporaries apologetically presented the equal system as a practical necessity, but Stevin held that its ratios, irrational though they may be, were "true" and that the simple, rational values such as 3:2 for the fifth were the approximations! In his day only a mathematician (and perhaps only a mathematician not fully cognizant of contemporary musical practice) could have made such a statement. It is refreshingly modern, agreeing completely with the views of Schönberg and other advanced theorists and composers of our day.

The most complete and important discussion of tuning and temperament occurs in the works of Mersenne. There, in addition to his valuable contributions to acoustics and his descriptions of instruments, Mersenne ran the whole gamut of tuning theory. He expressed equal temperament in numbers, indicated geometrical and mechanical solutions for it, and finally put it upon the practical basis of tuning by beats as used today. Fully as catholic is his list of instrumental groups for which this temperament should be used: all fretted instruments, all wind instruments, all keyboard instruments, and even percussion instruments (bells).[6] The widespread influence of Mersenne's greatest work, Harmonie universelle (Paris, 1636 – 37), undoubtedly helped greatly to popularize a tuning that was then still considered as suitable for lutes and viols only.

The first really practical approximation for equal tempera-

---

[6]Johann Philip Albrecht Fischer, Verhandlung van de Klokken en het Klokke-Spel (Utrecht, 1738), p. 19, gave a bell temperament, with C equal to 192.000. This was equal temperament, with a few minor errors.

ment had been presented by Vincenzo Galilei half a century before Mersenne. He showed that the ratio of 18:17 was convenient in fretting the lute. Since references to this size of semitone cover two and a half centuries, it is probable that it has been used even longer by makers of lutes, guitars, and the like. Of course the repeated use of the 18:17 ratio would not give an absolutely pure octave, but a slight adjustment in the intervals would correct the error. Galilei's explanation of the reason for equal semitones on the lute is logical and correct: Since the frets are placed straight across the six strings, the order of diatonic and chromatic semitones is the same on all strings. Hence, in playing chords, $C^{\#}$ might be sounded on one string and $D^{\flat}$ on another, and this will be a very false octave unless the instrument is in equal temperament.

Vicentino had referred to a serious difficulty that arose from the common practice of having one kind of tuning (meantone) for keyboard instruments and another (equal) for fretted instruments. Since the pitches were so divergent, there was dissonance whenever the two groups were used together. By 1600, theorists like Artusi and Bottrigari said that these different groups of instruments were not used simultaneously because of the pitch difficulties. That is why such large instrumental groups were needed as those employed in the Ballet Comique de la Reine or in Monteverdi's Orfeo — selected groups of like instruments sounded well, but the mixture of different tunings made tuttis impracticable. It would seem that this consideration would have brought about the universal adoption of equal temperament long before it did come. However, after the unfretted violins became the backbone of the seventeenth century orchestra, their flexibility of intonation made this problem less pressing than when lutes and viols had been opposed to organs and claviers.

Before we leave the sixteenth century, we should examine the contribution to tuning history for which Vicentino is especially known. His archicembalo was an instrument with six keyboards, with a total of thirty-one different pitches in the octave. He described its tuning as that of the "usage and tuning common to all the keyboard instruments, as organs, cembali, clavichords, and

---

the like."[7] This would have been the ordinary meantone temperament, in which the fifths were tempered by 1/4 comma. Huyghens, a century and a half after Vicentino, showed that there was very close correspondence between a system in which the octave is divided into thirty-one logarithmically equal parts and the meantone system, similarly extended to thirty-one parts.

A simpler type of multiple division was the cembalo with nineteen notes in the octave. Both Zarlino and Salinas intended their variants of the meantone temperament (with fifths tempered by 2/7 and by 1/3 comma respectively) for such an instrument, and the latter's temperament would result in an almost precisely equal division. Praetorius described such an instrument also, and it has received favor with some twentieth century writers, especially Yasser.

The best system of multiple division within the limits of practicability divides the octave into fifty-three parts. This is literally a scale of commas, and, as such, was suggested by the ancient Greek writers on the Pythagorean system. Mersenne and Kircher in the seventeenth century mentioned the system. Mercator realized its advantages for measuring intervals. But especial honor should be paid to the nineteenth century Englishman Bosanquet for devising an harmonium with a "generalized keyboard" upon which the 53-system could be performed.

Other varieties of equal multiple division will be discussed in Chapter VI, together with a number of unequal divisions, most of which are extensions of just intonation. Practical musicians have rejected all of them, chiefly because they are more difficult to play, as well as being more expensive, than our ordinary keyboards.

Just intonation, as has already been mentioned, has had few devotees since the early seventeenth century. The history of the meantone temperament makes more interesting reading, since various theorists in addition to Zarlino and Salinas had conflicting ideas as to the amount by which the fifths should be tempered. Silbermann's temperament of 1/6 comma for the fifths is the most significant for us, because he represents the more con-

---

[7]Nicola Vicentino, L'antica musica ridotta alla moderna prattica (Rome, 1555), Book 5, Chapter 6.

servative practice during the time of Bach and Handel. In his temperament the thirds are slightly sharp, but the wolves are almost as ravenous as in the Aron 1/4 comma system.

To some extent the final adoption of equal temperament for an individual organ or clavier might have meant substituting this temperament for some type of meantone temperament. We are told that organs in England were still generally in meantone temperament until the middle of the nineteenth century. England must have lagged behind the Continent in this respect, and it is quite possible that the change, when it did come, was radical.

But it is more likely that in most cases the change to equal temperament was made more smoothly than this. The importance of unequal systems of twelve notes to the octave has been generally neglected by the casual historians of tuning, to whom only the Big Four (Pythagorean, just, meantone, and equal) are of moment. It is my opinion, however, that the unequal systems were of the greatest possible significance in bringing about the supremacy of our present tuning system. Reference has already been made to the early sixteenth century irregular systems of Schlick and Grammateus. The former resembled the meantone temperament; the latter was derived from the Pythagorean tuning. Bermudo repeated Grammateus' tuning, and his own second method was basically Pythagorean also. Ramis and Agricola crossed just intonation with the Pythagorean tuning, with fairly happy issue. Ganassi and Artusi treated just intonation and the meantone temperament much as Grammateus and Bermudo had treated the Pythagorean tuning.

Only a few years later than Grammateus, Aron described for organs the meantone temperament, mentioned above. In it every fifth save one was tempered by such an amount (1/4 comma, or about 1/18 semitone) that four fifths less two octaves would produce a pure major third. Thus arose the system that, with various modifications, was to be the strongest opponent of equal temperament, so far as keyboard instruments were concerned, for two or three hundred years. In the meantone temperament a sharped note, as $G^{\#}$, is lower in pitch than the equivalent flattened note, as A^{b}, by the great diesis, which is almost half as large as a semitone.

10

After Aron's time the meantone temperament, or some similar system, was generally accepted for organ and clavier. But there were a few dissenting voices. One was that of his exact contemporary Lanfranco, whose practical tuning rules for keyboard instruments seem to agree with no system other than equal temperament. Another was that of Fogliano, who was apparently the first sixteenth century writer to follow Ramis' lead and use in a tuning system both the pure fifths and the pure thirds of just intonation. But there is a difference; for he realized that the triads on D and B^b would be hopelessly out of tune in such a system, and therefore recommended that there be a mean D and B^b, each differing by half a comma from a pair of just pitches. These two mean pitches hint at Aron's meantone system. Otherwise this is what we ordinarily understand just intonation to be. Ironically enough, Fogliano's method, although containing more perfect thirds than Ramis' did, is far inferior to it if one goes beyond the ordinary bounds of two flats and three sharps. Beyond these bounds lay in wait the howling wolves, to muffle whose voices was the task of many a later worker in this field.

Fogliano had no immediate followers as an advocate of just intonation, since the following generation was more concerned with temperament. But almost a century later, certain mathematicians — as Galileo, de Caus, and Kepler — proclaimed again the validity of pure thirds and fifths. Occasional lone figures, both mathematicians and music theorists, were to speak in favor of just intonation, even until our own day. But it is significant that the great music theorists, such as Zarlino, Mersenne, and Rameau, presented just intonation as the theoretical basis of the scale, but temperament as a practical necessity. Equally great mathematicians with some understanding of music, from Stevin to Max Planck, have hailed temperament.

From the middle of the sixteenth century, all the theorists agreed that the fretted instruments, lutes and viols, were tuned in equal temperament. Vicentino made the first known reference to this fact, going so far as to state that both types of instrument had been so tuned from their invention. If we may believe pictorial evidence, especially that of the Flemish painters, so meticulous about detail, frets were adjusted to equal temperament as early as 1500, although there is not complete agreement on this point.

In the National Gallery in London, for example, there are several paintings in which the position of frets is shown plainly. A Concert, by Ercole de Roberti (1450–96), contains a nine-stringed lute and a small four-stringed viol, both apparently in equal temperament. Marco Marziale's Madonna and Child Enthroned with Saints, painted between 1492 and 1507, has an eleven-stringed lute with intervals equally proportional. And The Ambassadors, painted by Hans Holbein the Younger in 1533, has a six-stringed lute, again in equal temperament. Negative evidence is furnished by a painting by the early sixteenth century painter Ambrogio de Predis, whose Angel Playing on a Musical Instrument is playing a nine-stringed lute on which the semitones run large, small, small, large, and then three equal, as if the notes might have been C, C$^{\#}$, D, E^{b}, E, etc.

Because of the ease of tuning perfect fifths, the Pythagorean tuning has been the foundation of many of the later irregular systems, including that of Kirnberger. It also had some importance for such sophisticated writers as Werckmeister, Neidhardt, and Marpurg, whose systems with subtly divided commas were directed to the intellect rather than to the ear of the practical musician.

It becomes apparent, however, from the works of the men just mentioned that an instrument that was "well tempered" was not necessarily tempered equally. The title of Bach's famous "48" meant simply that the clavier was playable in all keys. Werckmeister and Neidhardt explained clearly that in their systems the key of C would be the best and D^{b} the worst, with the consonance of the other keys somewhere between these extremes.

Mersenne's and Rameau's modification of the 1/4 comma meantone temperament resembles somewhat the "good" temperaments of Werckmeister and Neidhardt, and Gallimard, with the aid of logarithms, reached a very similar goal. Perhaps the best of these many irregular systems was Thomas Young's second method, in which six fifths are perfect, and the other six are tuned flat by 1/6 Pythagorean comma, as in Silbermann's tuning. This would have been simpler to construct by ear than most of the systems, and does have an orderly progression from good to poor tuning as one departs from the most common keys.

In almost all of these irregular systems, from Grammateus to Young, all the major thirds were sharp to some extent, thus differing from just intonation and the meantone temperament, in which the usable thirds were perfect and the others very harsh. For the practical musician it would have been an easy matter, as time went on, to tune the "common" thirds still sharper, so that all the thirds would be equally sharp, and his instrument would be substantially in equal temperament. Probably this is exactly what did happen.

The recorded opposition to equal temperament on the part of such men as Werckmeister and even Sebastian Bach was to the rigorous mathematical treatment implied by the name "gleichschwebend." Theirs was a practical approximation to equality, and, from the keyboard compositions of Bach, it is evident that his practice must have been as satisfactory as that of our present-day tuners, else the great majority of his compositions would have been unbearable.

Greek music theory is highly complex and difficult, with its al-
phabetical notation, the dependence of musical rhythm upon poetic
meter, and all the rest of it. Our confusion is not lessened by
the fact that scholars quarrel about the exact interpretation of
the modal scales and that a pitifully scant remnant of the music
itself is available for study today. Fortunately it is possible to
understand the essentials of Greek tuning theories without enter-
ing into the other and more controversial aspects of Greek musical science. Moreover, it is advisable that the Greek tuning
lore be presented in some detail in order that the attitude of many
sixteenth and seventeenth century theorists may be clarified.
   The foundation of the Greek scale was the tetrachord, a de-
scending series of four notes in the compass of the modern perfect fourth. Most typical was the Dorian tetrachord, with two
tones and then a semitone, as A G F E or E D C B. Two or more
tetrachords could be combined by conjunction, as the above tetrachords would be with E a common note. Or they might be combined by disjunction, as the above tetrachords would be in reverse
order, with a whole tone between B and A. Tetrachords combined
alternately by conjunction and by disjunction correspond to our
natural heptatonic scale.
   The Greeks had three genera—diatonic, chromatic, and enharmonic. A diatonic tetrachord contained two tones and a semitone, variously arranged, the Dorian tetrachord having the order
shown above, as A G F E. In the chromatic tetrachord the second
string (as G) was lowered until the two lower intervals in the
tetrachord were equal. Thus A G$^\flat$ F E represents the process
of formation better than the more commonly shown A F$^\sharp$ F E.
In the enharmonic tetrachord the second string was lowered still
further until it was in unison with the third string; the third string
was then tuned half way between the second and fourth strings.
In notes the enharmonic tetrachord would be A G$^{\flat\flat}$ F̣ E or A F
F̣ E. Thus in the chromatic tetrachord there were the consecutive semitones that we associate with the modern chromatic
genus; but the enharmonic tetrachord contained real quarter
tones, whereas our enharmonically equivalent notes, as F$^\flat$ and
E, differ by a comma, 1/9 tone, or at most by a diesis, 1/5 tone.

Claudius Ptolemy has presented the most complete list of tunings advocated by various theorists, including himself.[1] These (with one exception to be discussed later) were shown by the ratios of the three consecutive intervals that constituted the tetrachord, and also by string-lengths for the octave lying between 120 and 60, using sexagesimal fractions where necessary. The octave is the Dorian octave, as from E to E, with B–A the disjunctive tone, always with 9:8 ratio. Ptolemy's tables are given here (Tables 1–21) with comments following. The fractions have been changed into decimal notation.

Greek Enharmonic Tunings

Table 1. Archytas' Enharmonic

Lengths	60.00	75.00	77.14	80.00	90.00	112.50	115.71	120.00
Names	E	C	$\overset{\flat}{C}$	B	A	F	$\overset{\flat}{F}$	E
Ratios		5/4	36/35	28/27	9/8	5/4	36/35	28/27
Cents	1200	814	765	702	498	112	63	0

Table 2. Aristoxenus' Enharmonic

Lengths	60.00	76.00	78.00	80.00	90.00	114.00	117.00	120.00
Names	E	C	$\overset{\flat}{C}$	B	A	F	$\overset{\flat}{F}$	E
Parts		16	2	2	10	24	3	3
Cents	1200	791	746	702	498	89	44	0

Table 3. Eratosthenes' Enharmonic

Lengths	60.00	75.00	77.50	80.00	90.00	112.50	116.25	120.00
Names	E	C	$\overset{\flat}{C}$	B	A	F	$\overset{\flat}{F}$	E
Ratios		5/4	24/23	46/45	9/8	5/4	24/23	46/45
Cents	1200	814	740	702	498	112	38	0

[1] Claudii Ptolemaei <u>Harmonicorum</u> <u>libri</u> <u>tres</u>. Latin translation by John Wallis (London, 1699).

Greek Chromatic Tunings

Table 4. Archytas' Chromatic

Lengths	60.00	71.11	77.14	80.00	90.00	106.67	115.71	120.00
Names	E	D^b	C	B	A	G^b	F	E
Ratios		32/27	243/224	28/27	9/8	32/27	243/224	28/27
Cents	1200	906	765	702	498	204	63	0

Table 5. Aristoxenus' Chromatic Malakon

Lengths	60.00	74.67	77.33	80.00	90.00	112.00	116.00	120.00
Names	E	D^b	C	B	A	G^b	F	E
Parts		$14\frac{2}{3}$	$2\frac{2}{3}$	$2\frac{2}{3}$	10	22	4	4
Cents	1200	821	761	702	498	119	59	0

Table 6. Aristoxenus' Chromatic Hemiolion

Lengths	60.00	74.00	77.00	80.00	90.00	111.00	115.50	120.00
Names	E	D^b	C	B	A	G^b	F	E
Parts		14	3	3	10	21	$4\frac{1}{2}$	$4\frac{1}{2}$
Cents	1200	837	768	702	498	135	66	0

Table 7. Aristoxenus' Chromatic Tonikon

Lengths	60.00	72.00	76.00	80.00	90.00	108.00	114.00	120.00
Names	E	D^b	C	B	A	G^b	F	E
Parts		12	4	4	10	18	6	6
Cents	1200	884	791	702	498	182	89	0

17

Table 8. Eratosthenes' Chromatic

Lengths	60.00	72.00	76.00	80.00	90.00	108.00	114.00	120.00
Names	E	D^b	C	B	A	G^b	F	E
Ratios		6/5	19/18	20/19	9/8	6/5	19/18	20/19
Cents	1200	884	791	702	498	182	89	0

Table 9. Didymus' Chromatic

Lengths	60.00	72.00	75.00	80.00	90.00	108.00	112.50	120.00
Names	E	D^b	C	B	A	G^b	F	E
Ratios		6/5	25/24	16/15	9/8	6/5	25/24	16/15
Cents	1200	884	814	702	498	182	112	0

Table 10. Ptolemy's Chromatic Malakon

Lengths	60.00	72.00	77.14	80.00	90.00	108.00	115.71	120.00
Names	E	D^b	C	B	A	G^b	F	E
Ratios		6/5	15/14	28/27	9/8	6/5	15/14	28/27
Cents	1200	884	765	702	498	182	63	0

Table 11. Ptolemy's Chromatic Syntonon

Lengths	60.00	70.00	76.36	80.00	90.00	105.00	114.55	120.00
Names	E	D^b	C	B	A	G^b	F	E
Ratios		7/6	12/11	22/21	9/8	7/6	12/11	22/21
Cents	1200	933	783	702	498	231	81	0

Greek Diatonic Tunings

Table 12. Archytas' Diatonic

Lengths	60.00	67.50	77.14	80.00	90.00	101.25	115.71	120.00
Names	E	D	C	B	A	G	F	E
Ratios		9/8	8/7	28/27	9/8	9/8	8/7	28/27
Cents	1200	996	765	702	498	294	63	0

Table 13. Aristoxenus' Diatonic Malakon

Lengths	60.00	70.00	76.00	80.00	90.00	105.00	114.00	120.00
Names	E	D	C	B	A	G	F	E
Parts		10	6	4	10	15	9	6
Cents	1200	933	791	702	498	231	89	0

Table 14. Aristoxenus' Diatonic Syntonon

Lengths	60.00	68.00	76.00	80.00	90.00	102.00	114.00	120.00
Names	E	D	C	B	A	G	F	E
Parts		8	8	4	10	12	12	6
Cents	1200	983	791	702	498	281	89	0

Table 15. Eratosthenes' Diatonic

Lengths	60.00	67.50	75.94	80.00	90.00	101.25	113.91	120.00
Names	E	D	C	B	A	G	F	E
Ratios		9/8	9/8	256/243	9/8	9/8	9/8	256/243
Cents	1200	996	792	702	498	294	90	0

19

Table 16. Didymus' Diatonic

Lengths	60.00	67.50	75.00	80.00	90.00	101.25	112.50	120.00
Names	E	D	C	B	A	G	F	E
Ratios		9/8	10/9	16/15	9/8	9/8	10/9	16/15
Cents	1200	996	814	702	498	294	112	0

Table 17. Ptolemy's Diatonic Malakon

Lengths	60.00	68.57	76.19	80.00	90.00	102.86	114.27	120.00
Names	E	D	C	B	A	G	F	E
Ratios		8/7	10/9	21/20	9/8	8/7	10/9	21/20
Cents	1200	969	787	702	498	265	85	0

Table 18. Ptolemy's Diatonic Toniaion

Lengths	60.00	67.30	77.14	80.00	90.00	101.25	115.71	120.00
Names	E	D	C	B	A	G	F	E
Ratios		9/8	8/7	28/27	9/8	9/8	8/7	28/27
Cents	1200	996	765	702	498	294	63	0

Table 19. Ptolemy's Diatonic Ditoniaion

Lengths	60.00	67.50	75.94	80.00	90.00	101.25	113.91	120.00
Names	E	D	C	B	A	G	F	E
Ratios		9/8	9/8	256/243	9/8	9/8	9/8	256/243
Cents	1200	996	792	702	498	294	90	0

Table 20. Ptolemy's Diatonic Syntonon

Lengths	60.00	66.67	75.00	80.00	90.00	100.00	112.50	120.00
Names	E	D	C	B	A	G	F	E
Ratios		10/9	9/8	16/15	9/8	10/9	9/8	16/15
Cents	1200	1018	814	702	498	316	112	0

20

Table 21. Ptolemy's Diatonic Hemiolon

Lengths	60.00	66.67	73.33	80.00	90.00	100.00	110.00	120.00
Names	E	D	C	B	A	G	F	E
Ratios		10/9	11/10	12/11	9/8	10/9	11/10	12/11
Cents	1200	1018	853	702	498	316	151	0

Only two of these seventeen or eighteen independent tunings have had any great influence upon modern music theory—the third and fourth of Ptolemy's diatonic scales, commonly called the "ditonic" and the "syntonic." The former is the same as Eratosthenes' diatonic, and is the old Pythagorean tuning. It gains its name from the fact that its major third (ditone) consists of a pair of equal tones. The latter, the "tightly stretched" in contrast to the "soft" (malakon), is what we know as just intonation. Didymus' diatonic contains the same intervals as Ptolemy's syntonic diatonic, but with the minor tone (10:9) below the major tone (9:8) instead of the reverse. Didymus' arrangement is the more logical for constructing a monochord; Ptolemy's in terms of the harmonic series.

The theorists of the sixteenth and seventeenth centuries, eager to bolster their ideas with classical prototypes, pointed out that the just tuning was that of Didymus and Ptolemy. But they ignored the other diatonic tunings of Ptolemy. They liked to point out further that in three of the enharmonic tunings the pure major third (5:4) appears, and in four of the chromatic tunings the pure minor third (6:5). But only Didymus used enharmonic and chromatic tunings that really resembled just intonation. His chromatic is tuned precisely as E, C$^{\#}$, C, etc., would be in just intonation, using the chromatic semitone, 25:24, which appears in no other tuning. In his enharmonic, not only does the major third have the ratio 5:4, but the small intervals are "equal" quarter tones, resulting from an arithmetical division of the 16:15 semitone.* The other nine enharmonic and chromatic tunings depart more or less from Didymus' standard.

21

Let us examine more of the peculiarities of these Greek tunings. Archytas has used the same ratio (28:27) for the lowest interval in each genus, thus having an interval (63 cents) that is much larger than most of the semitones and smaller than the quarter tones. The ditonic semitone, 256:243, is about the same size as Ptolemy's "soft" semitone, 21:20, being a comma smaller than the syntonic semitone, 16:15. The tones range from minimum, 11:10, through minor, 10:9, and major, 9:8, to maximum, 8:7. Archytas' minor third, 32:27, is a comma larger than the syntonic third, 6:5, and more than a comma smaller than Ptolemy's minor third, 7:6. Eratosthenes' major third, 19:15, is about the same size as the Pythagorean ditone, 81:64, and is about a ditonic comma larger than the syntonic third, 5:4.

Ever since his own age a great controversy has raged about the teachings of Aristoxenus. Instead of using ratios, he divided the tetrachord into 30 parts, of which, in his diatonic syntonon, each tone has 12 parts, each semitone 6. Thus, if we are to take him at his word, Aristoxenus was here describing equal temperament. The sixteenth and seventeenth century theorists were of the opinion that such was his intention, the advocates of equal temperament opposing the name of Aristoxenus to that of Ptolemy.

Ptolemy himself did not so understand Aristoxenus' doctrines. With a fundamental of 120 units, the perfect fourth above has 90 units. Thus, as shown in the tables, Ptolemy subtracted Aristoxenus' "parts" from 120. His enharmonic then agrees with that of Eratosthenes, and his chromatic tonikon with the latter's chromatic. But Aristoxenus' diatonic syntonon does not then quite agree with the Pythagorean (ditonic) diatonic, although the latter is the only Greek tuning that contains two equal tones. His diatonic malakon, as Ptolemy has shown it, is unlike any of the other tunings; whereas in its succession of intervals—large, medium, small — it resembles Ptolemy's diatonic malakon or chromatic syntonon.

So it seems quite likely that Aristoxenus did not intend to express any new tunings by his adding together of parts of a tone, but simply to indicate in a general way the impression that current tunings made upon the ear. But his vagueness has made possible all sorts of wild speculations. It is even possible, by an improper manipulation of the figures, to argue that Aristoxenus was a proponent of just intonation. Take his enharmonic: 24 + 3 + 3. Add these numbers to 90 in reverse order as before, getting 90 93 96 120. Then consider these numbers to be frequencies rather than string-lengths. The result is practically the same as Didymus': 5/4 x 32/31 x 31/30. Or take Aristoxenus' diatonic syntonon: 12 + 12 + 6. Treat it as we have just treated his enharmonic, getting 90 96 108 120. If these are then taken as frequencies, we have Ptolemy's syntonic, 10/9 x 9/8 x 16/15.

The paramount principle in Ptolemy's tunings was the use of superparticular proportion, a ratio in which the antecedent exceeds the consequent by unity. (The Latin prefix "sesqui" is conveniently used to describe these ratios, e.g., "sesquiquarta," meaning 5/4.) Ptolemy used 5/4, 6/5, 7/6, 8/7, etc. Seven of the eight tunings that bear his own name are constructed entirely of superparticular proportions, the eighth being the ditonic, or Pythagorean. Seven tunings that he has ascribed to other writers also use these ratios exclusively, including all of Didymus' tunings, Archytas' enharmonic and diatonic, and Eratosthenes' chromatic (Aristoxenus' chromatic tonikon). In just intonation the ratios are, of course, superparticular, and this feature only would have appealed to Ptolemy and his contemporaries. For, despite the many apparently just intervals used in the given tunings, Ptolemy recognized no consonances other than those of the Pythagorean tuning—fourth, fifth, octave, eleventh, twelfth, and fifteenth.

It is easy to obtain, by algebra, all the possible divisions of the tetrachord built up entirely by superparticular proportions. (A theory for the superparticular division of tones is shown in connection with Colonna, in Chapter VII.) Eliminating those in which one interval is considerably smaller than the smallest enharmonic quarter tone (46:45), we find that, collectively, the Greeks had not omitted many possibilities. Other enharmonic tunings similar to Ptolemy's would be 5/4 x 22/21 x 56/55 and 5/4 x 26/25 x 40/39. Chromatic tunings would include 6/5 x 13/12 x 40/39; 7/6 x 9/8 x 64/63; 7/6 x 10/9 x 36/35; and 7/6 x 15/14 x 16/15. Two others are difficult to classify: 8/7 x 13/12 x 14/13 might best be considered a chromatic tuning, something like 14 + 8 + 8 in Aristoxenus' parts. And 8/7 x 8/7 x 49/48 is undoubtedly a variant of the ditonic tuning, but with a quarter tone instead of a semitone at the bottom, perhaps 14 + 14 + 2.

In later chapters we shall see many echoes of Greek tuning methods, not only in such well-known systems as the Pythagorean and the just, but also in the modified systems, such as Ganassi's, and in irregular systems, such as Dowland's. Unusual super-particular intervals are used by Colonna in the poorest tuning system shown in this book, and also by Awraamoff, whose system is even worse.

Chapter III. MEANTONE TEMPERAMENT

It is not definitely known when temperament was first used. Vicentino stated that the fretted instruments had always been in equal temperament. As· for the keyboard instruments, Zarlino declared that temperament was as old as the complete chromatic keyboard. It may well be that some organs in the fifteenth century had had temperament of a sort, although the Pythagorean tuning continued to have too many advocates not to have been dominant in the earlier period. However that may be, Riemann discovered the first mention of temperament in a passage from Gafurius' Practica musica (1496).[1] There, among the eight rules of counterpoint, Gafurius said that organists assert that fifths undergo a small, indefinite amount of diminution called temperament (participata). Since he was reporting a contemporary fact, rather than advocating an innovation, the practice may have begun decades earlier than his time.

Notice that Gafurius stated that there was nothing regular about the temperament of his day, nor were the fifths diminished by any large amount. It seems reasonable to believe that when organists first became dissatisfied with the extremely sharp thirds of the Pythagorean tuning, they would go about any alteration of the fifths in a gingerly manner, lopping off a bit here and a bit there. Grammateus' division of Pythagorean tones into equal semitones came only twenty-two years after Gafurius' observation,[2] and ranks very high among irregular systems that approach equal temperament. It is easy to believe, therefore, that organs were tuned as well in 1500 as they generally are today.

Dechales had no authority for stating that Guido of Arezzo was the father of temperament.[3] The association of Ramis[4] with

---

[1] Hugo Riemann, Geschichte der Musiktheorie (Berlin, 1898), p. 327.

[2] See Chapter VII for Grammateus.

[3] R. ℞ Claudius Franciscus Milliet Dechales, Cursus seu mundus mathematicus (Lugduni, 1674), Tomus Tertius, pp. 15–17.

[4] See Preface and Chapter V.

temperament is one of the most common misconceptions in the history of tuning. And, although Schlick's system[5] undoubtedly can properly be described as a temperament, it is just as surely of an irregular variety. It is well to mention these names, and discard each of them, before saying that full credit for describing the meantone temperament must go to Pietro Aron.

In Aron's Toscanello[6] there is a chapter entitled "Concerning the temperament (participation) and way of tuning the instrument." The tuning is to be made in three successive stages (see Table 22). First, the major third, C–E, is to be made "sonorous and just." But the fifth C–G is to be made "a little flat." The fifth G–D is to be similarly flattened, and then A is to be tuned so that the fifths D–A and A–E are equal. The idea, of course, is to ensure an equality of these four fifths, so far as it can be accomplished by ear.

Table 22. Aron's Meantone Temperament (1/4 Comma)

Names	C^0	$C\#^{-\frac{7}{4}}$	$D^{-\frac{1}{2}}$	$Eb^{+\frac{3}{4}}$	E^{-1}	$F^{+\frac{1}{4}}$	$F\#^{-\frac{3}{2}}$	$G^{-\frac{1}{4}}$	$G\#^{-2}$	$A^{-\frac{3}{4}}$	$Bb^{+\frac{1}{2}}$	$B^{-\frac{5}{4}}$	C^0
Cents	0	76	193	310	386	503	579	697	773	890	1007	1083	1200

M.D. 20.0; S.D. 20.2

In the second stage of tuning, the fifths F–C, B^b–F, and E^b–B^b are tempered exactly the same as the diatonic fifths had been. Finally, in the third stage, $C^\#$ and $F^\#$ are tuned as pure thirds to A and D respectively. Aron says nothing about $G^\#$. With Kinkeldey we can say that this note "probably belongs to the third group,"[7] and would be tuned as a pure third to E.

The name "meantone" was applied to this temperament because the tone, as C–D, is precisely half of the pure third, as

---

[5]See Chapter VII.

[6]Toscanello in musica (Venice, 1523); revised edition of 1529 was consulted.

[7]Otto Kinkeldey, Orgel und Klavier in der Musik des 16. Jahrhunderts (Leipzig, 1910), p. 76.

26

C-E. Aron said nothing about the division of the comma. But since the pure E is a syntonic comma lower than the Pythagorean E, and each fifth is to be tempered by the same amount, the fifths will all be tempered by 1/4 comma. It is easy to calculate the ratio of the meantone fifth: the major third has the ratio 5:4; hence the ratio of the tone will be the square root of this, or $\sqrt{5}{:}2$. The ratio of the major ninth will be twice the ratio of the tone, or $\sqrt{5}{:}1$. The ratio of the fifth will be the square root of the ratio of the ninth, or $\sqrt[4]{5}{:}1$. If we consider the syntonic comma to be 21.5 cents, a fifth diminished by 1/4 comma will be 702.0 - 5.4 = 696.6 cents.

The deviation for the meantone temperament is nearly as large as for just intonation. That would seem to indicate that temperament makes for little improvement. Strangely enough, this is absolutely true, so far as the remote keys are concerned. However, if the deviation were to be measured only from E^b to $G^{\#}$, without allowing for the enharmonic uses of notes, the meantone temperament would be an easy victor over just intonation. That is, if we were computing the deviation of eleven fifths only, omitting the wolf fifth of 737 cents, the standard deviation for the meantone temperament would be much smaller than that for just intonation. But, since our ideal is equal temperament, the deviation as computed shows accurately enough how very unsatisfactory this tuning is when its narrow bounds are overstepped.

The meantone temperament was used from the beginning upon keyboard instruments only. It was the temperament that Vicentino intended for his Archicembalo when he said that it may be tuned "justly with the temperament of the flattened fifth, according to the usage and tuning common to all the keyboard instruments, as organs, cembali, clavichords, and the like."[8] Zarlino called the meantone temperament a "new temperament" and said that it is "very pleasing for all purposes" when used on keyboard instruments.[9] To divide the major third into two mean tones, Zarlino advocated the Euclidean construction for a mean

[8]See Chapter VI.

[9]Gioseffo Zarlino, Dimostrationi armoniche (Venice, 1571), p. 267.

27

proportional, and of course the fifth could be constructed from the major ninth by the same means.

Verheijen's reply to Stevin's discussion of equal temperament explained the meantone temperament in detail [10] He even included a monochord for it (Table 23), and thus has the distinction of being the first person, so far as we know, to put its ratios into figures (cents values as in Aron, Table 22, beginning with F as 503).

Table 23. Verheijen's Monochord for Meantone Temperament

Lengths	10000	9750	8944	8560	8000	7477	7155	6687	6400	5961
Names	F^0	$F\#^{-\frac{7}{4}}$	$G^{-\frac{1}{2}}$	$G\#^{-\frac{9}{4}}$	A^{-1}	$Bb^{+\frac{1}{4}}$	$B^{-\frac{3}{2}}$	$C^{-\frac{1}{4}}$	$C\#^{-2}$	$D^{-\frac{3}{4}}$

	5590	5350	5000
	$Eb^{+\frac{1}{2}}$	$E^{-\frac{5}{4}}$	F^0

In Spain, Sancta María described a practical tuning system that may have been the same as the meantone tuning.[11] He said that on the clavichord and the vihuela (the Spanish lute) each fifth is to be "a little flat." In fact, the diminution is to be "so small that it can scarcely be noticed." Since he did not say whether the thirds were to be pure or a little sharp, we cannot know whether his system was the real meantone or came nearer equal temperament. However, he held that a tone cannot be divided into two equal semitones, and consistently made the diatonic semitone larger than the chromatic semitone, as it would be in just intonation or the meantone temperament.

The first German writer to describe the meantone temperament was more explicit. This was Michael Praetorius,[12] in a

---

[10]Simon Stevin, Van de Spiegeling der Singconst, ed. D. Bierens de Haan (Amsterdam, 1884). Verheijen's letter is in Appendice A. Both discussion and reply remained in manuscript for almost three hundred years.

[11]Tomás de Sancta María, Arte de tañer fantasia (Valladolid, 1565), Chapter 53.

[12]Syntagma musicum (Wolfenbüttel, 1618), Vol. II; new edition, 1884–94, published as Publikation älterer praktischen und theoretischen Musikwerke, Band 13, pp. 178 ff.

chapter on the tuning of the "Regal, Clavicymbel, Symphonien und dergleichen Instrument." His was a practical system, with major thirds and octaves pure, and fifths flat. Praetorius explained carefully how various intervals are altered by fractional parts of the comma. Otto Gibelius[13] showed a method for obtaining an approximately correct monochord for the meantone temperament. First he made a table in which were shown pairs of numbers differing by the syntonic comma for every note in a 14-note octave, extending from A^b to $D^\#$. Then he made an arithmetical division of each comma, with 3/4, 1/2, or 1/4 comma subtracted from the larger number, to obtain the tempered value. C, E, $G^\#$, and A^b needed no temperament (see Table 24). His results check closely with numbers obtained by taking roots.[14] For example, his D is 193200; it should be 193196. His G is 144450 instead of 144447. Since the comma is small relative to the intervals of the scale and since as much as a quarter or a half of it is used, the error could not be great. An arithmetical division of the ditonic comma into twelfths in the construction of equal temperament would create greater errors than this for certain notes of the division.

Table 24. Gibelius' Monochord for Meantone Temperament

Lengths	216000	206720	193200	184896	180562.5	172800	161500	154560
Names	C^0	$C^{\#\,-\frac{7}{4}}$	$D^{-\frac{1}{2}}$	$D^{\#\,-\frac{9}{4}}$	$E^{b\,+\frac{3}{4}}$	E^{-1}	$F^{+\frac{1}{4}}$	$F^{\#\,-\frac{3}{2}}$

	144450	138240	135000	129200	120750	115560	108000
	$G^{-\frac{1}{4}}$	$G^{\#\,-2}$	$A^{b\,+1}$	$A^{-\frac{3}{4}}$	$B^{b\,+\frac{1}{2}}$	$B^{-\frac{5}{4}}$	C^0

Lemme Rossi,[15] writing in the same year as Gibelius, would have approved the latter's approximation for the meantone tem-

---

[13]Propositiones mathematico-musicae (Münden, 1666), copperplate opposite page 14.

[14]Wolffgang Caspar Printz, Phrynis Mytilenaeus oder der satyrische Componist (Dresden and Leipzig, 1696), p. 73.

[15]Sistema musico (Perugia, 1666), p. 59.

perament, for he himself said that the arithmetical division of the comma differs "insensibly" from a geometrical division. In the example that he gave, the geometrical mean between the two numbers, 31104 and 30720, in the ratio of 81 to 80, is 30911, and the arithmetical mean is 30912, certainly a negligible difference. But, he said, the correct string-lengths for the meantone temperament can be obtained both "easily and quickly with the table of logarithms."

Our final monochord for the meantone temperament proper will be Rossi's "Numeri del sistema participato."[16] He has given it for a 19-note octave commencing on A (see Table 25). Since C itself is a tempered value here, we have transposed the system up a minor third from A to C, selecting those notes that would belong to the ordinary meantone scale. The number used for his fundamental had been previously used in a table of just intonation.

Table 25. Rossi's Monochord for Meantone Temperament

Lengths	41472	39690	37095	34668	33178	31008	29676	27734	26542
Names	C^0	$C^{\#-\frac{7}{4}}$	$D^{-\frac{1}{2}}$	$E^{b+\frac{3}{4}}$	E^{-1}	$F^{+\frac{1}{4}}$	$F^{\#-\frac{3}{2}}$	$G^{-\frac{1}{4}}$	$G^{\#-2}$

	24806	23184	22187	20736
	$A^{-\frac{3}{4}}$	$B^{b+\frac{1}{2}}$	$B^{-\frac{5}{4}}$	C^0

Another sort of approximation connected with the meantone temperament was given by Claas Douwes.[17] In describing the bonded clavichord he gave simple ratios (most of them superparticular) for various intervals that would occur on the same string. For example, the highest string has C, B, B^b, and A. C–A is 6:5; B–A, 19:17; B^b–A, 15:14. On the next string, G$^\#$–F is 7:6. Two octaves lower, the ninth string has only two notes, G$^\#$ and G, with the ratio 24:23.

Dou⸏⸏s had explained that his was a tempered system. His rational ratios are good approximations to the surds of the mean-

[16]Ibid., p. 83.

[17]Grondig Ondersoek van de Toonen der Musijk (Franeker, 1699), pp. 98–104.

tone temperament. His minor third, with ratio 6:5, is 316 cents; the meantone minor third is 310. His augmented second, 7:6, is 267 cents; the meantone augmented second is 270. His tone, 19:17, is almost 193 cents; the meantone tone is practically the same. His diatonic semitone, 15:14, is 119 cents; the meantone diatonic semitone, 117. His chromatic semitone, 24:23, is 74 cents; the meantone chromatic semitone, 76. His system agrees with itself as well as with the ordinary meantone system. For example, the tone should be the sum of the diatonic and the chromatic semitones, or 15/14 x 24/23. This product is 3420:3059; his ratio for the tone, 19:17, equals 3420:3060, a close correspondence.

In tracing the later history of the meantone temperament, it would be easy to name theorists in all the principal European countries who continued to favor an unequal tuning of keyboard instruments later than the first quarter of the eighteenth century. But, unless, like Galin in 1818, they specifically say that they favor the tuning in which the fifths are tempered by 1/4 syntonic comma or its equivalent (31-division),[18] we have no right to call their methods the meantone temperament. This is the fallacy of so much that has been written on this subject.

Other Varieties of Meantone Temperament

Strictly, there is only one meantone temperament. But theorists have been inclined to lump together under that head all sorts of systems intended for keyboard instruments. For example, the statement often appears in print that in England the meantone temperament was used for organs until the middle of the nineteenth century. William Crotch,[19] writing early in that century, wrote: "As organs are at present tuned, (with unequal temperament), keys which have many flats or sharps will not have a good effect, especially if the time be slow." That statement is enough to cause a host of later English writers to say

[18]Pierre Galin, Exposition d'une nouvelle méthode pour l'enseignement de la musique (3rd edition, Bordeaux and Paris, 1862; 1st edition, 1818).

[19]Elements of Musical Composition (London, 1812), p. 112.

that Crotch reported the meantone temperament to be in use in his age.

But later in his book Crotch had this to say: "Unequal temperament is that wherein some of the fifths, and consequently some of the thirds, are made more perfect than on the equal temperament, which necessarily renders others less perfect. Of this there are many systems, which the student is now capable of examining for himself."[20] In other words, Crotch is saying that there was a great diversity in the tuning of organs in his day.

In Chapter VII, "Irregular Systems," twenty-odd men are mentioned who collectively have described fifty of the "many systems," none of which is the meantone temperament. In the present chapter we propose to describe still other systems of temperament, systems formed on the same general pattern as meantone temperament. Bosanquet called "regular" a temperament constructed with one size of fifth.[21] The Pythagorean tuning, equal temperament, meantone temperament—all are regular systems. The systems that follow are also regular, with values for the fifth smaller than that of equal temperament and (usually) larger than that of the meantone temperament. Since their construction is similar, it is easy to describe them as varieties of the meantone temperament. In all of them, the tone is precisely half of the major third. No harm will be done by such a nomenclature if we realize that these are regular temperaments which the earlier theorists themselves considered of the same type as the 1/4-comma temperament and some of which they preferred to it.

The first regular temperament to be advocated after the description of the ordinary meantone temperament was that described by Zarlino in which "each fifth remains diminished and imperfect by 2/7 comma."[22] Although Zarlino showed a monochord with this tuning for the diatonic genus only, he intended it

[20]Ibid., p. 135.

[21]R.H M. Bosanquet, An Elementary Treatise on Musical Intervals and Temperament (London, 1876), Chapter VIII.

[22]Gioseffo Zarlino, Istitutioni armoniche (Venice, 1558), pp. 126 ff.

also for the chromatic genus—by which he meant the ordinary black keys. He also described an enharmonic genus, having 19 notes to the octave, as applied to a cembalo which Master Domenico Pesarese had made for him. This must have had the same tuning, although Zarlino did not clearly say so. Most of these varieties of the meantone temperament will have a smaller deviation when applied to a keyboard with 19 or more notes to the octave than upon the usual keyboard. Zarlino's temperament corresponds to the 50-division, and, as such, will be discussed in the chapter on multiple division.

In Table 26, we see the 2/7-comma temperament applied to a keyboard with 12 notes to the octave. Since the amount of tempering is greater than 1/4 comma, the deviation is greater than for Aron's system. It is, in fact, a very poor system, and Zarlino later admitted it to be inferior to the 1/4-comma system. The only just interval in it is the chromatic semitone. Tanaka liked it "because all the imperfect consonances are impure alike,"[23] that is, the major and minor thirds are 1/7 comma flat (3 cents), and the major and minor sixths are sharp by the same amount. To construct it on a monochord, Zarlino would use the questionable virtues of the mesolabium.[24]

Table 26. Zarlino's 2/7 - Comma Temperament

Names	C^0	$C^{\#-2}$	$D^{-\frac{4}{7}}$	$E^{b+\frac{6}{7}}$	$E^{-\frac{8}{7}}$	$F^{+\frac{2}{7}}$	$F^{\#-\frac{12}{7}}$	$G^{-\frac{2}{7}}$	$G^{\#-\frac{16}{7}}$	$A^{-\frac{6}{7}}$	$B^{b+\frac{4}{7}}$	$B^{-\frac{10}{7}}$	C^0
Cents	0	70	191	313	383	504	574	696	817	887	1008	1078	1200

M.D. 25.0; S.D. 25.3

The next variety of meantone temperament is also highly unsatisfactory when applied to an octave of twelve semitones. This is the 1/3-comma temperament, the invention of Francisco Salinas, which he described as follows: "The first of them [the other two were the 2/7-comma and the 1/4-comma temperaments] has the comma divided into three parts equally proportional, of which

[23]Shohé Tanaka, "Studien im Gebiete der reinen Stimmung," Vierteljahrsschrift für Musikwissenschaft, VI (1890), 65.

[24]For an account of the mesolabium, see the second part of Chapter IV.

the minor tone is increased by one part and the major tone is decreased by two parts."[25] Salinas showed that his method results in pure minor thirds, tritone, and major sixth. But the fifth is diminished by 1/3 comma, and so is the major third. On the whole this tuning does not compare favorably with the others, but Salinas added: "Although this imperfection is seen to be greater than that which is found in the other two temperaments, nevertheless it is endurable."

Salinas intended his temperament for an octave containing 19 notes, divided into the three genera—diatonic, chromatic, and enharmonic. His special reason for advocating this tuning was the ease of realizing it upon the monochord. Seven of the notes can be obtained by a series of just minor thirds below and above the fundamental. Thus we obtain C, $D^\#$, E^b, $F^\#$, G^b, A, and $B^\#$, and Salinas has given their string-lengths for the octave 22500 to 11250.

To find the notes D and E, two mean proportionals must be inserted in the tritone, $C-F^\#$. This "will be very easy to those who know the use of a certain instrument invented by Archimedes, which is called mesolabium, from finding mean lines by it." The remainder of the notes can then be obtained by minor thirds from D and E.

We agree with Salinas that the thirds and especially the fifths of the 1/3-comma temperament are less pleasing than those of the other two. But, in addition to its being capable of quicker tuning than the Zarlinian 2/7-comma method, it has an advantage possessed by neither of the other methods: it is practically a closed or cyclic system. Among its 19 notes there is no fifth containing a wolf; nor are there any discordant thirds. It is an equal temperament of 19 notes.

In recent times the 19-division has had eloquent advocates, to whom reference is made in the chapter on multiple division. Let us see how well the 1/3-comma system is adapted to a 12-note keyboard. As Table 27 shows, this is the poorest tuning of all—like Zarlino's method, it is worse than just intonation. However, too many theorists who have described these two systems have neglected to add that they are excellent for a 19-note octave.

[25]De musica libri VII, p. 143.

Table 27. Salinas' 1/3 - Comma Temperament

Names	C^0	$C\#^{-\frac{7}{3}}$	$D^{-\frac{2}{3}}$	E^{b+1}	$E^{-\frac{4}{3}}$	$F^{+\frac{1}{3}}$	$F\#^{-2}$	$G^{-\frac{1}{3}}$	$G\#^{-\frac{8}{3}}$	A^{-1}	$B^{b+\frac{2}{3}}$	$B^{-\frac{5}{3}}$	C^0
Cents	0	64	190	316	379	505	569	695	758	884	1010	1074	1200

M.D. 30.3; S.D. 30.7

It would help us in portraying an orderly development of the 12-note temperaments if we could show that little by little the temperament of the fifth was reduced from the 1/4 comma of the meantone temperament to the 1/11 comma (1/12 ditonic comma equals 1/11 syntonic comma) of equal temperament. Probably there was such a tendency. But it is only a fortunate accident that Verheijen included the ratio of the fifth for the 1/5-comma temperament, together with the ratios for the three temperaments discussed by Zarlino and Salinas.[26] Verheijen's first ratio for the fifth is the cube root of 10:3 (1/3-comma temperament); then the fourth root of 5:1 (1/4-comma); the fifth root of 15:2 (1/5-comma); the seventh root of 50:3 (2/7-comma). Verheijen's casual reference to the 1/5-comma temperament indicates that even then some people were using it. Rossi, a couple of generations later, also referred briefly to the 1/5-comma temperament, including it as one of the regular types then in use.[27]

The temperament shown in Table 28 has in its favor, like the 1/3-comma temperament, the equal distortion of the fifths and the major thirds, the former being 1/5 comma flat, the latter sharp by the same amount. In it the diatonic semitone is pure.

Table 28. 1/5 - Comma Temperament (Verheijen, Rossi)

Names	C^0	$C\#^{-\frac{7}{5}}$	$D^{-\frac{2}{5}}$	$E^{b+\frac{3}{5}}$	$E^{-\frac{4}{5}}$	$F^{+\frac{1}{5}}$	$F\#^{-\frac{6}{5}}$	$G^{-\frac{1}{5}}$	$G\#^{-\frac{8}{5}}$	$A^{-\frac{3}{5}}$	$B^{b+\frac{2}{5}}$	B^{-1}	C^0
Cents	0	83	195	307	390	502	586	698	781	893	1005	1088	1200

M.D. 14.0; S.D. 14.2

[26]Simon Stevin, Van de Spiegeling der Singconst, Appendice D.
[27]Sistema musico, p. 58.

The deviation of this temperament is only about two-thirds that of the 1/4-comma system.

There is an odd reference to the 1/5-comma temperament. Dechales[28] gave a monochord which he called the "Diatonic scale of Guido of Arezzo." It is, however, a chromatic scale, and, so far as can be ascertained, has nothing in common with any of the ideas expressed by Guido.

It seems evident that Dechales has intended the monochord in Table 29 for the 1/5-comma temperament. Its ninth note differs greatly from the cents value given in the previous table; but the note is A^b in Dechales' monochord and would naturally be more than a comma higher than the G$^\#$ more commonly used. Other divergences can be explained by the fact that Dechales has not expressed his numbers with great accuracy. However, the mean value for his diatonic semitone is 111.4, against 112.0 for the 1/5-comma temperament; for his chromatic semitone, 84.0 cents against 83.2. How he reached the conclusion that Guido favored such a temperament remains a mystery. Actually Dechales himself ascribed the 1/4-comma temperament to Guido (rather than the 1/5-comma), contrary to the evidence of this monochord.

Table 29. Dechales' "Guidonian" Temperament (1/5 - Comma)

Lengths	60	$57\frac{1}{8}$	$53\frac{5}{8}$	$50\frac{1}{10}$	$47\frac{3}{4}$	$44\frac{9}{10}$	$42\frac{3}{4}$	$40\frac{1}{8}$	$37\frac{5}{8}$	$35\frac{3}{16}$	$33\frac{1}{2}$	$31\frac{31}{32}$	30
Names	C	C$^\#$	D	E^b	E	F	F$^\#$	G	A^b	A	B^b	B	C
Cents	0	85	194	312	395	502	587	696	808	893	1009	1090	1200

M.D. 13.3; S.D. 13.8

The 1/5-comma variety of meantone temperament comes close to the 43-division. As such, it is discussed briefly in Chapter VI, with the principal reference to Sauveur.

Another temperament discussed by Rossi[29] has its fifths flattened by 2/9 comma (see Table 30). He merely called it "another tempered system," without ascribing it to any theorist. Romieu identified this temperament with the 31-division, and thus

[28]Cursus seu mundus mathematicus, p. 20.

[29]Sistema musico, p. 64.

Table 30. Rossi's 2/9 - Comma Temperament

Names	C^0	$C^{\#-\frac{14}{9}}$	$D^{-\frac{4}{9}}$	$E^{b+\frac{2}{3}}$	$E^{-\frac{8}{9}}$	$F^{+\frac{2}{9}}$	$F^{\#-\frac{4}{3}}$	$G^{-\frac{2}{9}}$	$G^{\#-\frac{16}{9}}$	$A^{-\frac{2}{3}}$	$B^{b+\frac{4}{9}}$	$B^{-\frac{10}{9}}$	C^0
Cents	0	79	194	308	389	503	582	697	777	892	1006	1085	1200

M.D. 17.0; S.D. 17.2

credited it to Huyghens.[30] Actually, as we have already said, the 1/4-comma temperament comes closest to the 31-division. But perhaps other writers before Romieu confused these temperaments. For example, Printz[31] spoke of a "still earlier" temperament that takes 2/9 comma from each fifth—earlier, perhaps, than Zarlino's 2/7-comma temperament, which he had been previously discussing. He also might have meant Vicentino's 31-division, since there are no early references to the 2/9-comma temperament.

Since 2/9 is the harmonic mean between 1/4 and 1/5, the deviation for this temperament is approximately the mean of the deviations of the other two temperaments. Like Zarlino's 2/7-comma temperament, its third is altered half as much as its fifth, being 1/9 comma sharp. Its augmented second, as F–G#, is pure. The 74-division corresponds to the 2/9-comma temperament, and Drobisch liked this division best of all systems that form their major thirds regularly.

Schneegass gave an interesting geometrical construction for what was much like the common meantone temperament, but more like the 2/9-comma temperament.[32] His contention was that the diatonic semitone contains 3 1/4 "commas" and the chromatic semitone 2 1/4. (These commas of 35.3 cents have nothing in common with either the ditonic [23.5] or the syntonic [21.5] comma). Thus the tone contains 5 1/2 commas, and the octave 5 x 5 1/2 + 2 x 3 1/4 = 34 commas. As is shown in Chapter VI, the 34-division has fifths that are almost 4 cents too large

[30]Jean-Baptiste Romieu, "Mémoire théorique & pratique sur les systèmes tempérés de musique," Mémoires de l'académie royale des sciences, 1758, p. 837.

[31]Phrynis Mytilenaeus oder der satyrische Componist, p. 88.

[32]Cyriac Schneegass, Nova & exquisita monochordi dimensio (Erfurt, 1590), Chapter III.

and thirds that are 2 cents too large. But this was not what Schneegass had in mind. His theoretical fifth had the ratio 160:107, or 696.6 cents, which is precisely the size of the mean-tone fifth, and he directed that this ratio be used twice to form the tone.

Then came the application of the doctrine about commas: A right triangle was to be constructed, with the space of the tone, G–A, as base, and thrice this length for the altitude (see Figure A). Note that "space" here does not refer to the total length of a line, but rather to the distance from one point of division to another   Since 3 1/4:2 1/4 = 13:9, the acute angle at the top was to be divided in the ratio of 13:9, with the larger angle toward A. The point where this line cut the base was to be G$^{\#}$. Now $\tan^{-1}1/3 = 18^{o}\ 26'$, and 13/22 of this angle is $10^{o}\ 53'$. The space between G$^{\#}$ and A, then, would be $3 \tan 10^{o}\ 53' = .57681$ of the space between G and A. From the figures in his table, the division was made with extreme care. The ratio in the table of the space from G$^{\#}$ to A to the space from G to A is 15/26 or .57692. By a series of lines parallel to the base, he cleverly divided the other tones (B^{b}–C, C–D, E^{b}–F, and F–G) into chromatic and diatonic semitones proportional to the division of G–A.

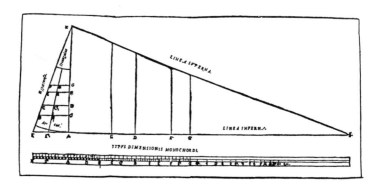

Fig. A. Schneegass' Division of the Monochord
Reproduced by courtesy of the Sibley Library of the Eastman School of Music

To examine the assumption that Schneegass made, let us designate as α the angle 10° 53' and as β the angle 18° 26', and as L the length for the note A. Then the length for $G^{\#}$ was L + tan α, and for G it was L + tan β . His assumption:

$$\log\left(\frac{L + \tan\beta}{L}\right): \log\left(\frac{L + \tan\alpha}{L}\right) = \beta : \alpha$$

In general this would be only a rough approximation. In this case, where $\beta : \alpha$ = 22:13, it works very well indeed.

Schneegass' actual fifth, G–D, of 698.1 cents is a little larger than his theoretical fifth of 696.6, and the mean of all 11 good fifths is 697.2 cents. This last figure is precisely the fifth of the 2/9-comma temperament. The mean value of his tones is 194.0 cents, as compared with 194.4 cents of the 2/9-comma temperament, and his geometrical division of the tones yields semitones of 113.9 and 80.1 cents, compared with 114.0 and 80.4 cents.

Schneegass' actual fifth has approximately the ratio 226:151, instead of his theoretical 160:107. It is idle to speculate why his figures fail to correspond with his theory, or why they agree so beautifully with the 2/9-comma temperament. The significant thing is that they agree so well with themselves, which is an indication of the soundness of his mathematics! There is, however, one puzzling clue to his division of the tone. Suppose the space of the tone G–A had been divided arithmetically in the ratio of 13:9, instead of the more complicated division of the angle actually used. Then Schneegass' $G^{\#}$ would have been at 86.100 instead of at 85.967. This would have made the $G^{\#}$ 3.3 cents lower than in the table, and his tone would have been divided into semitones of 117.7 and 76.0 cents. Now the semitones of the 1/4-comma temperament are of 117.1 and 76.0 cents respectively. Thus an arithmetical division of his tones would have come close to the temperament which is suggested by his theoretical fifth. However, his actual division (Table 31) with a 15:11 ratio, is very consistent with itself, as well as with the 2/9-comma temperament.

Table 31. Schneegass' Variety of Meantone Temperament

Lengths	90.000	85.967	80.467	75.267	71.867	67.267	64.200	60.133
Names	G	G$^\#$	A	B^b	B	C	C$^\#$	D
Cents	0	79	194	309	389	504	585	698

56.300	53.750	50.367	48.083	45.000
E^b	E	F	F$^\#$	G
812	892	1005	1085	1200

M.D. 16.7; S.D. 16.9

Robert Smith[33] is responsible for three wholly unsatisfactory varieties of the meantone temperament. He told first of a Mr. Harrison, who tuned his viol by "taking the interval of the major third to that of the octave, as the diameter of a circle to its circumference....It follows from Mr. Harrison's assumption, that his 3rd major is tempered flat by a full fifth of a comma." If the ratio of the major third to the octave is 1:π , the third will have 382.0 cents, or be 1/5 comma flat, as Smith said. The fifth will then be tempered by 3/10 comma. Romieu[34] barely mentioned 3/10- and 3/11-comma temperaments, but did not discuss them on the ground that they were too like temperaments with unity in the numerator. Except for a few references to Smith and this tuning by π, the 3/10-comma temperament has escaped further notice (see Table 32).

Table 32. Harrison's 3/10 - Comma Temperament

Names	C^0	C$^{\#-\frac{21}{10}}$	D$^{-\frac{3}{5}}$	E$^{b+\frac{9}{10}}$	E$^{-\frac{6}{5}}$	F$^{+\frac{3}{10}}$	F$^{\#-\frac{2}{5}}$	G$^{-\frac{3}{10}}$	G$^{\#-\frac{12}{5}}$	A$^{-\frac{9}{10}}$	B$^{b+\frac{3}{5}}$	B$^{-\frac{3}{2}}$	C^0
Cents	0	69	191	314	382	504	573	696	764	887	1009	1078	1200

M.D. 26.2; S.D. 26.6

Since 3/10 is about the same as 2/7, the deviation for this temperament is approximately the same as for Zarlino's, both

[33]Harmonics, or the Philosophy of Musical Sounds (Cambridge, 1749), pp. xi, xii.

[34]In Mémoires de l'académie royale des sciences, 1758, p. 827.

being inferior to just intonation. It has no special features to recommend it, since its one natural feature, the π ratio, is something to be determined by ear or by logarithms, and would not make the construction of a monochord any simpler.

After referring to Harrison's system, as quoted above, Smith continued, "My third determined by theory, upon the principle of making all the concords within the extent of every three octaves as equally harmonious as possible, is tempered flat by one ninth of a comma; or almost one eighth, when no more concords are taken into the calculation than what are contained within one octave." Later he showed that "to have all the concords in four octaves made equally harmonious," the thirds will be 1/10 comma flat.[35]

With the third flat by 1/9 comma, the fifth will be tempered by 5/18 comma, a quantity impossible to judge by ear. In the second temperament, with the third 1/10 comma flat, the fifth will be 11/40 comma flat. The difference between these values of the fifth is only 1/360 comma. Therefore the temperaments would not vary for any note by as much as one cent. For this reason only the first of Smith's temperaments is shown in Table 33.

Table 33. Smith's 5/18 - Comma Temperament

Names	C^0	$C^{\#-\frac{35}{18}}$	$D^{-\frac{5}{9}}$	$E^{b+\frac{5}{8}}$	$E^{-\frac{10}{9}}$	$F^{+\frac{5}{18}}$	$F^{\#-\frac{5}{3}}$	$G^{-\frac{5}{18}}$	$G^{\#-\frac{20}{9}}$	$A^{-\frac{5}{6}}$	$B^{b+\frac{5}{9}}$	$B^{-\frac{25}{18}}$	C^0
Cents	0	72	192	312	384	504	576	696	768	888	1008	1080	1200

M.D. 23.3; S.D. 23.7

Since 5/18 is also approximately the same as 2/7, Smith's temperament is only a little better than Zarlino's. We have previously indicated that the 50-division has usually been considered the equivalent of the 2/7-comma temperament. Smith asserts, however, that his temperament corresponds to the 50-division, the error of the fifth in the latter being 41/148 comma. He is entirely correct in his claim.

Smith did not suggest, however, that the octave be divided into fifty parts—merely that "a system of rational intervals deduced

---

[35]Smith, Harmonics, p. 171.

from dividing the octave into 50 equal parts,...will differ insensibly from the system of equal harmony." His desire is more modest—to have at least 21 different pitches in the octave, properly to differentiate the sharps, naturals, and flats. On the organ and harpsichord this could be done by adding extra pipes and strings. Performance would be facilitated by having "seven couples of secondary notes," governed by stops, so that the appropriate notes for a particular piece could be chosen. Of course, upon an instrument with 19 notes to the octave (the other two would be of little use), Smith's temperament, like Zarlino's and Salinas', would be far more acceptable than on the ordinary keyboard. Smith himself considered that ordinary equal temperament "far exceeds" both the 31- and 50-divisions, because of the cumbersomeness of the latter systems.

The only other important variety of the meantone temperament was that practiced by Silbermann and his contemporaries. According to Sorge, Silbermann tempered his fifths by 1/6 comma.[36] Since Sorge himself made no distinction between the syntonic and ditonic commas, we might divide either. If we divide the ditonic comma, the deviation is precisely the same as for the Pythagorean tuning, M.D. 11.7, S.D. 11.8. But, for better comparison with the other varieties of meantone temperament, let us divide the syntonic comma. Then the major third is 1/3 comma sharp, and the tritone is pure (see Table 34).

Table 34. Silbermann's 1/6 - Comma Temperament

Names	C^0	C#$^{-\frac{7}{6}}$	D$^{-\frac{1}{3}}$	E$^{b+\frac{1}{2}}$	E$^{-\frac{2}{3}}$	F$^{+\frac{1}{6}}$	F#$^{-1}$	G$^{-\frac{1}{6}}$	G#$^{-\frac{4}{3}}$	A$^{-\frac{1}{2}}$	B$^{b+\frac{1}{3}}$	B$^{-\frac{5}{6}}$	C^0
Cents	0	89	197	305	394	502	590	698	787	895	1003	1092	1200

M.D. 9.3; S.D. 9.5

Romieu[37] adopted the 1/6-comma temperament as his "tempérament anacratique," showing its correspondence to the 55-division. A generation after Romieu, Barca called this tempera-

[36]Georg Andreas Sorge, Gespräch zwischen einem Musico theoretico und einem Studioso musices (Lobenstein, 1748), p. 20.

[37]In Mémoires de l'académie royale des sciences, 1758, pp. 856f.

ment the "temperamento per comune opinione perfettisimo,"[38] and showed that it could be approximated by multiplying both terms of the ratio 81:80 by 6 and then tempering the fifth by the mean ratio 483:482, which gives 241:161 for the tempered fifth. (A better approximation is 220:147.) From additional references to the 55-division in Chapter VI, it would appear that this method of tuning was in use for well over a century. As a system upon which modulations might be made to any key, it was much better than the 1/4-comma meantone system, although inferior to most of the irregular systems discussed in Chapter VII.

Romieu mentioned temperaments of 1/7, 1/8, 1/9, and 1/10 commas, but did not consider them sufficiently important to discuss. The 1/10-comma temperament was included among Marpurg's many temperaments.[39] Otherwise none of these temperaments has been advocated by any of our theorists. They should be presented, however, in order to complete our study of regular temperaments approaching equal temperament (see Tables 35–38). The syntonic comma has been divided in each case.

Table 35. 1/7 - Comma Temperament

Names	C^0	$C^{\#-1}$	$D^{-\frac{2}{7}}$	$Eb^{+\frac{3}{7}}$	$E^{-\frac{4}{7}}$	$F^{+\frac{1}{7}}$	$F^{\#-\frac{6}{7}}$	$G^{-\frac{1}{7}}$	$G^{\#-\frac{8}{7}}$	$A^{-\frac{3}{7}}$	$Bb^{+\frac{2}{7}}$	$B^{-\frac{5}{7}}$	C^0
Cents	0	92	198	303	396	501	593	699	791	897	1002	1095	1200

M.D. 6.3; S.D. 6.4

Table 36. 1/8 - Comma Temperament

Names	C^0	$C^{\#-\frac{7}{8}}$	$D^{-\frac{1}{4}}$	$Eb^{+\frac{3}{8}}$	$E^{-\frac{1}{2}}$	$F^{+\frac{1}{8}}$	$F^{\#-\frac{3}{4}}$	$G^{-\frac{1}{8}}$	$G^{\#-1}$	$A^{-\frac{3}{8}}$	$Bb^{+\frac{1}{4}}$	$B^{-\frac{5}{8}}$	C^0
Cents	0	95	199	302	397	501	596	699	794	898	1001	1097	1200

M.D. 4.0; S.D. 4.1

[38]Alessandro Barca, "Introduzione a una nuova teoria di musica, memoria prima," Accademia di scienze, lettere ed arti in Padova. Saggi scientifici e lettari (Padova, 1786), pp. 365–418.

[39]F. W. Marpurg, Versuch über die musikalische Temperatur (Breslau, 1776), p. 163.

With the exception of some of Marpurg's symmetrical versions of Neidhardt's unequal temperaments, the temperaments shown in Tables 37 and 38 come closer to equal temperament than any divisions that were not practical approximations to it.

Table 37. 1/9 - Comma Temperament

Names	C^o	$C\#^{-\frac{7}{9}}$	$D^{-\frac{2}{9}}$	$Eb^{+\frac{1}{3}}$	$E^{-\frac{4}{9}}$	$F^{+\frac{1}{9}}$	$F\#^{-\frac{2}{3}}$	$G^{-\frac{1}{9}}$	$G\#^{-\frac{8}{9}}$	$A^{-\frac{1}{3}}$	$Bb^{+\frac{2}{9}}$	$B^{-\frac{5}{9}}$	C^o
Cents	0	97	199	301	398	500	598	700	797	899	1001	1098	1200

M.D. 2.3; S.D. 2.4

Table 38. 1/10 – Comma Temperament

Names	C^o	$C\#^{-\frac{7}{10}}$	$D^{-\frac{1}{5}}$	$Eb^{+\frac{3}{10}}$	$E^{-\frac{2}{5}}$	$F^{+\frac{1}{10}}$	$F\#^{-\frac{3}{5}}$	$G^{-\frac{1}{10}}$	$G\#^{-\frac{4}{5}}$	$A^{-\frac{3}{10}}$	$Bb^{+\frac{1}{5}}$	$B^{-\frac{1}{2}}$	C^o
Cents	0	99	200	301	399	500	599	700	798	899	1000	1099	1200

M.D. 1.2; S.D. 1.2

Chapter IV. EQUAL TEMPERAMENT

The first tuning rules that might be interpreted as equal temperament were given by Giovanni Maria Lanfranco.[1] As stated, these rules were for clavichords and organs (<u>Monochordi & Organi</u>), but Lanfranco extended them also to the common stringed instruments of his time. Thus there is none of the confusion that arose later when the keyboard instruments were tuned in one manner, the fretted instruments in another.

Lanfranco's essential rules concern the tempering of the fifths and the thirds: the fifths are to be tuned so flat "that the ear is not well pleased with them," and the thirds as sharp as can be endured. There seems to be a distinction here: for a fifth might be tuned only slightly flat and the ear would not then be wholly pleased with it; but the thirds are to be only a shade less harsh than those which cannot be endured at all.

Most of Lanfranco's contemporaries still knew no tuning but the Pythagorean, with its pure fifths and impossibly sharp thirds. Lanfranco's rules seem to represent a temperament of the Pythagorean tuning, rather than of just intonation. Equal temperament then fits his directions excellently. As further evidence, Lanfranco divided the notes to be tuned into two classes, sharps and flats. As with the meantone temperament, the sharps included $F^{\#}$, $C^{\#}$, and $G^{\#}$, "although most of these are also common to the flat class, if not in tuning, at least in playing." But, although the flats proper included only B^{b} and E^{b}, this class "occasionally needs in playing the black keys $F^{\#}$ (G^{b}) and $C^{\#}$ (D^{b})." As Kinkeldey says, "the enlargement of the major third, the diminution of the minor third, the equivalence of the notes $C^{\#}$ and D^{b}, $F^{\#}$ and G^{b}—these are essential departures from his contemporaries."[2]

Aurelio Marinati[3] honored Lanfranco by inserting in his "ex-

[1]<u>Scintille de musica</u> (Brescia, 1533), p. 132.

[2]Otto Kinkeldey, <u>Orgel und Klavier in der Musik des 16. Jahrhunderts</u>, pp. 77f.

[3]<u>Somma di tutte le scienza</u> (Rome, 1587), pp. 95–98.

ample of the tuning of clavichords and organs" a word-for-word account of Lanfranco's system, complete even to the title—without, however, giving him credit for it. Another plagiarist, Cerone, sufficiently appreciated Lanfranco to copy out his system for the benefit of organ-builders.[4] At the time when these men were writing, the meantone temperament was the recognized tuning norm for keyboard instruments. It is rather surprising that Cerone in particular, who had presented Zarlino's 2/7-comma system in detail, did not seem to realize that there was a conflict between Zarlino's flat and Lanfranco's sharp major thirds.

Lodovico Zacconi[5] was more astute. He presented no tuning rules of his own, saying that it is "better that those who wish to know and to see should look to the source and to the original authors." For keyboard instruments he recommended Aron's meantone temperament. "As for the other instruments, such as the viole da braccio, viole da gamba, violins, and others, you can look at the end of Giovanni Maria Lanfranco's book, which indicates clearly how each one is to be tuned."

In Zacconi's day and long before it, the fretted instruments were said to have equal semitones. To Zarlino, Salinas, and Galilei this meant equal temperament, with all semitones equal. To Grammateus and Bermudo, only ten semitones were equal, the others being smaller; to Artusi, and presumably also to Bottrigari and Cerone, there were ten equal semitones, the other two being larger. But, of these three types of temperament—equal, modified Pythagorean, and modified meantone—only equal temperament had both flat fifths and sharp thirds in addition to equal semitones. Therefore, Zacconi, writing only sixty years after Lanfranco, is practically saying that the latter's rules represent equal temperament. In view of the excellent tuning methods of Lanfranco's immediate predecessors, Grammateus and Schlick, it is very likely that Lanfranco did intend equal temperament for all instruments, including clavichords and organs.

Later writers who gave practical tuning rules for equal temperament were often no more precise than Lanfranco had been.

[4]See Kindeldey, op. cit., p. 80.

[5]Prattica di musica (Venice, 1592), Part I, p. 218.

Jean Denis,[6] for example, said nothing about the size of the thirds. But all the fifths are to be lowered a trifle (d'un poinct), "and all the fifths ought to be tempered equally." Denis may even have had some variety of meantone temperament in mind, for he directed that the tuning should begin with E^b and end with $G^{\#}$. But if his "toutes" means what it says, his was equal temperament.

Godfrey Keller's tuning rules for harpsichord or spinet were widely circulated, having been reprinted in the appendix to William Holder's Treatise . . . of Harmony (London, 1731), and in Part VI of Pierre Prelleur's long popular Modern Musick-Master.[7] Although they can refer to nothing but equal temperament, they are by no means accurate: "Observe all the Sharp Thirds must be as sharp as the Ear will permit; and all Fifths as flat as the Ear will permit. Now and then by way of Tryal touch Unison, Third, Fifth, and Eighth; and afterward Unison, Fourth, and Sixth." It is impossible for the thirds to be very sharp and the fifths simultaneously very flat; for in the 1/5-comma variety of meantone temperament, in which the error of the fifths and the thirds is equal, the error is not large. Keller's rules would read better if he had said that the fifths were to be only slightly flat.

Barthold Fritz[8] gave tuning rules for equal temperament that merited the approval of Emanuel Bach, to whom he had dedicated his little book. Bach said that "in my [Fritz's] few pages everything had been said that was necessary and possible, and that would satisfy far more needs than the sundry computations with which many a man has racked his brains; since the latter method

---

[6]Traité de l'accord de l'espinette (Paris, 1650), pp. 10f.

[7]Keller's book had the title A Compleat Method . . . (London: Richard Meares). The British Museum has a copy dated 1707, but with a different printer. The Library of Congress copy does not contain the tuning rules; its copy of the Prelleur book is the 4th edition, dated 1738. The British Museum has an edition of the latter dated 1731. Part VI was printed separately with the title The Compleat Tutor for the Harpsichord or Spinet, and passed through several editions, with various printers, in the 1750's and '60's.

[8]Anweisung wie man Claviere, Clavicins, und Orgeln, nach einer mechanischen Art, in allen zwölf Tönen gleich rein stimmen könne, . . . (3rd edition; Leipzig, 1780).

of instruction was only for very few people, but mine was for everybody, the computers not excepted, because they depend upon the judgment of the ear as well as the others."[9]

Fritz's rules were very simple. After going from F to A by four tempered fifths, he said, "I now have the already pure F as a major third to this A, and, by touching the A and by testing it with F, can hear whether it sounds sharp enough or so much upwards that the beats are about the rapidity of eighth notes in common time."[10]

Fritz began his tuning in the octave below middle C. From William Braid White's table,[11] the tempered F - A in this octave will beat about 7 times per second, or over 400 times in a minute. Even allowing for the somewhat lower pitch of the eighteenth century, Fritz's eighth notes would be very fast, unless by "common time" he meant alla breve.

Mersenne[12] also gave a practical tuning hint for equal temperament when he said, "Certain people believe that they can find the preceding accord of the equal semitones by beginning ut, re, mi, fa, etc. on each key of the spinet, or by the number of tremblings or beats which the fifth and other tempered consonances make: for example, the fifth beats once in each second when it is tempered as it should be (as much for the organ as for the spinet); whereas when it is just it does not beat at all." From White's table, Mersenne's rule would apply best to the fifth D–A in the octave above middle C, and approximately to other fifths in that vicinity.

Alexander Ellis' practical rules for the formation of equal temperament[13] may be paraphrased as follows: If one tunes by upward fifths and downward fourths within the octave above middle C, each fifth should beat once per second, and each fourth

[9]Ibid., Preface to 2nd edition.

[10]Ibid., p. 14.

[11]Piano Tuning and Allied Arts (4th edition; Boston, 1943), p. 68.

[12]Harmonie universelle (Paris, 1636–37), Nouvelles observations physiques & mathematiques, p. 20.

[13]H. L. F. Helmholtz, Sensations of Tone (2nd English edition, translated by Alexander J. Ellis; London, 1885), pp. 489 f.

three times in two seconds. Ellis stated that if this rule is followed accurately, the error for no pitch will be greater than two cents. Again using White's useful table, we find that the mean value of the beats of the tempered fifths in the C–C octave is 1.02 and of the tempered fourths, 1.47, proving that Ellis' rule is correct.

White himself "lays the bearings" in the F–F octave,[14] just as Fritz did. Since the ratio of a tempered fifth is approximately 3:2, one might suppose that he would advocate beating rates that are 2/3 of Ellis' values: fourths once per second, and fifths twice in three seconds. However, he recommends that the fifths beat three times in five seconds, or 36 times per minute, and suggests setting a metronome at 72, with the bell ringing at every second tick. Since, from his own table, the mean value of the beats of his tempered fifths is .68 rather than .60, he would get better results from setting the metronome at 80.

Bossler's method[15] for achieving equal temperament is reminiscent of Aron's method for the meantone tuning. Aron, it may be remembered, first tuned his major third pure and then tuned equally flat the four fifths that were used in constructing the major third. Bossler first divided the octave by ear into three equal parts—C-E-G#-C. Then he tuned a group of four fifths, as C-G-D-A-E, slightly flat, so that the last would give the sharp major third already found. The method would be continued until the entire octave was tuned. Having these first three notes fixed gave him points of reference, so that he could never go far wrong. But he realized that the human ear is fallible, for he recommended that the tuner buy "steel forks from Frankfurt or Leipzig for all twelve notes."

Geometrical and Mechanical Approximations

One of the famous problems of antiquity was the duplication of the cube. It had been proved that the construction of the cube root of 2 could not be accomplished by Euclidean geometry, that

---

[14]Op. cit., p. 85.

[15]H. P. Bossler, Elementarbuch der Tonkunst (Speier, 1782), pp. xxiv–xxvi.

is, by compass and ruler. This is the precise problem involved in the solution of equal temperament by geometry, if Bossler, for example, had desired to construct a monochord upon which would be located his C-E-G#-C.

The first sixteenth century writer to suggest a geometrical or mechanical means of solving equal temperament was Francisco Salinas.[16] Let him explain his method: "We judge this one thing must be observed by makers of viols, namely, that the octave must be divided into 12 parts equally proportional, which 12 will be the equal semitones. And since they cannot accomplish this by the 9th of the 6th book [the mean proportional construction] or by any other proposition of Euclid, it will be the task to use the instrument which we said was called the mesolabium, invented (as they believe) by Archimedes: by which they will be able to obtain a line divided into as many equal parts as they wish. We have not bothered to append the rule of its construction here, because mention is made of its principle by Vitruvius in his 9th book on architecture; from whom and from his expositors they will be able to obtain the method of constructing it: for it is to practical men for framing most matters not only useful, but wellnigh indispensible."

The mesolabium had been previously advocated by Zarlino for constructing his 2/7-comma meantone temperament, and later Zarlino was to follow Salinas' lead in recommending it for equal temperament. Hutton defined the word as follows: "Mesolabe, or Mesolabium, a mathematical instrument invented by the ancients, for finding two mean proportionals mechanically, which they could not perform geometrically. It consists of three parallelograms, moving in a groove to certain intersections. Its figure is described by Eutocius, in his Commentary on Archimedes. See also Pappius, Lib. 3."[17]

With the aid of a clear diagram (Figure B) James Gow[18] has explained the operation of the mesolabium as follows: "If AB, GH be the two lines between which it is required to find two mean

[16]De musica libri VII, p. 173.

[17]Charles Hutton, Mathematical Dictionary (new ed.; London, 1815).

[18]A Short History of Greek Mathematics (Cambridge, 1884; reprinted, New York, 1923), pp. 245f.

proportionals, then slide the second frame under the first and the third under the second so that AG shall pass through the points C, E, at which the diameters of the second and third frames, respectively, cease to be visible. Then CD, EF are the required two mean proportionals."

Fig. B. The Mesolabium (From James Gow, A Short History of Greek Mathematics [c. 1884])

Although Zarlino contended that the mesolabium might be used for finding any number of means, by increasing the number of parallelograms, his diagram is for two means only. Of course for equal temperament or for the 1/3-comma meantone temperament, two means would suffice. But Salinas also advocates it for an unlimited number of means, and Rossi would find the thirty means for Vicentino's division by its aid. Mersenne,[19] however, in commenting upon Salinas' construction for equal temperament, said it was incorrect if he intended to use the mesolabium for more than two means, because the instrument mentioned by Vitruvius "is of no use except for finding two means between two given lines." We shall not attempt to pass judgment upon these conflicting opinions, but it would seem that the difficulty of the process would be increased greatly with an increasing number of means.

Zarlino[20] has given three methods by which "to divide the octave directly into 12 equal and proportional parts or semitones." The first used the mesolabium, as already mentioned. The second used the method of Philo of Bysantium (second century, B.C.), which consisted of a circle and a variable secant

[19]Harmonie universelle, p. 224.

[20]Gioseffo Zarlino, Sopplimenti musicali (Venice, 1588), Chap. 30.

through a point on its circumference. The third is a variation of the first, in that the string-length for one note is found by the mesolabium, and then the lengths for the other notes are found by similar proportions.

Mersenne,[21] too, has contributed non-Euclidean methods for finding two geometric means. The first, ascribed to Molthée, used straight lines only, in the form of intersecting triangles. The other method (Figure C) was furnished by Roberval and used

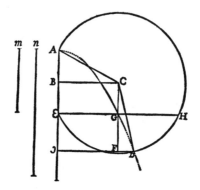

Fig. C. Roberval's Method for Finding
Two Geometric Mean Pro-
portionals (From Mersenne's
Harmonie universelle)
Reproduced by courtesy of
the Library of Congress

a parabola and a circle.[22] Kircher[23] combined the Euclidean method for finding one mean proportional with a mechanical method for finding two means. This latter is by still another method, consisting of two lines at right angles and two sliding

[21]Op. cit., p. 68.

[22]Ibid, p. 408.

[23]Athanasius Kircher, Musurgia universalis (Rome, 1650), I, 207.

52

L -shaped pieces, like carpenters' squares (Figure D). According to Rossi,[24] Kircher's is the method of Nicomedes, and Rossi considered it "more expeditious" than others that have been mentioned. Marpurg[25] ascribed Kircher's method to Plato, and added methods by Hero and by Newton, together with Descartes' method for finding any number of mean proportionals. Thus we have more than half a dozen geometrical and mechanical methods, proposed particularly for constructing a monochord in equal temperament.

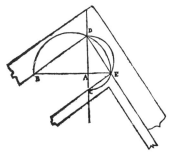

Fig. D. Nicomedes' Method for Finding
Two Geometric Mean Pro-
portionals (From Kircher's
Musurgia universalis)
Reproduced by courtesy of
the Library of Congress

Since these mechanical methods for finding two mean proportionals are rather awkward, the attempt has been made to use a satisfactory ratio for the major third or minor sixth, so that the remainder of the division could be made by the Euclidean construction for finding a single mean. Mersenne[26] has given two such methods. In the second, which he said is "the easiest of all possible ways," the just value of the minor sixth (8:5) is used. By mean proportionals, eight equal semitones are found

[24]Sistema musico, pp. 95f.

[25]Versuch über die musikalische Temperatur, 19. Abschnitt.

[26]Harmonie universelle, p. 69.

between the fundamental and the minor sixth, and then, in like manner, the remaining four semitones between the minor sixth and the octave.

As can be seen from Table 39, this method is not extremely close to correct equal temperament, because the just value of the minor sixth is about 14 cents higher than its value in the equal division. One might have expected the usually astute Mersenne to have chosen a tempered value in the first place. The equally tempered minor sixth is very nearly 100:63, as can be readily seen in Boulliau's table given by Mersenne, where it bears exactly this value. If this fraction is too difficult to work with, 27:17 will serve almost as well, and 19:12 comes rather close also. Any of these other ratios would have given a more satisfactory monochord than his. In Table 40, 19:12 is used for the minor sixth.

Table 39. Mersenne's Second Geometrical Approximation

Names	C	x	D	x	E	F	x	G	x	A	x	B	C
Cents	0	102	203	305	407	508	610	712	814	910	1007	1103	1200

M.D. 2.3; S. D. 2.5

Table 40. Geometrical Approximation (19:12 for Minor Sixth)

Names	C	x	D	x	E	F	x	G
Cents	0	99.5	198.9	298.4	397.8	497.3	596.7	696.2
Names	x	A	x	B	C			
Cents	795.6	896.7	997.8	1098.9	1200.0			

M.D. .76; S.D. .78

But we cannot be supercilious regarding Mersenne's other practical method for obtaining two mean proportionals. Mersenne himself correctly said, "It serves for finding the mechanical duplication of the cube, to about 1/329 part."[27] By the familiar Euclidean method he found the mean proportional between a line and its double, subtracted the original line from the mean,

[27]Ibid., p. 68.

54

and then subtracted this difference from the doubled line. The length thus found was the larger of the desired means—that is, the string-length for the major third. In numbers, this ratio is $(3 - \sqrt{2}) : 2$, or .79289, which represents 401.8 cents. The result is shown in Table 41, the remaining values being found by mean proportionals as in Mersenne's second approximation. This is an extremely fine geometrical way to approximate equal temperament.

Table 41. Mersenne's First Geometrical Approximation

Names	C	x	D	x	E	F	x	G
Cents	0	100.4	200.9	301.3	401.8	501.6	601.3	701.1
Names	x		A		x		B	C
Cents	800.9		900.6		1000.4		1100.2	1200.0

M.D. .30; S.D. .32

Table 42. Hô Tchhêng-thyēn's Approximation

Lengths	900	849	802	758	715	677	638	601	570	536	509.5	479	450
Names	C	C#	D	D#	E	E#	F#	G	G#	A	A#	B	C
Cents	0	101	200	297	398	493	596	699	791	897	985	1091	1200

M.D. 4.8; S.D. 5.8

Numerical Approximations

The earliest numerical approximation for equal temperament comes from China. About 400 A.D., Hô Tchhêng-thyēn gave three monochords for the chromatic octave, with identical ratios, but with the fundamental taken as 9.00, 81.00, and 100.0 respectively.[28] (String-lengths are given for the first of these tables only, since they illustrate the manner of its formation better than the other two.)

Table 42 shows a remarkable temperament for the time when it was constructed, comparable to the brilliant solution of the

[28]Maurice Courant, "Chine et Corée," Encyclopédie de la musique et dictionnaire du conservatoire (Paris, 1913), Part 1, Vol. I, p. 90.

problem of equal temperament by Prince Tsai-yü over a thousand years later. At the time of Tchhêng-thyēn the Pythagorean tuning was the accepted system in China. If we assume the calculation to begin with the higher C at 450 and proceed in strict Pythagorean manner to B$^\#$ in the lower octave, the B$^\#$ will be at 888 instead of 900. This is 12 units too short. Let us, therefore, add 1 unit to 600, the value for G; 2 units to 800, the value for D; 3 units to 533, the value for A; and so forth, along a sequence of fifths, until we reach the correct value for C at 900. Tchhêng-thyēn's figures agree precisely with our hypothesis.

A linear correction, such as Tchhêng-thyēn made, often provides a good approximation, as we shall see elsewhere in this chapter. The difficulty with his correction is that if he had started with the lower C and had continued until he had reached the higher B$^\#$, the latter would have been only 6 units too short instead of 12. By adding 10 parts for A$^\#$, 8 for G$^\#$, etc., he obtained pitches that were much too low. If he had added 12 parts to 444 for the higher B$^\#$, the corrected length, 456, would have been at 1177, instead of 1200 cents, 23 cents flat! Let us consider the effect of adding precisely half the correction for each note. This would work well for the odd semitones, C D E F$^\#$ G$^\#$ A$^\#$ B$^\#$, as might have been expected; but the lower three even semitones, C$^\#$ D$^\#$ E$^\#$, are then as sharp as the higher odd semitones were flat before! We shall have better success if we continue the series of whole tones from G to Fx, the latter at 296 needing a correction of 4.2 to make a perfect octave to G, 600.5. Then the intermediate notes can be given a proportional linear correction, which would be doubled for the three notes C$^\#$ D$^\#$ E$^\#$ when transposed to the lower octave. This improved temperament is shown in Table 43. The greatest error is at C$^\#$.

Table 43. Hô Tchhêng-thyēn's Temperament, Improved

Lengths	900	846.6	801	754.8	713	763	635	600.5
Names	C	x	D	x	E	F	x	G
Cents	0	106	202	305	403	503	604	701
Lengths	566	534.1	504.5	475.7	450			
Names	x	A	x	B	C			
Cents	803	903	1004	1101	1200			

M.D. 2.2; S.D. 2.7

The arithmetical division of the 9:8 tone into 17:16 and 18:17 semitones was known to all sixteenth century writers through Ptolemy's demonstration that Aristoxenus could not have obtained equal semitones in this way. But Cardano (1501–76) may have been referring to some practical use of the 18:17 semitone when he wrote: "And there is another division of the tone into semitones, which is varied by putting the tone between 18 and 16; the middle voice is 17; the major semitone is between 17 and 16, but the minor between 18 and 17, the difference of which is 1/288. It is surprising how the minor semitone should be introduced so pleasingly in concerted music, but the major semitone never."[29]

The simplest way to construct a monochord in equal temperament is to choose a correct ratio for the semitone and then apply it twelve times, a construction that can be performed very easily by similar proportion. Vincenzo Galilei[30] must be given the credit for explaining a practical, but highly effective, method of this type. For placing the frets on the lute he used the ratio 18:17 for the semitone, saying that the twelfth fret would be at the midpoint of the string. He went on to say that no other fraction would serve; for 17:16, etc., would give too few frets, and 19:18, etc., too many. Since 18:17 represents 99 cents, 17:16, 105 cents, and 19:18, 94 cents, Galilei was correct in his contention. But he did not give a mathematical demonstration of his method. It remained

Table 44. Galilei's Approximation

Lengths	100000	94444	89197	84242	79562	75142	70967
Names	C	x	D	x	E	F	x
Cents	0	99	198	297	396	495	594
Lengths	67024	63301	59784	56463	53326	50000	
Names	G	x	A	x	B	C	
Cents	693	792	891	990	1089	1200	

M.D. 1.8; S.D. 3.3

[29]Girolamo Cardano, Opera omnia, ed. Sponius (Lyons, 1663), p. 549.

[30]Dialogo della musica antica e moderna (Florence, 1581), p. 49.

57

for him a proof by intuition. The string-lengths in Table 44 were calculated by Kepler.[31]

Mersenne[32] testified that Galilei's method was favored by "many makers of instruments." The Portugese writer Domingos de S. Jose Varella[33] gave a "way to divide the fingerboards of viols and guitars." This is precisely Galilei's method, and Varella told how the construction could be continued by similar proportion after the first 18:17 semitone had been formed. Likewise Delezenne[34] showed that 18:17 is very near the value for the correct equal semitone, and gave a geometrical construction for it used by Delannoy, the instrument maker, in placing the frets upon his guitars.

Two other early nineteenth century references to what Garnault[35] called the "secret compass" of the makers of fretted instruments were given in his tiny and not very trustworthy monograph on temperament. The first was from the Robet-Maugin Manuel du Luthier (1834), which stated that if the string is 2 feet in length, the first semitone will be at a distance of 16 lines from the end; this represents $16/2 \times 12 \times 12 = 1/18$ the length of the string, thus giving 18:17 for the ratio of each semitone.

Garnault's second reference was to the Bernard Romberg 'cello method (1839),[36] which he said had been adopted by Cherubini for use in the Paris Conservatoire. Romberg's directions

[31]Johannes Kepler, Harmonices mundi (Augsburg, 1619; edited by Ch. Frisch, Frankfort am Main, 1864), p. 164.

[32]Harmonie universelle, p. 48.

[33]Compendio de musica (Porto, 1806), p. 51.

[34]C. E. J. Delezenne, "Mémoire sur les valeurs numériques des notes de la gamme," Recueil des travaux de la société des sciences,...de Lille, 1826-27 p. 49, note (a), and p. 50.

[35]Paul Garnault, Le tempérament, son histoire, son application aux claviers, aux violes de gambe et guitares, son influence sur la musique du xviiie siècle (Nice, 1929), pp. 29 ff.

[36]In the German translation (original?), Violoncell Schull (Berlin, 1840 [?]), the directions are given on page 17; in the English translation, A Complete Theoretical and Practical School for the Violoncello, they are omitted.

were much the same as those given previously. Although Garnault does not mention this, Romberg added that the directions given were for equal temperament, but the more advanced player would often make the sharped notes sharper and the flatted notes flatter than these pitches—another confirmation of the quasi-Pythagorean tuning of instruments of the violin family.

These references to the 18:17 semitone cover two and a half centuries. It is probable that they could be brought much nearer our own times if the makers of fretted instruments were given a chance to express themselves. We must accept Galilei's method, therefore, as representing the contemporary practice. A player on a lute was not going to bother with the mesolabium or with a monochord on which were numbers representing the successive powers of the 12th root of 2. But he could place his frets by a simple numerical ratio such as 18:17, and we are glad that the frets thus placed served their purpose so well.

Critics of Galilei were not slow to show that the 12th fret would not coincide precisely with the midpoint of the string. Passing by the inconveniently large numbers of Zarlino's ratios, we come to Kepler's result: if the entire string is 100,000 units in length, Galilei's 12th fret will be at 50,363 instead of 50,000. As we have already stated, his semitone has only 99 cents, so that the octave contains 1188 instead of 1200.

There are various ways of correcting the octave distortion arising from the use of the 18:17 semitone. An obvious way is suggested by Mersenne's approximations: form only 4 semitones with the 18:17 ratio; then apply Mersenne's mean-proportional method to the remaining 8 semitones. The monochord thus constructed (Table 45) is as good as Mersenne's first method.

Table 45. Approximation à la Galilei and Mersenne

Names	C	x	D	x	E	F	x	G
Cents	0	99	198	297	396	496.5	597	697.5
Names	x	A	x	B	C			
Cents	798	898.5	999	1099.5	1200			

M.D. .67; S.D. .71

59

An even simpler correction uses linear divisions only: since the length for the 12th fret is 363 units too great, divide 363 into 12 equal parts and subtract 30 units for the first fret, 61 for the second, 91 for the third, etc. As is always the case with this type of correction, there is a slight bulge in the middle of the octave, but the largest error is only 1.8 cents.

The correction shown in Table 46 lends itself well to numerical computation, since the fundamental and its octave are in round numbers. But in practice, with a geometrical, not a numerical, construction, the following would be simpler and is even a trifle better: if 50,363 be considered the real middle of the string, the octave will be perfect. To make it the middle, shorten the entire string by twice the difference between 50,000 and 50,363, that is, by 726. Then every one of the lengths as given by Kepler will be diminished by 726, and the 12th fret, 49,637, will be the exact middle of the string, 99,274. Note again the slight bulge in the middle of the division (Table 47), with the greatest distortion 1.0 cent.

Table 46. Galilei's Temperament, with Linear Correction, No. 1

Lengths	100000	94414	89136	84151	79441	74991	70785
Names	C	x	D	x	E	F˙	x
Cents	0	99.5	199.1	298.8	398.5	498.3	598.2
Lengths	66812	63059	59512	56160	52993	50000	
Names	G	x	A	x	B	C	
Cents	698.3	798.4	898.5	998.9	1099.4	1200	

M.D. .26; S.D. .31

Table 47. Galilei's Temperament, with Linear Correction, No. 2

Lengths	100000	99274	88471	83516	78836	74416	70241
Names	C	x	D	x	E	F	x
Cents	0	99.7	199.4	299.3	399.1	499.0	599.0
Lengths	66298	62575	59058	55737	52600	49637	
Names	G	x	A	x	B	C	
Cents	699.0	799.0	899.2	999.3	1099.7	1200	

M.D. .17; S.D. .21

The improvements upon Galilei's tuning shown in Tables 46 and 47 could have been made by practical tuners. They are better divisions than many of the numerical expressions of equal temperament which will be shown later. They are better also than the temperament our contemporary tuners give our own pianos and organs. So there is nothing more that needs to be said, as far as practice is concerned. There are, however, several other and more subtle ways of improving Galilei's tuning which we should like to mention. These are of speculative interest solely.

Let us return to the false octave generated by the 18:17 semitone. Mersenne suggested that "if the makers should increase slightly each 18:17 interval, they would arrive at the justness of the octave." The 11th fret is at 53326, leaving a ratio of 53326: 50000 for the remaining semitone. This, as its cents value indicates (111 cents), is about the size of the just 16:15 semitone. Let us pretend that the final digit in the antecedent is 5, and reduce the ratio to 2133:2000. Now let us average this semitone with the eleven 18:17 semitones, using the arithmetical division generally followed by sixteenth century writers. Our desired semitone is $\frac{2000/2133 + 187/18}{12} = \frac{48319}{51192}$. In decimal form this is .9438779, as compared with the true equal semitone, .9438743. The successive powers of this decimal would deviate more and more from those of the 12th root of 2, but even then the octave would be only .1 cent flat.

Another way of correcting Galilei's tuning is based upon the fact that his octave would be 12 cents, that is, half a Pythagorean comma, flat. A somewhat crude, but practical, manner of adjusting the octave would be to form four 18:17 semitones, from C to E, then take the next five notes, F through A, as perfect fourths to the first five, and then the two remaining notes, B^b and B, as perfect fourths to F and $F^{\#}$. A satisfactory monochord is shown in Table 48. Note particularly how much smaller its standard deviation is than that of Galilei's actual tuning.

As an approach to a finer division using Pythagorean intervals, let us turn to Pablo Nassarre.[37]

[37]Escuela musica (Zaragoza, 1724), Part I, pp. 462 f.

Table 48. Galilei's Temperament Combined with Pythagorean

Names	C	x	D	x	E	F	x	G
Cents	0	99	198	297	396	498	597	696
Names	x	A	x	B	C			
Cents	795	894	996	1095	1200			

M.D. 1.5; S.D. 1.6

He had discussed equal semitones upon fretted instruments, using much the same language as Praetorius,[38] to the effect that a 16:15 diatonic semitone contains 5 commas and a 25:24 chromatic semitone 4 commas, but that these semitones have the peculiarity that they are all equal, containing 4 1/2 commas. They are obtained by a linear division of the 9:8 tone into 18:17 and 17:16 semitones. To place the frets, three or four 9:8 tones are constructed, and the distance between each pair of frets divided equally to form the semitones. Of course an arithmetical division of tones will not form precisely equal semitones. Furthermore, there is a fairly large distortion for the last semitone if the process is carried out through twelve semitones. Of course, as with Galilei's method, no single string would have had twelve frets. In Table 49 the division is made for the entire octave. The length for B was taken as the arithmetical mean between A$^\#$ and the middle of the string.

Table 49. Nassarre's Equal Semitones

Names	C^o	x	D^o	x	E^o	(F)	F$^{\#o}$	(G)
Cents	0	99	204	303	408	507	612	711
Names	G$^{\#o}$	(A)	A$^{\#o}$	(B)	C^o			
Cents	816	915	1020	1107	1200			

M.D. 4.2; S.D. 5.4

If Nassarre had divided each 9:8 tone into precisely equal semitones by a mean proportional, his errors would have been smaller.

[38]Syntagma musicum, Vol. 2, p. 66.

Table 50. Nassarre's Temperament Idealized

Lengths	100000	94281	88889	83805	79012	74494	70233
Names	C⁰	x	D⁰	x	E⁰	(F)	F#⁰
Cents	0	102	204	306	408	510	612

Lengths	66216	62429	58859	55493	52319	50000
Names	(G)	G#⁰	(A)	A#⁰	(B)	C⁰
Cents	714	816	918	1020	1110	1200

M.D. 3.7; S.D. 6.7

It is not particularly difficult to set down this temperament in figures, since the square root need be performed only for $C^\#$, after which a second series of 9:8 tones can be formed, starting with this note. If B is taken as the geometric mean between $A^\#$ and C, its length is 52675, or 1110 cents, making the mean deviation 3.3, and the standard deviation 4.5. However, for the sake of an approximation to be made in Table 50, B is taken as the geometric mean between $A^\#$ and $B^\#$, with a relatively high standard deviation.

If we now compare the cents values of the temperament shown in Table 50 with those of Galilei's tuning, we shall find that the error of the former is opposite to and twice as great as that of the latter. Therefore, for every pair of string-lengths, subtract the smaller (Nassarre) from the larger (Galilei), and then subtract 1/3 the difference from the larger number. The excellent monochord shown in Table 51 results.

Table 51. Temperament à la Galilei and Nassarre

Lengths	100000	94390	89094	84096	79379	74926	70722
Names	C	x	D	x	E	F	x
Cents	0	99.9	199.9	299.9	399.8	499.8	599.7

Lengths	66755	63010	59476	56140	52990	50000
Names	G	x	A	x	B	C
Cents	699.7	799.7	899.6	999.6	1099.6	1200

M.D. .07; S.D. .13

If the idealized Nassarre temperament had been extended one more semitone, the string-length for the octave would have been 49,328. When this number is adjusted with the 50,363 of Galilei's tuning, the octave proper to the above temperament becomes 50,018 or 1199.5 cents. Let us now make the same type of octave adjustment as with the original Galilei tuning, by subtracting 18 from the 12th semitone, and 1 or 2 less for each succeeding semitone. Then no length varies by more than 2 or 3 units from the correct value, that is, the maximum variation is less than .1 cent.

This procedure sounds somewhat complicated. It is not necessary to go through the entire process three times, as shown above, in order to obtain the final monochord. The ratio for the semitone will be $\dfrac{17/9 + 2\sqrt{2}/3}{3} = \dfrac{17 + 6\sqrt{2}}{27}$. Including the octave correction, the formula for the string-length of the nth semitone is: $100{,}000 \left(\dfrac{17 + 6\sqrt{2}}{27}\right) - \dfrac{3(n-1)}{2}$. Perhaps it would be simpler after all to stick to cube roots, especially when fortified with a table of logarithms!

Johann Philipp Kirnberger,[39] however, used a very roundabout method of attaining equal temperament, believing it to be simpler in practice than tuning by beating fifths. He showed that the ratio 10935:8192 closely approaches the value of the fourth used in equal temperament. In practice this value would be obtained by tuning upward seven pure fifths and then a major third. In other words, if C^0 is the lower note, $E^{\#-1}$ is regarded to be the equivalent of F^{+1}, the tempered fourth. The basis for this equivalence lies in the fact that the schisma, the difference between the syntonic and the ditonic commas, is almost exactly 1/12 ditonic comma, the amount by which the fourth must be tempered. The ratio given above becomes, in decimal form, .7491541 . . ., whereas the true tempered value is .7491535 . . . . The result is an extremely close approximation.

---

[39]Die Kunst des reinen Satzes in der Musik, 2nd part (Berlin, 1779), 3rd Division, pp. 179 f.

Kirnberger spoke of Euler's approval of his method, and of Sulzer's and Lambert's publication of it. Marpurg[40] showed that Lambert's method, when applied to an entire octave, will differ for no note by more than .00001. He praised it as a method that needs no monochord, and believed that the tuning of the just intervals used in it could be made more quickly and accurately than the estimation by ear of the tempering needed for the fourth or the fifth. However, the tuning of a pure major third is so difficult that Alexander Ellis thought that better thirds can be obtained from four beating fifths than by tuning the thirds directly. If this be true, a type of tuning in which the essential feature is a pure major third could not be very accurate, without considering the labor of tuning eight pure intervals in order to have only one tempered interval!

Kirnberger's approximation for equal temperament was next heard of in England, where John Farey[41] seems to have discovered it independently. In Dr. Rees's New Cyclopedia[42] we are shown how Farey's method "differs only in an insensible degree" from correct equal temperament.

Among the monochords shown by Marpurg is one by Daniel P. Strähle,[43] allegedly in equal temperament, but actually unequal, as can be seen in Table 52. This is a geometric construction of a curious sort, for which Jacob Faggot computed the string-lengths by trigonometry (see Figure E). In brief, it went like this: upon the line QR, 12 units in length, erect an isosceles triangle, QOR, its equal legs being 24 units in length. Join O to the eleven points of division in the base. On QO locate P, 7 units from Q, and draw RP, extending it its own length to M. Then if RM represents the fundamental pitch and PM its octave, the

[40]Versuch über die musikalische Temperatur, p. 148.

[41]"On a New Mode of Equally Tempering the Musical Scale," Philosophical Magazine, XXVII (1807), pp. 65–66.

[42]1st American edition, Vol. 14, Part 1, article on Equal Temperament.

[43]"Nytt påfund, til at finna temperaturen, i stämningen för thonerne på claveretock dylika instrumenter," Proceedings of the Swedish Academy, IV (1743), 281–291.. The second part of the article, "Trigonometrisk uträkning," appears under Faggot's name.

points of intersection of RP with the 11 rays from O will be the 11 semitones within the octave.

Table 52. Faggot's Figures for Strähle's Temperament

Lengths	10000	9379	8811	8290	7809	7365	6953
Names	C	x	D	x	E	F	x
Cents	0	111	219	325	428	529	629
Lengths	6570	6213	5881	5568	5274	5000	
Names	G	x	A	x	B	C	
Cents	727	824	919	1014	1108	1200	

M.D. 4.8; S.D. 5.7

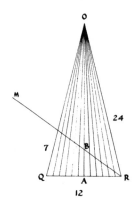

Fig. E. Strähle's Geometrical Approximation for Equal Temperament
Reproduced by courtesy of the Library of the University of Michigan

It is obvious from the construction that the distance between two consecutive points of division will be greater near R than near P, and hence that, superficially at least, the division will resemble a series of proportional lines, as in true equal tem-
66

perament. But, as Table 52 shows, there is a large bulge in the middle of the octave, and $F^{\#}$, which should be $5000\sqrt{2} = 7071$, is distorted very greatly. Now, if QR is given, the points of division are functions of QO (or RO), but they are also functions of QP. It is primarily the size of the angle QRP that determines the ratios of the string-lengths. Strähle's choice of 7 units for QP was unfortunate, or the distortion would not have been so great.

To reduce the errors in this construction, let us attempt to find a value for the angle QRP for which the length for $F^{\#}$ is correct, $\dfrac{\sqrt{2}RM}{2}$. Let A be the midpoint of QR and B the point where OA cuts RM; so that BM is the length for $F^{\#}$. Then

1. $RB = \sqrt{2}BP = \dfrac{\sqrt{2}RP}{1+\sqrt{2}}$

2. $OQR = \cos^{-1} 1/4 = 75^{O}\ 31'$.

By the sine law and from 1. and 2.,

3. $\dfrac{\sin RPQ}{\sin PQR} = \dfrac{12}{RP}$, or $\dfrac{\sin RPQ}{\sqrt{15}/4} = \dfrac{12}{RB\left(\dfrac{1 + \sqrt{2}}{\sqrt{2}}\right)}$

4. $\cos QRP = 6/RB$.

From 3. and 4.,

5. $\sin RPQ = \dfrac{\sqrt{30}\ \cos QRP}{2(1+\sqrt{2})} = 1.1344\ \cos QRP$

From 2.,

6. $QRP + RPQ = 104^{O}\ 29'$.

As an approximate solution to 5. and 6.,

7. $QRP = 33^{O}\ 36'$ and $RPQ = 70^{O}\ 53'$.

From 7., PQ = 7.028. But this is almost exactly Strähle's figure! A check reveals that Faggot made a serious error in computing the angles QRP and RPQ; so that his value for PQ was actually 8.605 rather than 7. Table 53 gives the correct figures for Strähle's temperament.

67

Table 53. Correct Figures for Strähle's Temperament

Lengths	100000	9432	8899	8400	7931	7490	7073
Names	C	x	D	x	E	F	x
Cents	0	101	202	302	401	500	600
Lengths	6676	6308	5955	5621	5303	5000	
Names	G	x	A	x	B	C	
Cents	699	798	897	997	1098	1200	

M.D. .83; S.D. 1.00

It is, therefore, possible to achieve superfine results by following a method essentially the same as Strähle's. Although unaware of the possibilities in Strähle's method, Marpurg has collected many unusual and interesting temperaments by other men.[44] He presented two monochords by Schröter, both of which are excellent approximations to equal temperament constructed from tabular differences. In the first (Table 54), Schröter anchored his column of differences upon the notes of the just minor triad, as C E^b G C, with ratio 6:5:4:3. The intermediate notes were obtained by arithmetical divisions. This column of differences is worth showing as a monochord in its own right, for the method of construction resembles that of Ganassi and Reinhard. The mean deviation is about the same as for the Pythagorean tuning, but the standard deviation is larger because the semitone B–C, with ratio 28:27, is much smaller than the others.

Table 54. Schröter's Column of Differences, No. 1

Lengths	54	51	48	45	42	40	38	36
Names	C	x	D	x	E	F	x	G
Cents	0	99	204	317	435	520	608	702
Lengths	34	32	30	28	27			
Names	x	A	x	B	C			
Cents	804	906	1018	1137	1200			

M.D. 11.9; S.D. 15.3

[44]Versuch über die musikalische Temperatur, pp. 179 ff.

In Schröter's monochord proper (Table 55) the upper fundamental (451) is the sum of all the differences in the above table, save the first number to the left (54). Thus the lower fundamental (902) will be a true octave. This monochord is a highly satisfactory approximation to equal temperament.

Table 55. Schröter's Approximation, No. 1

Lengths	902	851	803	758	716	676	638
Names	C	x	D	x	E	F	x
Cents	0	100.7	201.3	301.1	399.9	499.3	599.7
Lengths	602	568	536	506	478	451	
Names	G	x	A	x	B	C	
Cents	700.0	800.7	901.1	1000.8	1099.4	1200	

M.D. .52; S.D. .59

Schröter's column of differences for the second approximation (Table 56), while also containing arithmetical divisions, is constructed more carefully than the first. The minor thirds D–F and A–C have the unusual ratio 19:16 or 297 cents. All the notes in the tetrachord G–C are pure fifths above the notes in the tetrachord C–F. Here the deviation is about the same as in Grammateus' tuning, thus ranking among the best of the irregular systems.[45]

Table 56. Schröter's Column of Differences, No. 2

Lengths	384	363	342	324	306	288	272	256	242
Names	C	x	D	x	E	F	x	G	x
Cents	0	97	201	294	393	496	597	702	799
Lengths	228	216	204	192					
Names	A	x	B	C					
Cents	903	996	1095	1200					

M.D. 3.8; S.D. 4.3

[45]For Grammateus see the second part of Chapter VII.

69

Schröter's second approximation (Table 57) is constructed from the above column of differences in the same manner as was his first. Its deviations, like those of the column of differences upon which it was based, are about 1/3 as large as those of the first monochord.

Table 57. Schröter's Approximation, No. 2

Lengths	6850	6466	6103	5761	5437	5131	4843
Names	C	x	D	x	E	F	x
Cents	0	99.9	199.9	299.7	400.0	500.2	600.3
Lengths	4571	4315	4073	3845	3629	3425	
Names	G	x	A	x	B	C	
Cents	700.3	800.1	900.0	999.7	1099.9	1200	

M.D. .15; S.D. .18

Schröter's success in building up a monochord by using well-chosen tabular differences suggests that the same method be applied to Ganassi's tuning, which is rather similar to his first column of differences.[46] The sum of the twelve numbers of Ganassi's monochord is 805, which is chosen, therefore, for the higher fundamental. As might have been expected, the monochord (Table 58) is very good.

Table 58. Approximation Based on Ganassi's Monochord

Lengths	1610	1520	1435	1355	1279	1207	1139
Names	C	x	D	x	E	F	x
Cents	0	99.6	199.3	298 6	398.5	498.8	599.2
Lengths	1075	1015	958	904	853	805	
Names	G	x	A	x	B	C	
Cents	699.3	798.8	898.8	999.3	1099.9	1200	

M.D. .42; S.D. .51

[46]See Chapter VII for Ganassi's tuning.

70

Table 59. Monochord from Difference Column, No. 1

Lengths	24	23	22	21	20	19	18	17	16
Names	C	x	D	x	E	F	x	G	x
Cents	0	74	151	232	316	405	498	597	702
Lengths	15	14	13	12					
Names	A	x	B	C					
Cents	815	933	1062	1200					

M.D. 18.2; S.D. 19.7

These rather amusing improvements in poor or fair tuning systems suggest that the method be really put to the test by choosing for the original monochord an entirely unsatisfactory tuning. Accordingly, the thirteen numbers from 12 through 24 were chosen (Table 59). This is so perverted a tuning system that the major third (E), the fourth (F), and the fifth (G) are precisely a semitone flat according to just intonation. However, a benighted anonymous writer in the Mercure de France in 1771 declared that if the entire string were divided into 24 parts, the numbers 12 through 24 would give all the semitones.[47] Thanks to the regularity of its construction, the deviation of this system ranks it somewhere near the meantone tuning!

In the next monochord (Table 60) the deviation is of the same class as that of Galilei's tuning. Its higher fundamental, 210, is the sum of the numbers 12 to 23 inclusive.

Table 60. Monochord from Difference Column, No. 2

Lengths	420	397	375	354	334	315	297
Names	C	x	D	x	E	F	x
Cents	0	97.5	196.2	296.0	397.7	498.1	599.9
Lengths	280	264	249	235	222	210	
Names	G	x	A	x	B	C	
Cents	702.0	803.9	905.2	1005.4	1103 9	1200	

M.D. 1.6; S.D. 1.9

[47]Lionel de La Laurencie, Le violon de Lully à Viotti (Paris, 1924), Tome III, p. 74.

For our third monochord (Table 61) we use the lengths of Table 60 as differences. Here the deviation is about the same as in Schröter's second approximation.

In the fourth and last approximation (Table 62) the errors have become too small to be recorded correctly when five-place logarithms are used. Apparently, however, the deviation is again about 1/10 that of the previous monochord.

Table 61. Monochord from Difference Column, No. 3

Lengths	7064	6667	6292	5938	5614	5289	4992
Names	C	x	D	x	E	F	x
Cents	0	100.1	200.2	300.6	400.9	501.0	601.1
Lengths	4712	4448	4199	3964	3742	3532	
Names	G	x	A	x	B	C	
Cents	701.0	800.9	900.6	1000.3	1100.1	1200	

M.D. .18; S. D. .21

Table 62. Monochord from Difference Column, No. 4.

Lengths	118758	112091	105799	99861	94257	88968	83976
Names	C	x	D	x	E	F	x
Cents	0	100	200	300	400	500	600
Lengths	79264	74816	70617	66653	62911	59379	
Names	G	x	A	x	B	C	
Cents	700	800	900	1000	1100	1200	

Objection may be made to Schröter's approximations, and to ours as well, on the ground that the fundamentals are not round numbers such as most of the theorists used for the representation of equal temperament. Let us see whether we can supply this lack. In our third monochord (Table 61) the length for F# is 4992. Let this be our higher fundamental. Add 8 to it, and 16 to its double, the lower fundamental. We could then make an arithmetical division to correct the intermediate numbers. It is little more trouble, however, to take the two left-hand digits of the numbers in this same monochord, starting with the value for

72

B^b, 40. Multiply these and those for B, 37, by .4, as 16.0, 14.8, and all the pairs of digits to the left of B^b by .2. Add these numbers to the appropriate numbers in Monochord No. 3, and we have a corrected monochord, in which the maximum error is 4 units, or about 1 cent (see Table 63). Deviation is as in the original Monochord No. 3 (Table 61).

Table 63. Monochord No. 3, Adjusted

Lengths	10000	9439	8910	8411	7940	7496	7075
Names	C	x	D	x	E	F	x
Lengths	6678	6302	5947	5613	5297	5000	
Names	G	x	A	x	B	C	

Fortunately, it is possible to make a similar adjustment of our five-digit monochord, No. 4 (Table 62). Here we shall take as our lower fundamental the length for E^b, 99861. We need 139 to make a round number. This is about twice the length for G in Monochord No. 2. So we divide the numbers in the second monochord by 2 or by 4, and add to the appropriate numbers in Monochord No. 4. The maximum error is 6 units, or about 1/6 cent.

A very useful approximation for equal temperament is to express all its irrational ratios as comparatively small fractions. Alexander Ellis[48] has made a table of about 150 intervals within the octave, which he has represented by logarithms, cents, and ratios, actual or approximate. Since all the intervals of equal temperament are contained in this table, it is easy to list them separately, as in Table 65.

Table 64. Monochord No. 4, Adjusted

Lengths	100,000	94,388	89,092	84,093	79,375	74,921	70,716
Names	C	x	D	x	E	F	x
Lengths	66,747	62,999	59,462	56,124	52,974	50,000	
Names	G	x	A	x	B	C	

[48]H. L. F. Helmholtz, Sensations of Tone, pp. 453–456.

Table 65. Ellis' Fractional Approximations

Ratios	1	89:84	449:400	44:37	63:50	303:227	140:99	433:289
Names	C	x	D	x	E	F	x	G
Ratios	100:63	37:22	98:55	168:89	2			
Names	x	A	x	B	C			

Charles Williamson[49] has given the material in Table 65, wrongly ascribing it to Helmholtz rather than to Ellis. By continued fractions he himself found that the majority of Ellis' ratios were correct. He objected to the ratio for the major second (449:400), stating that this interval can be represented more accurately as the inversion of a minor seventh. The ratios for the fourth (303:227) and fifth (433:289) he thought were not sufficiently close either, and should likewise be paired. Ellis' ratio for the tritone (140:99) was good, but Williamson preferred to use the ratio for its inversion (99:70), which is no better.

Williamson remarked that his ratio for the tone (55:49) occurs in Cahill's patent for the Telharmonium, and for the tritone (99:70) in Laurens Hammond's patent for the Hammond Electric Organ. He had not previously run across 295:221 or 442:295. It is interesting to note that here, as in many other instances, Pere Mersenne[50] has anticipated the modern students of temperament. Mersenne stated that the minor third of equal temperament is approximately $6/5 \times 112/113 = 672/565$. Convergents to this ratio are 44:37 and 157:132, the first of these occurring in both tables above. Mersenne's ratio for the major third was $5/4 \times 127/126 = 635/504$, convergents to which are 63:50 (as above) and 286:227. For the perfect fifth he gave the ratio $32 \times 886/887 = 1329/887$, the convergent to which is 442:295, used by Williamson.

Williamson's reference to Hammond's patent[51] suggests that the latter's ratios be examined in their entirety. (It must be remembered that these ratios are based on the practical con-

[49] "Frequency Ratios of the Tempered Scale," Journal of the Acoustical Society of America, X (1938), 135.

[50] Harmonie universelle, Nouvelles observations physiques & mathematiques, p. 19.

[51] L. Hammond's Patent, 1,956,350, April 24, 1934, Sheet 18.

sideration of cutting teeth on gears.) The difficulty is that, although it is easy enough to reduce Hammond's frequencies to ratios with no more than two digits in numerator and denominator, no one note appears as unity. (The ratios times 320 are the frequencies from middle C to its octave.) We cannot well compare this with Table 65. If either F or A, which have the simplest ratios in Table 66, is given the value of 1, more than half of the ratios will have three digits. Hence the composite table, Table 67, with decimal equivalents, gives a better idea of how the three systems compare.

Table 66. Hammond's Fractional Approximations

Ratios	85:104	71:82	67:73	35:36	69:67	12:11	37:32
Names	C	x	D	x	E	F	x
Ratios	49:40	48:37	11:8	67:46	54:35	85.52	
Names	G	x	A	x	B	C	

Table 67. Comparison of Three Approximations

	Ellis	Williamson	Hammond	Equal Temperament
C	200000	200000	200000	200000
B	188652	188652	188697	188775
x	178182	178182	178182	178180
A	168182	168182	168182	168179
x	158730	158730	158677	158740
G	149827	149831	149796	149831
x	141414	141429	141414	141421
F	133480	133484	133499	133484
E	126000	126000	125942	125992
x	118919	118919	118881	118921
D	112250	112245	112207	112246
x	105952	105952	105928	105946
C	100000	100000	100000	100000

Hammond has utilized some of the same ratios as Ellis and Williamson. His tone G–A is 55:49; his minor thirds F–A^b and F$^#$–A are 44:37; his major third E^b–G is 63:50; his tritones E^b–A and F–B are 99:70. He had another major third (B^b–D) with small ratio, 73:46, but this is a poorer approximation than 63:50. Note that many of Hammond's ratios are related in pairs, but not in the same way as Williamson's. The product of the ratios for $F^\#$ and $G^\#$, F and A, E and B^b, and B and $D^\#$ is equal to 3:2. C and D are not so related. Of course the axis G is approximately the square root of 3:2, and $C^\#$, the other axis, the square root of 3:4.

Let us compare these three approximations with the true values for equal temperament to six places (see Table 67). For Ellis and Williamson these are the decimal equivalents of the fractions as given. For Hammond the note A was taken as the fundamental, and his frequencies as given in the patent have been divided by 1.1.

In our absorption with quasi-equal temperaments that excel many presumably correct versions, we should not neglect the pioneers who first set down in figures the monochords constructed upon the 12th root of 2. The first European known to have formed such a monochord is Simon Stevin,[52] about 1596, who said that since there are twelve proportional semitones in the octave, the problem is to "find 11 mean proportional parts between 2 and 1, which can be learned through the 45th proposition of my French arithmetic." There he had explained that mean proportionals can be found by extracting roots of the product of the extremes. He now applied this principle, by representing each semitone as the 12th root of some power of 2 (see Table 68).

Table 68. Stevin's Monochord, No. 1

Lengths	10000	9440	8911	8408	7937	7493	7071
Names	C	x	D	x	E	F	x
Cents	0	99.7	199.6	300.2	400.0	499.6	600.0
Lengths	6675	6301	5945	5612	5298	5000	
Names	G	x	A	x	B	C	
Cents	699.8	799.6	900.3	1000.1	1099.7	1200	

[52]Van de Spiegeling der Singconst, pp. 26 ff.

In his actual calculations Stevin first computed notes 7, 4, and 5, that is, $F^{\#}$, E^b, and E. These involve no more difficult roots than cubic and quartic. There is now sufficient material to compute the remaining notes by proportion, "the rule of three." Thus the fifth note (7937), divided by the fourth (8408), gives the second (5440). This method is much easier than to extract the roots for each individual note, which runs into difficulties with the roots of prime powers, as for notes 2, 6, 8, and 12 ($C^{\#}$, F, G, B), where the 12th root itself must be extracted. But the method by proportion lacks in accuracy, for an error for any note is magnified in succeeding notes. Even so, the maximum error is only .4 cent. The deviation for Stevin's monochord lies between those for Schröter's two monochords.

Stevin has worked out a second monochord for equal temperament upon the same principle as the first, but with a different order of notes.[53] Here the maximum error, for E, is 1 cent. The fact that the two monochords do differ indicates that proportion is not the ideal method (see Table 69).

At the same time that Stevin was setting down the figures for equal temperament, or perhaps a few years earlier (1595), Prince Tsai-yü in China was making a much more elaborate and careful calculation of the same roots of 2.[54] We are not told how he performed his calculation, but, since it is correct to nine places, he must have extracted the appropriate root for each note separately—and without the aid of logarithms, which were to simplify

Table 69. Stevin's Monochord, No. 2

Lengths	10000	9438	8908	8404	7936	7491	7071
Names	E	F	x	G	x	A	x
Lengths	6674	6298	5944	5611	5296	5000	
Names	B	C	x	D	x	E	

[53]Ibid., p. 72.

[54]Pere Joseph Maria Amiot, De la musique des Chinois (Mèmoires concernant l'histoire, ... des Chinois," Vol. VI [Paris, 1780]), Part 2, Fig. 18, Plate 21. See also J. Murray Barbour, "A Sixteenth Century Approximation for π," American Mathematical Monthly, XL (1933), 69–73.

the problem so greatly for men who attempted it a few decades later. In some cases, since the tenth digit will be 5 or larger, modern computers would round off the number at the ninth digit by substituting the next higher digit. This is a convention of our mathematics, intended to reduce the error arising from rounding off a number. Tsai-yü never did this.

Probably the first printed solution of equal temperament in numbers was made in Europe in 1630, a generation after Tsai-yü's time, when Johann Faulhaber solved a problem propounded by Dr. Johann Melder of Ulm.[55] The problem was to divide a monochord 20000 units in length, so that all intervals of the same size should be equal. Faulhaber did not explain to his readers how he had arrived at his result (Table 71), presenting it rather as a riddle. His monochord was for equal temperament, but contained several errors of 1 in the unit's place. This is the sort of error likely to occur when logarithms are used, and we might suppose Faulhaber had made use of the logarithmic tables printed in his book.

Table 70. Tsai-yü's Monochord

C	500,000,000	F	749,153,538
B	529,731,547	E	793,700,525
x	561,231,024	x	840,896,415
A	594,603,557	D	890,898,718
x	629,960,524	x	943,874,312
G	667,419,927	C	1,000,000,000
x	707,106,781		

Table 71. Faulhaber's Monochord

Lengths	20000	18877	17817	16817	15874	14982	14141
Names	C	x	D	x	E	F	x
Lengths	13347	12598	11891	11224	10594	10000	
Names	G	x	A	x	B	C	

[55]Johann George Neidhardt, Sectio canonis harmonici (Königsberg, 1724), p. 23.

Mersenne has given a number of different tables of equal temperament. The most characteristic, to six places, was furnished by Beaugrand, "very excellent geometer."[56] Mersenne also printed a table of first differences for the numbers in this monochord, to be used in connection with a method by Beaugrand for constructing the equal semitones. A comparison with Tsai-yü's table shows this one to be very inaccurate, the errors being much larger than if logarithms had been used. A much more ambitious table was contributed by Gallé.[57] In this table the lengths were given to eleven places. Beside it Mersenne printed a table with 144,000,000 as fundamental, so that the numbers might readily be compared with those of "the perfect clavier with 32 keys or steps to the octave," which had been presented in the book on the organ. This table will not be included here, for it seems likely that Mersenne himself computed these numbers from Gallé's larger table, by multiplying them by .00144. Of the numbers in the table, the length for D is correct to only five places. The others agree fairly well with Tsai-yü to the ninth place, although there are some slight divergences. Beyond the ninth place no digits are correct. If Gallé was using logarithms, he made some serious errors in interpolation. But if he was extracting roots, it is difficult to see how he failed to find correctly the middle number, the length for $F^{\#}$, which represents 10^{11} times the square root of $1/2$. It should be ten units larger. The length for E^{b} (10^{11} times the fourth root of $1/2$) agrees neither with the correct value nor with the square root of the length for $F^{\#}$.

Our final table from Mersenne[58] was supplied by Boulliau, "one of the most excellent astronomers of our age." In it he expressed the string-lengths for equal temperament in degrees, minutes, and seconds. This is equivalent to having a fundamental of 14400 in decimal notation, and the errors should be no greater than for such a table. However, the errors are greater than in Stevin's four-place table, with a mean deviation of about 1 cent. We can only surmise how Boulliau computed his figures. Evi-

[56]Mersenne, Harmonie universelle, p. 38.

[57]Ibid., Nouvelles observations, p. 21.

[58]Ibid., pp. 384 f.

dently the sexagesimal notation is somehow linked with his method of extracting the roots. Neidhardt printed six-place tables in equal temperament from Faulhaber, Mersenne, and Bümler, as well as several of his own.[59] His first original method was to divide the syntonic comma arithmetically, thus giving rise to a twofold error. The arithmetical division makes little difference, but the fact that the syntonic comma is about two cents smaller than the ditonic comma means that each fifth will be about .2 cent sharper than in correct equal temperament. Such a division is fairly easy to make, and, as the cents values indicate, the errors are small. The mean deviation is about 1 cent.

Later, Neidhardt[60] was to divide the ditonic comma, both arithmetically and geometrically, the latter method being genuine equal temperament. He contended, however, that the differences between these two methods were negligible. Since the greatest variation is 5 units, in tables containing 6 digits, his contention was correct. Note that the numbers for the arithmetical division are the larger throughout the table. The true values come closer to his geometrical division, but in every instance lie between the two.

Neidhardt's contemporary, Jakob Georg Meckenheuser,[61] printed a table, "as computed in the first Societäts-Frucht," evidently the proceedings of some learned society. From his figures, the syntonic comma is divided arithmetically, as in Neidhardt's first monochord. But evidently Meckenheuser's division ran to sharps, for seven of his notes were higher in pitch than the ·corresponding notes in Neidhardt's monochord. The higher C is not a true octave, but a B$^\#$ tempered by a full syntonic comma, just as his F is really a tempered E$^\#$. The ratio of these pairs of enharmonic notes is the schisma, about 2 cents. Thus even when two temperaments are constructed upon the same hypothesis and both are intended for equal temperament,

[59]Neidhardt, Sectio canonis harmonici, p. 32.

[60]Ibid., p. 19.

[61]Die sogenannte allerneueste musicalische Temperatur (Quedlinburg, 1727), p. 51.

Table 72. Beaugrand's Monochord

Lengths	200000	188770	178171	168178	158740	149829	141421
Names	C	x	D	x	E	F	x
Lengths	133480	125992	118920	112245	105945	100000	
Names	G	x	A	x	B	C	

Table 73. Gallé's Monochord

C	50,000,000,000	F	74,915,353,818
B	52,973,154,575	E	79,370,052,622
x	56,123,102,370	x	84,089,641,454
A	59,460,355,690	D	89,090,418,365
x	62,996,052,457	x	94,387,431,198
G	66,741,992,715	C	100,000,000,000
x	70,710,678,109		

Table 74. Boulliau's Monochord

Sexagesimal Notation	Decimal Notation	The Same, 20000 as Fundamental
C 2^0 $0'$ $0''$	7200	10000
B 2 7 12	7632	10600
x 2 14 52	8092	11239
A 2 22 53	8573	11907
x 2 31 12	9072	12600
G 2 40 5	9605	13340
x 2 49 39	10179	14138
F 2 59 32	10772	14961
E 3 10 5	11405	15840
x 3 21 50	12110	16819
D 3 33 43	12823	17810
x 3 46 20	13580	18861
C 4 0 0	14400	20000

Table 75. Neidhardt's Division of Syntonic Comma

Lengths	200000	188867	178148	168229	158683	149845	141344
Names	C	D^b	D	E^b	E	F	F$^\#$
Cents	0	99.1	200.3	299.5	400.6	499.9	601.0
Lengths	133472	126041	118888	112268	105898	100000	
Names	G	A^b	A	B^b	B	C	
Cents	700.2	799.3	900.5	999.7	1100.8	1200	

Table 76. Neidhardt's Division of Ditonic Comma

	Arithmetical	Geometrical
C	100000	100000
B	105948	105945
x	112247	112245
A	118922	118920
x	125994	125991
G	133484	133483
x	141424	141420
F	149831	149830
E	158743	158739
x	168182	168178
D	178182	178179
x	188779	188774
C	200000	200000

there may be a lack of agreement unless the process is followed through in exactly the same way for both. If it is true equal temperament, however, it does not matter in what order the notes are obtained, whether on the sharp or the flat side or mixed up in any way whatever. In Table 77, Meckenheuser's numbers have been divided by 18. This tends to conceal his rather obvious arithmetical division of the comma: in the original, every number except one (the length for D) ends in zero. There the value for G had been 240200000. This has been corrected to 240250000, since the number should be 240000000 tempered by $1/12 \times 1/80 = 1/960$.

Since the syntonic comma is much easier to form than the ditonic, it is easy to see why it should have been preferred as the quantity to be divided. However, since the ratio of the two commas is about 11:12, an excellent approximation for equal temperament can be made by tempering the fifths by 1/11 syntonic comma.[62] This was done arithmetically by Sorge, with the results shown in Table 78. The mean tempering of his fifths is 1/886, whence the ratio of the fifth will be .667419962..., instead of .667419927.... However, there are larger errors for most notes, since the temperament is not built solely by fifths, and the temperament as a whole is comparable to Neidhardt's arithmetical division of the ditonic comma.

Table 77. Meckenheuser's Division of Syntonic Comma

Lengths	200,000,000	188,658,258	178,148,341	168,045,776	158,684,002
Names	C	C#	D	D#	E
Cents	0	101.0	200.3	301.3	400.6
Lengths	149,685,380	141,346,458	133,472,222	125,903,184	118,889,159
Names	E#	F#	G	.G#	A
Cents	501.6	600.9	700.2	801.2	900.5
Lengths	112,147,215	105,899,532	99,894,201		
Names	A#	B	B#		
Cents	1001.5	1100.8	1201.8		

[62]Marpurg, Versuch über die musikalische Temperatur, p. 177.

Table 78. Sorge's Division of Syntonic Comma

Lengths	200000	188775	178182	168181	158743	149831	141422
Names	C	C$^{\#}$	D	D$^{\#}$	E	E$^{\#}$	F$^{\#}$
Lengths	133484	125994	118923	112247	105948	100000	
Names	G	G$^{\#}$	A	A$^{\#}$	B	C	

The impression is likely to become quite strong as one reads
the second half of this chapter that equal temperament is nothing
but a mass of figures of astronomical size. Actually, as far as
the ear is concerned, a wholly satisfactory monochord in equal
temperament (or any other tuning system) would be obtained from
the division of a string a meter long, marked off in millimeters.
Mersenne[63] gave such a table, considering it more practicable
than the very complicated tables of Beaugrand and Gallé. It could
easily have been constructed from one of the more elaborate
tables by rounding off the numbers at three places. Oddly, many
of Mersenne's figures are one unit too large. The correct monochord is shown in Table 79. It is instructive to note that the deviation for this monochord is larger than for one of Marpurg's
irregular tunings,[64] and about the same as that for a couple of
his other tunings. Thus, to three places, Marpurg's systems
would have coincided with equal temperament.

Table 79. Practical Equal Temperament, after Mersenne

Lengths	1000	944	891	841	794	749	707	667
Names	C	x	D	x	E	F	x	G
Cents	0	99.8	199.8	299.8	399.4	500.3	600.3	701.1
Lengths	630	595	561	530	500			
Names	x	A	x	B	C			
Cents	799.9	898.9	1000.7	1099.9	1200			

M.D. .60; S.D. .81

[63]Harmonie universelle, p. 339.

[64]Compare Marpurg's Temperaments E, B, and G in Chapter VII with the
cents values of Table 79.

84

In 1706 young Neidhardt, full of importance as the author of a new book on temperament, Beste und leichteste Temperatur des Monochordi, held a tuning contest with Sebastian Bach's cousin, Johann Nikolaus Bach, in Jena.[65] Neidhardt tuned one set of pipes by a monochord he had computed by making an arithmetical division of the syntonic comma. Therefore, although he had worked out this division to six places, it was about as accurate as the practical monochord given above. Bach tuned another set of pipes entirely by ear, and won the contest handily, for a singer found it easier to sing a chorale in B^b minor in Bach's tuning than in Neidhardt's.

Perhaps part of Neidhardt's difficulty lay in the fact that it is difficult to tune a pipe to a string. Many years later, Adlung wrote that this same Johann Nikolaus Bach had what might be called a "monopipe"—a variable organ pipe with a sliding cylinder upon which the numbers of the monochord were inscribed.[66] Because of the end correction for a pipe, this method is likely to be faulty. However, forty years before the date of the historic tuning contest in Jena, Otto Gibelius[67] described and pictured just such a pipe, intended for his meantone approximation discussed in Chapter III. He also gave an end correction, amounting to 8/3 the width of the mouth of the pipe. In his accurately drawn copperplate (see Figure F) the width of the mouth is 11 millimeters, making the end correction about 30 millimeters. Since the internal depth is about 15 millimeters, his rule corresponds very closely to our modern rule that the end correction for a rectangular pipe is twice the internal depth. The Dayton Miller Collection now at the Library of Congress contains several specimens of the "tuning pipe," most of them fairly small.

Since the "tuning pipe" was not widely disseminated, organ-

[65]Philipp Spitta, Johann Sebastian Bach, trans. Clara Bell and J. A. Fuller-Maitland (2 vols.; London, 1884), I, 137 f.

[66]Jacob Adlung, Anleitung zu den musikalischen Gelahrtheit (Erfurt, 1758), p. 311. In addition to the Neidhardt-Bach test, he described a similar experience that befell Meckenheuser in Riechenberg vor Goslar, where he tried for three days to tune the organ by his monochord, but in vain. See Jacob Adlung, Musica mechanica organoedi (Berlin, 1768), p. 56.

[67]Propositiones mathematico-musicae, pp. 1–11.

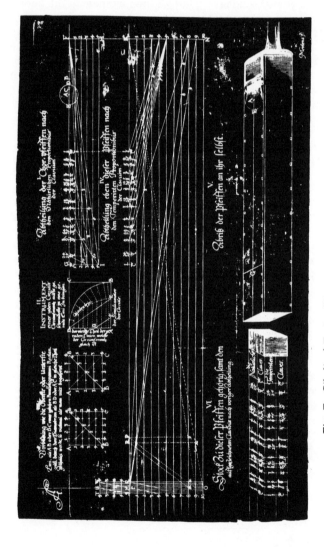

Fig. F. Gibelius' Tuning Pipe
Reproduced by courtesy of the Library of Congress

ists tuning by the aid of the monochord probably had no more success than Neidhardt had. It is probable, however, that, like Johann Nikolaus—and Sebastian, too—the organists did not bother with a monochord but relied upon their ears. Hence the tuning rules given in the beginning of this chapter were of the greatest possible importance in practice. Some of them seem so vague that they would have needed to be supplemented by oral directions. But if we could be sure that Mersenne's rule that a tempered fifth should beat once per second was to have been applied to the fifths in the vicinity of middle C, we would have as accurate a rule for equal temperament as that given by Alexander Ellis over two centuries later.

Unfortunately, the more mathematically minded writers on equal temperament have given the impression that extreme accuracy in figures is the all-important thing in equal temperament, even if it is patent that such accuracy cannot be obtained upon the longest feasible monochord. This is why Sebastian Bach and many others did not care for equal temperament. They were not opposed to the equal tuning itself, and their own tuning results were undoubtedly comparable to the best tuning accomplished today—upon the evidence of their compositions, as will be discussed in the final chapter. But they needed a Mersenne to tell them that the complicated tables could well have had half their digits chopped off before using, and that, after all, a person who tunes accurately by beats gets results that the ear cannot distinguish from the successive powers of the 12th root of 2.

Chapter V. JUST INTONATION

The seeds of just intonation had been sown early in the Christian era, when Didymus and Ptolemy presented monochords that contained pure fifths and major thirds (see Chapter II). But they remained dormant during the Middle Ages. Even after the seeds had sprouted near the beginning of the modern era, the plants were to bear fruit only occasionally and haphazardly.

Enough of our metaphor. We shall consider in this chapter all 12-note systems that contain some arrangement of pure fifths and major thirds. The Pythagorean tuning may be thought of as the limiting form of just intonation, since it has a great many pure fifths, but no pure major thirds. As the various chromatic notes were added to the scale during the latter Middle Ages, they were tuned by pure fifths or fourths to notes already present in the scale. Finally, fifteenth century writers were describing the formation of a complete chromatic monochord, using the Pythagorean intervals. Such a writer was Hugo de Reutlingen,[1] whose altered notes consisted of two sharps and three flats. Since the more typical tuning has $G^{\#}$ instead of A^b, that is shown in Table 80. Of course the deviation would be the same as for Hugo's tuning. The ratio for each diatonic semitone is 256:243, and for the chromatic semitone 2187:2048. Compare with these ratios the relative simplicity of the ratios for Marpurg's first tuning, the model form of just intonation. (The lengths are very much simpler also.)

The first known European writer to break away from the Pythagorean tuning for the tuning of the chromatic monochord was Bartolomeus Ramis de Pareja.[2] Ramis gave specific directions for tuning the monochord that resulted in a system in which the six notes A^{b0} -G^0 are joined by perfect fifths, as in the Pythagorean tuning, and the remaining six notes, D^{-1}-$F^{\#-1}$, also joined by fifths, lie a comma higher than the corresponding notes

[1]Flores musicae omnis cantus Gregoriani (Strassburg, 1488), Chapter II.

[2]Musica practica (Bologna, 1482); new edition, by Johannes Wolf (1901), published as Beiheft der Internationale Musikgesellschaft.

Table 80. Pythagorean Tuning

Lengths	629856	589824	559872	531441	497664	472392	442368
Names	C^0	$C^{\#0}$	D^0	E^{b0}	E^0	F^0	$F^{\#0}$
Cents	0	114	204	294	408	498	612
Lengths	419904	393216	373248	354294	321776	314928	
Names	G^0	$G^{\#0}$	A^0	B^{b0}	B^0	C^0	
Cents	702	816	906	996	1110	1200	

M.D. 11.7; S.D. 11.8

Table 81. Ramis' Monochord

Names	C^0	$C^{\#-1}$	D^{-1}	E^{b0}	E^{-1}	F^0	$F^{\#-1}$	G^0	A^{b0}	A^{-1}	B^{b0}	B^{-1}	C^0
Cents	0	92	182	294	386	498	590	702	792	884	996	1088	1200

M.D. 10.0; S.D. 10.1

in the Pythagorean tuning (see Table 81). Thus there are pure major thirds to only the four notes B^b-G.

Montucla,[3] writing a "history of music," gave string-lengths for a 17-note tuning, in which twelve notes are the same as in Ramis. The other five extend the scale to $A^{\#-1}$ and to G^{b-0}. This is a wholly useless extension because such enharmonic pairs as D^{b0} and $C^{\#-1}$ differ by the schisma, 2 cents. Helmholtz was more astute in constructing his 24-note harmonium in just intonation, in which the eight notes from C^0 through $C^{\#0}$ are joined by fifths; the next eight, E^{-1} through $E^{\#-1}$, furnish major thirds to notes in the first series; and the remaining eight, A^{b+1} through A^{+1}, are considered (by disregarding the schisma) as equivalent to the thirds above the notes in the second series, i. e., $G^{\#-2}$-Gx^{-2}.[4]

Ramis' monochord does not differ perceptibly from the Pythagorean tuning. If he had substituted D^{b0} and all the other Pythagorean enharmonic equivalents of the syntonic notes, he would

---

[3]Jean Etienne Montucla, Histoire des mathématiques (New ed.; Paris, 1802), IV, 650.

[4]H. L. F. Helmholtz, Sensations of Tone, pp. 316 f.

have had a monochord from E^{bb0} through G^0, in Pythagorean tuning. His reason for making the new division was solely to simplify the construction of the monochord. In his own words, the Pythagorean tuning, as given by Boethius, is "useful and pleasing for theorists, but tiresome for singers and irksome to the mind. But because we have promised to satisfy both [singers and theorists], we shall simplify the division of the monochord." Later he expressed the same idea in these words: "So therefore we have made all our divisions very easy, because the fractions are common and are not difficult."

Undoubtedly Ramis' method is easier. But if he had desired to obtain the equivalent of the Pythagorean tuning from A^b to $C^{\#}$, he would have commenced his tuning with $F^{\#}$ instead of with C, having notes with zero exponents from D^0 to $C^{\#0}$ and with -1 from $G^{\#-1}$ to Fx^{-1}. On such a monochord, however, as on the usual Pythagorean monochord, the eight most common thirds would have been very sharp and the four useless thirds, $E-A^b$, $B-E^b$, $F^{\#}-B^b$, and $C^{\#}-F$, would have been pure. The monochord, as Ramis actually tuned it, has as its four pure thirds, B^b-D, F-A, C-E, and G-B. Thus, although Ramis professed to be making his division of the octave solely for the sake of simplicity, the accidental result was that several pure triads were available in keys frequently used.

The bitter critics of Ramis in his own day failed to realize that his tuning was just what he had described: a simplified equivalent of the Pythagorean tuning — shifted, however, by six scale degrees to the flat side. To them, any tampering with the old intervals was sacrilege. Many later writers, misled by Ramis' announced intentions, have stated, without examining his monochord, that he had advocated temperament. As we have defined temperament and as the word is usually understood, this is a serious misconception. It has even been stated that Ramis advocated equal temperament! Since Ramis' book is accessible in a modern edition, there is no longer any excuse for repeating such myths.

It must be said, somewhat sadly, that Ramis was not aware himself of the peculiar properties of the monochord he had fathered. For example, he explained that although E^b does not form a major third to B, $D^\#$ is not really needed, for the minor triad B D $F^\#$ can be used in making a Phrygian cadence on E. But his interval B^{-1}-E^{b0} is slightly better than the Pythagorean thirds, A^{b0}-C^0 and E^{b0}-G^0, that were acceptable to him!

Ramis must have been a good practical musician. Although his system would not now be called a temperament, we might do well to take him at his own evaluation and hail him as the first of modern tuning reformers.

Corroboration of Ramis' tuning system is found in an interesting anonymous German manuscript of the second half of the fifteenth century, Pro clavichordiis faciendis, which Dupont[5] ran across in the Erlangen University Library. Starting with the note B, C is to be a just semitone (16:15) higher, E a perfect fourth, G a just minor sixth .(8:5), etc. A succession of pure fifths on the flat side extends to G^b, below which there is a just major third (5:4), E^{bb}, and the monochord is completed by adding B^{bb}, the fifth above E^{bb}! The complete monochord is shown in Table 82.

The deviation for this tuning is almost precisely the same as for that of Ramis, and it too contains many pure fifths and several pure thirds. However, it has one peculiar feature as Dupont has presented it. In every other tuning system we have examined, there has been an uninterrupted succession of notes connected by fifths from the flattest to the sharpest. In the Pythagorean and other regular tuning systems, such as the meantone, the wolf fifth would be very flat or sharp, and in the irregular systems there would be other divergences. But the note names persisted, usually from E^b to $G^\#$ inclusive.

Table 82. The Erlangen Monochord

Names	C^0	D^{b0}	$E^{bb^{+1}}$	E^{b0}	E^{-1}	F^0	G^{b0}	G^0	A^{b0}	$B^{bb^{+1}}$	B^{b0}	B^{-1}	C^0
Cents	0	90	202	294	386	498	588	702	792	904	996	1088	1200

M.D. 10.3; S.D. 10.5

[5]Wilhelm Dupont, Geschichte der musicalischen Temperatur (Erlangen, 1935), pp. 20-22.

But in the Erlangen monochord there is no D or A, and the notes that Dupont has given as their enharmonic equivalents, E^{bb} and B^{bb}, are not in a fifth-relation with any other notes in the monochord. Therefore it seems obvious that the anonymous writer intended these notes to be D^0 and A^0, each of which is higher by the schisma than E^{bb+1} and B^{bb+1} respectively. Then the notes that are pure thirds above D^0 and A^0 will be $F^{\#-1}$ and $C^{\#-1}$, notes that continue the fifth-series from B^{-1}. It would then be immaterial whether to call the semitone between G and A by the name A^{b0} or $G^{\#-1}$, since either would complete the scale correctly. The original writer, by the way, had not named the black keys, merely designating the semitone between C and D as the first, between D and E as the second, between F and G as the third, and between G and A as the fourth. In renaming some of the black keys, therefore, we are not violating his intent, but rather confirming it. The revised monochord, with schismatic alterations, is shown in Table 83.

These two pre-sixteenth-century tunings, the one in Spain and the other in Germany, are sufficient indication of the trend of men's thinking with regard to consonant thirds. Lodovico Fogliano,[6] half a century later than Ramis, offered no apologies for using the 5:4 ratio for the major third. But he was not content to present ordinary just intonation. Realizing that D^0 formed an imperfect fifth below A^{-1}, he advocated D^{-1} as a consonant fifth. This in turn led him to B^{b0} as a pure major third below D^{-1}, as well as the B^{b+1} as third below D^0. But he said the "practical musicians" used only one key each for D and B^b, "neither right nor left, but the mean between both." "Such a mean D or B^b, moreover, is nothing else than a point dividing the proportion of the comma into two halves."

Table 83. Erlangen Monochord, Revised

Names	C^0	$C^{\#-1}$	D^0	E^{b0}	E^{-1}	F^0	$F^{\#-1}$	G^0	$G^{\#-1}$	A^0	B^{b0}	B^{-1}	C^0
Cents	0	92	204	294	386	498	590	702	794	906	996	1088	1200

M.D. 10.0; S.D. 10.1

[6]Musica theorica (Venice, 1529), fol. 36.

To obtain the mean proportional by geometry, Fogliano used the familiar Euclidean construction, and appended a figure to show how the division was to be made. This alteration of pure values, he said is "what they [the practical musicians] call temperament." Here is the germ of the meantone temperament, which his countryman Aron had described in its complete form at about this same time.

For the sake of showing monochords in just intonation from the early sixteenth century, there are set down here three monochords after Fogliano, first with his one pair of D's and B♭'s, then with the second pair, and finally with the mean D and B♭. The first monochord (Table 84) is the best, having two groups of four notes each with like exponents. The second monochord (Table 85) would have had the same deviation as the first if it had had $F^{\#-1}$ (in place of $F^{\#-2}$) as third above D^0. (This is Marpurg's first monochord, Table 96.) The monochord with the two meantones (Table 86) ranks between the first two. If Fogliano had formed three meantones, including one on F#, the deviation would be slightly less than for the first monochord. The result is given in Table 87.

Table 84. Fogliano's Monochord, No. 1

Lengths	3600	3456	3240	3000	2880	2700	2592	2400
Names	C^0	$C^{\#-2}$	D^{-1}	E^{b+1}	E^{-1}	F^0	$F^{\#-2}$	G^0
Cents	0	70	182	316	386	498	568	702
Lengths	2304	2160	2025	1920	1800			
Names	$G^{\#-2}$	A^{-1}	B^{b0}	B^{-1}	C^0			
Cents	772	884	996	1088	1200			

M.D. 21.3; S.D. 23.6

JUST INTONATION

Table 85. Fogliano's Monochord, No. 2

Lengths	3600	3456	3200	3000	2880	2700	2592	2400
Names	C^0	$C^{\#-2}$	D^0	E^{b+1}	E^{-1}	F^0	$F^{\#-2}$	G^0
Cents	0	70	204	316	386	498	568	702
Lengths	2304	2160	2000	1920	1800			
Names	$G^{\#-2}$	A^{-1}	B^{b+1}	B^{-1}	C^0			
Cents	772	884	1018	1088	1200			

M.D. 25.0; S.D. 26.7

Table 86. Fogliano's Tempered Just Intonation

Lengths	3600	3456	[3220]	3000	2880	2700	2592	2400
Names	C^0	$C^{\#-2}$	$D^{-\frac{1}{2}}$	E^{b+1}	E^{-1}	F^0	$F^{\#-2}$	G^0
Cents	0	70	193	316	386	498	568	702
Lengths	2304	2160	[2012.5]	1920	1800			
Names	$G^{\#-2}$	A^{-1}	$B^{b+\frac{1}{2}}$	B^{-1}	C^0			
Cents	772	884	1007	1088	1200			

M.D. 23.2; S.D. 24.7

Table 87. Fogliano's Tempered Just Intonation, Revised

Lengths	3600	3456	[3220]	3000	2880	2700	[2576]
Names	C^0	$C^{\#-2}$	$D^{-\frac{1}{2}}$	E^{b+1}	E^{-1}	F^0	$F^{\#-\frac{3}{2}}$
Cents	0	70	193	316	386	498	579
Lengths	2400	2304	2160	[2012.5]	1920	1800	
Names	G^0	$G^{\#-2}$	A^{-1}	$B^{b+\frac{1}{2}}$	B^{-1}	C^0	
Cents	702	772	884	1007	1088	1200	

M.D. 21.3; S.D. 22.3

Martin Agricola[7] resembled Ramis in his tuning ideas. He gave a monochord in which the eight diatonic notes, including B^b, were joined by pure fifths, as in the Pythagorean tuning. Then he directed that the interval from B to the end of the string be divided into ten parts, with $C^{\#}$ at the first point of division, $D^{\#}$ at the second, and $G^{\#}$ at the fourth. Then $F^{\#}$ was to be a pure fourth to $C^{\#}$. Thus these black keys were given syntonic values, and the whole monochord is made up of notes with 0 and -1 exponents (see Table 88). Ramis' monochord is slightly better than Agricola's, with a ratio of 6:6 for the number of fifths in each group, in place of 8:4.

Table 88. Agricola's Monochord

Names.	C^0	$C^{\#-1}D^0$	$D^{\#-1}E^0$	F^0	$F^{\#-1}G^0$	$G^{\#-1}A^0$	B^{b0}	B^0	C^0
Cents	0	92 204	296 408	498	590 702	794 906	996	1110	1200

M.D. 10.3; S.D. 10.5

It will be observed that the better of Fogliano's untempered monochords has more than twice the deviation of Ramis'. Thus it might be thought that Fogliano had been unfortunate in his choice of intervals. Quite the contrary. The most symmetric form of just intonation for the series E^b-$G^{\#}$ has four notes with the same exponent, followed by four more with exponents that are one less. Of the remaining four notes, two would have +2 and two would have -2 as exponents. This is precisely Fogliano's second monochord, if we should substitute $F^{\#-1}$ in it. Fogliano's first monochord has the exponential pattern 1,4,4,3, which is just as satisfactory. (That is, the tuning contains one note with exponent +1, 4 with 0 and -1 exponents, and 3 with -2.) The difficulty, therefore, is inherent in just intonation itself, as will be discussed further a bit later.

Salomon de Caus[8] was one of several mathematicians of the early seventeenth century who were interested in just intonation.

---

[7]"De monochordi dimensione," in Rudimenta musices (Wittemberg, 1539)

[8]Les raisons des forces mouvantes avec diverses machines (Francfort, 1615) Book 3, Problem III.

If we follow his directions, we obtain the monochord shown in Table 89. Here there are three groups of four notes each with the same exponent — the most symmetric arrangement of all. The deviation is appreciably less than in Fogliano's arrangement.

Johannes Kepler[9] gave some genuine tuning lore together with an elaborate discussion of the harmony of the spheres. His two monochords in just intonation (Tables 90 and 91) are identical except that the second has a $G^{\#}$ in place of an A^{b}. Since Kepler had five notes with zero exponents in both monochords, the deviation for his systems is lower than most that have been presented in this chapter.

Table 89. De Caus's Monochord

Names	C^0	$C^{\#-2}$	D^{-1}	$D^{\#-2}$	E^{-1}	F^0	$F^{\#-2}$	G^0	$G^{\#-2}$	A^{-1}	B^{b0}	B^{-1}	C^0
Cents	0	70	182	274	386	498	568	702	772	884	996	1088	1200

M.D. 17.7; S.D. 20.1

Table 90. Kepler's Monochord, No. 1

Lengths	1620	1536	1440	1350	1296	1215	1152
Names	C^0	$C^{\#-1}$	D^0	E^{b+1}	E^{-1}	F^0	$F^{\#-1}$
Cents	0	92	204	316	386	498	590
Lengths	1080	1024	960	900	864	810	
Names	G^0	$G^{\#+1}$	A^0	B^{b+1}	B^{-1}	C^0	
Cents	702	794	906	1018	1088	1200	

M.D. 14.0; S.D. 15.8

[9]Harmonices mundi, p. 163.

Although Marin Mersenne was a zealous advocate of equal temperament in practice, he took pains to present literally dozens of tables in just intonation. He repeated, among others, Kepler's two monochords shown in Tables 90 and 91, together with tables for keyboards with split keys. Four of his monochords (Tables 92-95) are worth including here, as evidence of the variety that is possible in a type of tuning that is ordinarily thought to be fixed and uniform.[10] None is as good as either of Kepler's two.

Table 91. Kepler's Monochord, No. 2

Lengths	100000	93750	88889	833333	80000	75000	71111
Names	C^0	$C^{\#-1}$	D^0	E^{b+1}	E^{-1}	F^0	$F^{\#-1}$
Cents	0	92	204	316	386	498	590
Lengths	66667	62500	60000	56250	53333	50000	
Names	G^0	A^{b+1}	A^0	B^{b+1}	B^{-1}	C^0	
Cents	702	814	906	1018	1088	1200	

M.D. 14.0; S.D. 15.8

Table 92. Mersenne's Spinet Tuning, No. 1

Lengths	3600	3375	3240	3000	2880	2700	2531 1/4
Names	C^0	D^{b+1}	D^{-1}	E^{b+1}	E^{-1}	F^0	G^{b+1}
Cents	0	112	182	316	386	498	610
Lengths	2400	2250	2160	2025	1920	1800	
Names	G^0	A^{b+1}	A^{-1}	B^{b0}	B^{-1}	C^0	
Cents	702	814	884	996	1088	1200	

M.D. 17.7; S.D. 20.1

[10]Mersenne, Harmonie universelle, pp. 54, 117 f.

Table 93. Mersenne's Spinet Tuning, No. 2

Lengths	3600	3456	3200	3072	2880	2700	2592	2400
Names	C^0	$C^{\#-2}$	D^0	$D^{\#-2}$	E^{-1}	F^0	$F^{\#-2}$	G^0
Cents	0	70	204	274	386	498	568	702
Lengths	2304	2160	2025	1920	1800			
Names	$G^{\#-2}$	A^{-1}	$B^{\flat 0}$	B^{-1}	C^0			
Cents	772	884	996	1088	1200			

M.D. 21.3; S.D. 23.6

Table 94. Mersenne's Lute Tuning, No. 1

Names	C^0	$D^{\flat+1}$	D^{-1}	$E^{\flat+1}$	E^{-1}	F^0	$G^{\flat+1}$	G^0	$A^{\flat+1}$	A^{-1}	$B^{\flat+1}$	B^{-1}	C^0
Cents	0	112	182	316	386	498	610	702	814	884	1018	1088	1200

M.D. 21.3; S.D. 23.6

Table 95. Mersenne's Lute Tuning, No. 2

Names	C^0	$D^{\flat+1}$	D^0	$E^{\flat+1}$	E^{-1}	F^0	$G^{\flat+1}$	G^0	$A^{\flat+1}$	A^{-1}	$B^{\flat+1}$	B^{-1}	C^0
Cents	0	112	204	316	386	498	610	702	814	884	1018	1088	1200

M.D. 17.7; S.D. 20.1

Table 96. Marpurg's Monochord, No. 1

Lengths	900	864	800	750	720	675	640
Ratios	24/25	25/27	15/16	24/25	15/16	128/135	15/16
Names	C^0	$C^{\#-2}$	D^0	$E^{\flat+1}$	E^{-1}	F^0	$F^{\#-1}$
Cents	0	70	204	316	386	498	590
Lengths	600	576	540	500	480	450	
Ratios	24/25	15/16	25/27	24/25	15/16		
Names	G^0	$G^{\#-2}$	A^{-1}	$B^{\flat+1}$	B^{-1}	C^0	
Cents	702	772	884	1018	1088	1200	

M.D. 21.3; S.D. 23.6

Table 97. Marpurg's Monochord, No. 3

Names	C^0	$C^{\#-2}D^0$	E^{b+1}	E^{-1}	F^0	$F^{\#-1}$	G^0	$G^{\#-2}$	A^0	B^{b0}	B^{-1}	C^0
Cents	0	70 204	306	386	498	590	702	772	906	996	1088	1200

M.D. 19.3; S.D. 22.0

Table 98. Marpurg's Monochord, No. 4

Names	C^0	$C^{\#-2}D^{-1}$	E^{b+1}	E^{-1}	F^0	$F^{\#-2}G^0$	$G^{\#-2}A^{-1}$	B^{b+1}	B^{-1}	C^0
Cents	0	70 182	316	386	498	568 702	772 884	1018	1088	1200

M.D. 25.0; S.D. 26.7

Note that Mersenne's first spinet tuning (Table 92) has flats for its black keys and the second tuning (Table 93) has sharps except for B^b. The first tuning is constructed exactly the same as de Caus's tuning (Table 89), except that it begins a major third lower, with G^b instead of B^b. Mersenne's first lute tuning (Table 94) differs from his first spinet tuning (Table 92) at only one pitch (B^{b+1} instead of B^{b0}), but that is enough to 'increase its deviation to that of the second spinet tuning (Table 93). The second lute tuning (Table 95), although differing from the first spinet tuning (Table 92) at two places, has the same deviation.

Friedrich Wilhelm Marpurg,[11] who wrote brilliantly about temperament 140 years after Mersenne, included four monochords in just intonation. The second of these was Kepler's first, and need not be repeated here. The other three are shown in Tables 96-98. In each of them the notes, according to their exponents, are grouped into four classes. The first may be considered the model form of just intonation, the ideal form of Fogliano's second monochord (Table 85).

Opelt has shown two monochords in just intonation from Rousseau's Dictionary.[12] The first (Table 99) was by Alexander Malcolm, whose linear improvement upon just intonation is to be found in Chapter VII. This is the same as Kepler's second monochord (Table 91), transposed a fifth lower.

[11]Versuch über die musikalische Temperatur, pp. 118, 123.

[12]F. W. Opelt, Allgemeine Theorie der Musik (Leipzig, 1852), p. 46.

100

Rousseau tried to "improve" upon this tuning by substituting other just pitches in place of D^{b+1}, $F^{\#-1}$, and B^{b0}, with very unsatisfactory results, since his division of the major tone of 204 cents was into semitones of 70 and 134 cents! This monochord (Table 100) is the reverse of Marpurg's fourth (Table 98), with semitones paired in contrary motion, when Rousseau's A^{b+1} is made to coincide with Marpurg's $G^{\#-2}$.

Table 99. Malcolm's Monochord

Names	C^0	D^{b+1}	D^0	E^{b+1}	E^{-1}	F^0	$F^{\#-1}$	G^0	A^{b+1}	A^{-1}	B^{b0}	B^{-1}	C^0
Cents	0	112	204	316	386	498	590	702	814	884	996	1088	1200

M.D. 14.0; S.D. 15.8

Table 100. Rousseau's Monochord

Names	C^0	$C^{\#-2}$	D^0	E^{b+1}	E^{-1}	F^0	$F^{\#-2}$	G^0	A^{b+1}	A^{-1}	B^{b+1}	B^{-1}	C^0
Cents	0	70	204	316	386	498	568	702	814	884	954	1088	1200

M.D. 25.0; S.D. 26.7

Table 101. Euler's Monochord

Names	C^0	$C^{\#2}$	D^0	$D^{\#-2}$	E^{-1}	F^0	$F^{\#-1}$	G^0	$G^{\#-2}$	A^{-1}	$A^{\#2}$	B^{-1}	C^0
Cents	0	70	204	274	386	498	590	702	772	884	976	1088	1200

M.D. 17.1; S.D. 20.1

Table 102. Montvallon's Monochord

Names	C^0	$C^{\#-1}$	D^0	E^{b+1}	E^{-1}	F^0	$F^{\#-1}$	G^0	$G^{\#-1}$	A^{-1}	B^{b0}	B^{-1}	C^0
Cents	0	92	204	316	386	498	590	702	794	884	996	1088	1200

M.D. 12.0; S.D. 13.3

Table 103. Romieu's Monochord

Names	C⁰	C#⁻²	D⁰	E♭⁺¹	E⁻¹	F⁰	F#⁻¹	G⁰	G#⁻²	A⁻¹	B♭⁰	B⁻¹	C⁰
Cents	0	70	204	316	386	498	590	702	772	884	996	1088	1200

M.D. 17.7; S.D. 20.1

Euler's monochord ran entirely to sharps.[13] However, it has the same symmetric grouping of its notes as de Caus's (Table 89), only transposed a fifth higher.

Montvallon's monochord, given by Romieu,[14] follows a more familiar order in the selection of notes than Euler's did (see Table 102).

Romieu himself contributed an example (Table 103) of a "système juste."[15] It has a somewhat more complicated pattern than Euler's (Table 101), but the same deviation.

Theory of Just Intonation

In the foregoing pages there have been presented more than twenty different monochords in authentic just intonation, i. e., with pure fifths and major thirds. Their mean deviations have varied from 10.0 to 25.0. And yet each has a right to be called just intonation! This great divergence can be explained by mathematics. Let us consider first a monochord in the Pythagorean tuning. Its mean deviation is 11.7. A Pythagorean chromatic semitone, as C^0-$C^{\#0}$, is 114 cents; the diatonic semitone, as $C^{\#0}$-D^0, 90. Hence the deviation for the pair of semitones is 24 cents. When the just semitones are used, the chromatic semitone, C^0-$C^{\#-1}$, is 92 cents; the diatonic, $C^{\#-1}$-D^0, 112. The deviation for the pair of just semitones is 20 cents, or 4 cents less than for the pair of Pythagorean semitones. Therefore the substitution of each just note reduces the deviation by 4/12 or .3 cent.

[13]A. F. Häser, "Über wissenschaftliche Begründung der Musik durch Akustik," Allgemeine musikalische Zeitung, 1829, col. 145.

[14]"Mémoire théorique & pratique sur les systèmes tempérés de musique," Mémoires de l'académie royale des sciences, 1758, p. 867.

[15]Ibid., p. 865.

But the sixth note to be altered around the circle of fifths is adjacent to the first note to have been altered, and therefore the total deviation is unchanged. The same is true for the seventh note. The eighth note lies between two notes, each sharper by the syntonic comma. Therefore, when it too is raised, the syntonic semitones already present are changed to Pythagorean semitones, and the deviation is increased by .3 cent. This process continues until all twelve notes have been raised by a comma, and the monochord is again in Pythagorean tuning. If we call the number of notes with -1 exponent n_1, and with 0 exponent n_2, the following formula gives the mean deviation:

$$3\ D_2 = 29 + \left| n_1 - 6 \right| + \left[6 - \frac{\left| n_1 - 6 \right|}{6} \right]$$

The minimum deviation of 10.0 cents occurs when $(n_1, n_2) = (5,7)$, (6,6), or (7,5). Thus Ramis' monochord (Table 81) with 6,6 is one of the three best possible.

When there are notes with three different exponents, the change of a single note may cause a greater change in the deviation than was possible with two exponents only. Suppose a monochord contains the notes $C^0\ C^{\#-1}\ D^{-1}$, the total deviation being 18 cents for the two semitones. When $C^{\#-2}$ is used, the deviation becomes 42 cents, an increase of 24 cents. But if the notes had originally been $C^0\ C^{\#-1}\ D^0$, the change to $C^{\#-2}$ would increase the deviation from 20 cents to 64 cents, that is, by 44 cents, or two commas. Again, the deviation of the two semitones $C^{\#-1}\ D^0\ E^{b+1}$ is 24 cents; with D^{-1} it is 44 cents, an increase of 20 cents.

Thus when a note is changed by a comma, the change in the mean deviation may be 1/3 (as before) or 6/3 or 11/3 or 5/3. A much more complicated formula, therefore, is needed to express the deviation with the three exponents. If we call the number of notes with -1 exponent n_1, with 0, n_2, and with +1, n_3, the mean deviation is given by the formula:

$$3\ D_3 = 23 + \left| n_1 - 6 \right| + \left| n_3 - 6 \right| + \left[\frac{6 - \left| n_1 - 6 \right|}{6} \right] + \left[\frac{6 - \left| n_3 - 6 \right|}{6} \right] +$$

$7(k_2 - k_1) + 5(k_4 - k_3)$, where k_1 = the larger of n_2 and $(7 - n_1)$, k_2 = the smaller of 7 and $(12 - n_1)$, k_3 = the larger of n_2 and $(5 - n_1)$, and k_4 = the smaller of 5 and $(12 - n_1)$. The terms containing the k's are zero whenever $k_2 \leq k_1$ and $k_4 \leq k_3$.

Let us now compute the deviations for two of the tunings shown on previous pages. Mersenne's first spinet tuning (Table 92) has for its (n_1, n_2, n_3) the numbers $(4,4,4)$. Here $k_1 = n_2 = 4$, $k_2 = 7$, $k_3 = n_2 = 4$, $k_4 = 5$.

$3\ D_3 = 23 + 2 + 2 + 0 + 0 + 7 \times 3 + 5 \times 1 = 53$. $D_3 = 17.7$.

For Mersenne's second spinet (Table 93) or first lute tuning (Table 94) the exponential numbers are $(4,3,5)$.

$3\ D_3 = 23 + 2 + 1 + 0 + 0 + 7 \times 4 + 5 \times 2 + 64$. $D_3 = 21.3$.

When there are four different exponents, there is a very analogous formula for the deviation:

$$3\ D_4 = 23 - n_1 + \left| n_1 + n_2 - 6 \right| + \left| n_4 - 6 \right| + \left[\frac{6 - \left| n_1 + n_2 - 6 \right|}{6} \right] +$$

$$\left[\frac{6 - \left| n_4 - 6 \right|}{6} \right] + 7(k_2 - k_1) + 5(k_4 - k_3) + 7(L_2 - L_1) + 5(L_4 - L_3),$$

where k_1 = the larger of n_3 and $(7 - n_1 - n_2)$, k_2 = the smaller of 7 and $(12 - n_1 - n_2)$, k_3 = the larger of n_3 and $(5 - n_1 - n_2)$, k_4 = the smaller of 5 and $(12 - n_1 - n_2)$; L_1 = the larger of n_2 and $(7 - n_1)$, L_2 = the smaller of 7 and $(12 - n_1)$, L_3 = the larger of n_2 and $(5 - n_1)$, and L_4 = the smaller of 5 and $(12 - n_1)$. The terms containing the k's and L's are zero whenever $k_2 \leq k_1$, $k_4 \leq k_3$, $L_2 \leq L_1$, and $L_4 \leq L_3$.

As examples, let us compute the deviation for two of Marpurg's tunings. His first tuning (Table 96) is the model form of just intonation, with $(2,4,4,2)$ for its (n_1, n_2, n_3, n_4). Here $k_1 = 4$, $k_2 = 6$, $k_3 = 4$, $k_4 = 5$, $L_1 = 5$, $L_2 = 7$, $L_3 = 4$, and $\overset{.}{L}_4 = 5$. Hence $3\ D_4 = 23 - 2 + 0 + 4 + 1 + 0 + 7 \times 2 + 5 \times 1 + 7 \times 2 + 5 \times 1 = 64$. $D_4 = 21.3$. Marpurg's third tuning (Table 97) has for its exponents $(2,3,6,1)$. Here $k_2 = 6$, $k_3 = 7$, $k_4 = 6$, $k_4 = 5$, $L_1 = 5$, $L_2 = 7$, $L_3 = 4$, $L_4 = 5$. The deviation: $3\ D_4 = 23 - 2 + 1 + 5 + 0$

+ 0 + 7 x 1 + 0 + 7 x 2 + 5 x 2 = 58. D_4 = 19.3.

With all these complex mathematical formulas before us, we are likely to forget that we are ostensibly studying a form of tuning that to many people is a sort of ideal system. It is not likely that any sane person would advocate so perverted a tuning as that represented by (5,1,1,5), with a mean deviation of 43.3 cents. But the systems that have been shown on the previous pages have all been advocated by various writers, and they show great variety in their construction and almost as great a variety in their deviations, ranging from the 10.0 of Ramis to the 25.0 of Fogliano's second or Rousseau's or Marpurg's fourth. The model form, Marpurg's first, with a deviation of 21.3, comes nearer the maximum than the minimum. We shall speak again of just intonation in the final chapter. Let us close this chapter with a double paradox: there is no such thing as just intonation, but, rather, many different just intonations; of these, the best is that which comes closest to the Pythagorean tuning.

Chapter VI. MULTIPLE DIVISION

If a keyboard instrument is not in equal temperament, its intonation can be improved by a judicious increase in the number of notes in the octave. The first reference to split keys came from Italy, where before 1484 the organ of St. Martin's at Lucca had separate keys for E^b and $D^\#$ and also for $G^\#$ and A^b.[1] At this same time, Ramis[2] noted that split keys were being used in Spain, but objected to having separate keys for A^b and $G^\#$ and for $F^\#$ and G^b, on the ground that this would be mixing the chromatic with the diatonic genus. From Germany came further evidence of the divided keyboard from Arnold Schlick,[3] who referred to an organ constructed at the turn of the sixteenth century "that had double semitones on manual and pedal ... which were called half semitones or 'ignoten.'"

There are frequent references to multiple division during the sixteenth and seventeenth centuries, chiefly by Italian theorists. Jean Rousseau[4] in 1687 deplored the fact that the French clavecins did not have the "doubles feintes" common in Italy, and consequently had "mauvais effets dans les Tons transposez." But the split keys must have been very common in Germany during the latter part of the seventeenth and beginning of the eighteenth centuries, if we may judge by the copious references to "subsemitonia" by Werckmeister and his successors. Buttstett, it is true, said in 1733 that the sub- and supersemitonia were "mehr curieux als practicabel."[5] But six years later, in Holland, van Blankenburg was to show "'t Gesnede Clavier" with three extra

---

[1] Wilhelm Dupont, Geschichte der musicalischen Temperatur, p. 45.

[2] Musica practica, Tract. 2, Cap. 4.

[3] Spiegel der Orgelmacher und Organisten (Maintz, 1511), Chap. 8. Reprinted in Monatshefte für Musikgeschichte, 1869.

[4] Traité de la viole (Paris, 1687), p. 50.

[5] Johann Heinrich Buttstett, Kurze Anführung zum General-Bass (2nd edition; Leipzig, 1733), p. 20.

keys, as well as an "Archicymbalam" with eighteen notes in the octave.[6]

Handel played on English organs with split keys.[7] Father Smith's Temple Church organ in London, constructed in 1682-83, had the same pairs of divided keys as the Lucca organ, G#-A♭ and D#-E♭, and so did Durham Cathedral. The organ of the Foundling Hospital (1759) had an ingenious mechanism by which D♭ and A♭ could be substituted for C# and D#, or D# and A# for E♭ and B♭, thus increasing the compass to sixteen notes, without increasing the number of keys.

Many of the sources said nothing about the tuning of the extra notes, and we can freely assume that whatever variety of meantone temperament was used for the twelve regular notes was extended both clockwise and counterclockwise around the circle (or, rather, spiral) of fifths. More interesting to us are the systems that represent just intonation, as extended to the enharmonic scale. We have already noted that Fogliano (1529) had felt the need for two D's and two B♭'s, to ensure just triads, but was willing to settle for a mean D and a mean B♭. But van Blankenburg, mentioned above, included both pairs of notes in his Archicymbalam, and so did almost all of the men whose systems will be described below.

The "enharmonic genus" of Salinas[8] was one of the earliest and best of these systems. Although it contained twenty-four notes, it had nothing in common with a real enharmonic scale composed of quarter tones. It is just intonation extended to seven sharps and six flats. In tabular form it would appear as shown in Table 104.

Observe that all the notes in the right diagonal are duplicated on the left, a comma lower. Thus it is possible to play all major triads from G♭ through G#, and all minor triads from E♭ through E#. Mersenne's "parfait diapason"[9] is based upon Salinas' system, with the addition of seven more notes, or thirty-one in all

[6]Quirinus van Blankenburg, Elementa musica (The Hague, 1739), p. 112.

[7]Helmholtz, Sensations of Tone, p. 434.

[8]De musica libri VII, p. 122.

[9]Harmonie universelle, p. 338.

(see Figure G). These would be joined to Table 104 on the left side, as shown in Table 105.

Table 104. Salinas' Enharmonic Genus

$$A^{\#-2} \quad E^{\#-2} \quad B^{\#-2}$$
$$F^{\#-1} \quad C^{\#-1} \quad G^{\#-1} \quad D^{\#-1} \quad A^{\#-1}$$
$$D^0 \quad A^0 \quad E^0 \quad B^0 \quad F^{\#0}$$
$$B^{b+1} \quad F^{+1} \quad C^{+1} \quad G^{+1} \quad D^{+1}$$
$$G^{b+2} \quad D^{b+2} \quad A^{b+2} \quad E^{b+2} \quad B^{b+2}$$
$$G^{b+3}$$

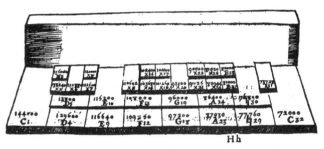

Fig. G. Mersenne's Keyboard with Thirty-One Notes in the Octave
(From Mersenne's Harmonie universelle)
Reproduced by courtesy of the Library of Congress

Table 105. Mersenne's Addition to Salinas' System

$$A^{-1} \quad E^{-1} \quad B^{-1}$$
$$F^0 \qquad G^0$$
$$A^{b+1} \quad E^{b+1}$$

This is not a particularly clever addition. Note that Mersenne did not have a C^0. Furthermore, for the sake of symmetry, there should have been D^{b+1} in the lowest line of Mersenne's additional notes, B^{bb+2}, F^{b+2}, and C^{b+2} in the line below it, and $C^{\#-2}$, $G^{\#-2}$, and $D^{\#-2}$ in the line above the highest line, or a total of thirty-nine notes.

109

The praiseworthy thing about Mersenne's addition is that it recognized the need for having more pairs of notes differing by a comma. Imperfect as his scheme was, it would be much more useful than the 34-note keyboard of Galeazzo Sabbatini, given by Kircher.[10] There were, as usual with Kircher, many errors in the figures, and an erratic manner of naming the notes. The actual notes of Sabbatini's keyboard are shown in Table 106.

Table 106. Sabbatini's Keyboard

$$
\begin{array}{ccccc}
 & & Cx^{-3} & Gx^{-3} & Dx^{-3} & Ax^{-3} \\
 & A^{\#-2} & E^{\#-2} & B^{\#-2} & [F^{\#-2}] \\
 & F^{\#-1} & C^{\#-1} & G^{\#-1} & D^{\#-1} \\
 D^{0} & A^{0} & E^{0} & B^{0} \\
 B^{b+1} & F^{+1} & C^{+1} & G^{+1} \\
[G^{b+2}] & D^{b+2} & A^{b+2} & E^{b+2} \\
E^{bb+3} & B^{bb+3} & F^{b+3} & C^{b+3} \\
C^{bb+4} & G^{bb+4} & D^{bb+4} & A^{bb+4} \\
E^{bbb+5} & B^{bbb+5} & [F^{bbb+5}] \\
 & D^{bbb+6}
\end{array}
$$

Except for the three notes in brackets which have been supplied, this is a beautifully symmetric scheme. But how different from that of Salinas! Here there are no notes differing by the syntonic comma, with the result that no major triad based on a note in the diagonal on the right will have a pure fifth, and there will be a similar series of defective minor triads. With this intonation it is not even possible to supply a missing note by its enharmonic equivalent, because no pair of notes differs by the ditonic comma either. The most characteristic small interval in it is the great diesis of 42 cents, as between $A^{\#-2}$ and B^{b+1}, whereas $A^{\#-1}$, needed as the fifth of the $D^{\#}$ triad, lies almost half way between these two notes, 22 cents higher than $A^{\#-2}$ and 20 cents lower than B^{b+1}. Other small intervals of little use contain 28, 14, and 8 cents. This, then, is an example of just

[10]Athanasius Kircher, Musurgia universalis, I, 460.

intonation carried to an absurd end. Doni's three-manual organ keyboard[11] (abacus Triharmonicus) was more elaborate than any system previously described, with sixty keys in the octave, but with only thirty-nine distinct pitches. The lowest keyboard was the Dorian, then the Phrygian, and finally the Lydian. The arrangement of the notes on each keyboard was identical, and the keyboards were tuned a major third apart, so that the Dorian E, the Phrygian C, and the Lydian A^b were the same pitch. The tuning was largely just, as can be seen from Table 107, which represents seventeen of the twenty notes on one keyboard.

Table 107. Doni's Keyboard

B^{-2}	$F^{\#-2}$	$C^{\#-2}$	$G^{\#-2}$	$D^{\#-2}$
D^{-1}	A^{-1}	E^{-1}	B^{-1}	
B^{b0} F^0	C^0	G^0	D^0	
G^{b+1}	A^{b+1}	E^{b+1}		

This arrangement is somewhat lacking in symmetry, and the additional three notes, which were real quarter tones, were of no use except to illustrate the scales of the Greeks, this being one of the uses of the organ. The enharmonic notes were formed, as Didymus formed his, by an arithmetical division of the syntonic semitone, 16:15, into 32:31 and 31:30 quarter tones.[12]

The nineteenth century was particularly rife with proposals to increase greatly the number of notes in the octave. Many of the instruments upon which the inventors practiced their ingenuity were harmoniums, intended for experimental purposes only. One of the more modest was Helmholtz's, already mentioned in Chapter V, with only twenty-four notes in the octave.[13] It followed a suggestion by Euler in 1739 that each manual be in the

[11]Giovanni Battista Doni, Compendio del trattato de' generi, e de' modi (Rome, 1635), Chap. 13.

[12]Shohé Tanaka (in Vierteljahrsschrift für Musikwissenschaft, VI [1890] , 85) was in error in showing these notes of Doni as only a comma higher than the lower note of the pair forming the semitone.

[13]Helmholtz, Sensations of Tone, p. 316 f.

111

Pythagorean tuning, the one manual a comma higher than the other. General Thompson followed Doni's lead by having three manuals on his Enharmonic Organ, with forty different pitches in the octave. Henry Poole's Euharmonic Organ had only two black keys on the keyboard; but through a series of eleven pedals all the notes could be transposed into five sharp and five flat keys, giving fifty distinct pitches in the octave.

Liston's organ also relied upon pedals to obtain a great variety of notes with the minimum number of keys.[14] With only twelve keys to the octave, tuned in just intonation, he was able by means of six pedals to add their enharmonic equivalents, thus having twenty-four notes in his normal scale. These are shown in Table 108. Then by three acute pedals all these notes could be raised in pitch by a comma. Two grave pedals similarly lowered nine or eleven of the normal notes by a comma. Thus Liston had a total of fifty-nine pitches available.

Of Liston's fifty-nine notes, there were ten pairs, such as D^{b0}-$C^{\#-2}$, which differed by the schisma, 2 cents. Furthermore, Cx^{-3} and $E^{\#-3}$ differed by only six cents from D^{b+1} and F^{b+3} respectively, and could be considered equivalent pairs also. Thus there were essentially only 47 separate pitches. These included four larger intervals: between C^{+1} and $C^{\#-2}$ and between Cx^{-4} and D^{-1} there were two commas; between $E^{\#-1}$ and $F^{\#-2}$ and between $A^{\#-1}$ and B^{-2} there were three. If these larger intervals had been divided, the octave would have contained 43 + 2 x 2 + 2 x 3 = 53 commas, which is the number one might have

Table 108. Liston's Enharmonic Organ

					$B^{\#-3}$		Fx^{-3}		Cx^{-3}	
				$G^{\#-2}$		$D^{\#-2}$		$A^{\#-2}$		$E^{\#-2}$
			A^{-1}		E^{-1}		B^{-1}		$F^{\#-1}$		$C^{\#-1}$
		B^{b0}		F^0		C^0		G^0		D^0	
C^{b+1}	G^{b+1}		D^{b+1}		A^{b+1}		E^{b+1}				
		B^{bb+2}		F^{b+2}						

[14]Henry Liston, An Essay upon Perfect Intonation (Edinburgh, 1812), pp. 3-7, 33-40.

anticipated. These "commas" are not all the same size. The ditonic comma does not occur at all except as the sum of the syntonic comma and the schisma. The syntonic comma is, as is evident from the scheme of pedals, the most common interval. But intervals of 20 cents, as $D^{\#-2}$ -E^{b0}, and of 26 cents, as G^{+1} -$G^{\#-3}$, also occur.

More ambitious was Steiner's system.[15] For the key of C he used 12 notes in just intonation, symmetrically arranged in three groups of 4 notes each. But these could be transposed mechanically into any of 12 different keys, the keynotes being tuned by perfect fifths. Thus there were 144 notes, but only 45 distinct pitches. Shohé Tanaka adopted Steiner's idea of having 12 keynotes in Pythagorean tuning, for mechanical transposition. But he extended his keyboard to 26 different notes, as shown in Table 109. Of the 312 notes to the octave of Tanaka's "Transponir-Harmonium" or "Enharmonium," there were only 70 unduplicated pitches, no more than on an organ described by Ellis which had a total of 14 x 11 or 154 notes to the octave, with 70 separate pitches.

Table 109. Tanaka's Enharmonium

	$F^{\#-2}$	$C^{\#-2}$	$G^{\#-2}$	$D^{\#-2}$	$A^{\#-2}$	$E^{\#-2}$
G^{-1}	D^{-1}	A^{-1}	E^{-1}	B^{-1}	$F^{\#-1}$	$C^{\#-1}$
B^{b0}	F^0	C^0	G^0	D^0	A^0	E^0
G^{b+1}	D^{b+1}	A^{b+1}	E^{b+1}	B^{b+1}	F^{+1}	

Equal Divisions

With Tanaka's Enharmonium we may safely drop the subject of just intonation extended. The theory is simple enough: provide at least four sets of notes, each set being in Pythagorean tuning and forming just major thirds with the notes in another set; construct a keyboard upon which these notes may be played with the minimum of inconvenience. Only in the design of the keyboards did the inventors show their ingenuity, an ingenuity that might better have been devoted to something more practical.

[15]Tanaka, op. cit., pp. 18 f. and 23 ff.

The other direction in which multiple division developed had far greater possibilities. This was the division of the octave into more than twelve acoustically equal parts.[16] Any regular system of tuning — a system constructed on a fixed value of the fifth — will eventually reach a point where its "comma," the error for the enharmonic equivalent of the keynote, is small enough to be disregarded. Thus we have closed systems that agree more or less closely with the various types of meantone temperament, etc.

If the Pythagorean tuning is extended to 17 notes, an interval of 66 cents is formed — a doubly diminished third, as Ax-C. Divided among 17 notes, the deficit is about 4 cents, the amount by which each fifth must be raised to have a closed system. The fifth (now taken as 10/17 octave) contains 706 cents, being raised by about the same amount that it is lowered in the Silbermann variety of meantone temperament. The major third (6/17 octave) contains 423 cents, being more than twice as sharp as it is in equal temperament, and the minor third is correspondingly very flat. If we take 5 parts for the third, this becomes a neutral third of 353 cents, such as the thirds found in some scales of the Orient.

In the 17-division, the tone is composed of 3 equal parts, of which the diatonic semitone comprises 1 part and the chromatic semitone 2 parts. Since the diatonic semitone, 70 cents, is even smaller than in the Pythagorean tuning, this system is well adapted to melody. It is, of course, wholly unacceptable for harmony because of its outsize thirds. It is notated with 5 sharps and 5 flats only, $D^{\#}$ and $A^{\#}$ being considered the equivalent of F^{b} and C^{b}, and G^{b} and D^{b} the equivalent of $E^{\#}$ and $B^{\#}$. The 17-division is the well-known Arabian scale of third-tones.[17]

A much more popular system is the 19-division. It arises in much the same way as the 17-division, except that, as in just in-

---

[16]For the sake of completeness two smaller divisions should be mentioned: the Javanese equal pentatonic and the Siamese equal heptatonic. For a strange reference to the latter see J. Murray Barbour, "Nierop's Hackebort," Musical Quarterly, XX (1934), 312-319.

[17]Joseph Sauveur ("Système général des intervalles des sons," Mémoires de l'académie royale des sciences, 1701, pp. 445 f.) made an early reference to this scale, and of course it is discussed in all modern accounts of Arabian theory.

114

tonation, the diatonic semitone is considered the larger, with 2 parts to 1 for the chromatic semitone. Since the octave contains 5 tones and 2 semitones, it will have $5 \times 3 + 2 \times 2 = 19$ parts. The history of the 19-division goes back to the middle of the sixteenth century, when Zarlino and Salinas discussed, among types of meantone tuning, one in which the fifth was tempered by 1/3 comma. Like the other two types (1/4 and 2/7 comma) it was intended for a cembalo with 19 notes to the octave.[18] Salinas' claim as inventor has not been disputed. He was rather apologetic concerning it, because of its greater deviation from pure intervals than the other two. He apparently did not realize that this could not be distinguished from an equal division into 19 parts, and that thus, as a closed system, it possessed a great advantage. It can be notated with 6 sharps and 6 flats, C^b being the equivalent of $B^\#$ and $E^\#$ of F^b.

We have plenty of evidence from past centuries of cembali with 19 notes in the octave, for which this division would have been the ideal tuning. Zarlino[19] described such a cembalo that Master Domenico Pesarese had made for him. Elsasz is frequently but erroneously called the inventor of the 19-note cembalo, because his instrument is described in Praetorius' Syntagma.

After having been neglected during the nineteenth century for the more elaborate systems such as have been described in the previous section of this chapter, the 19-division was revived in the second quarter of the twentieth century. It has had eloquent contemporary advocates in Ariel, Kornerup, and Yasser. Of all these enthusiasts, Yasser has gone to the greatest pains to show the construction of the system and its possibilities.[20] He differs radically from its other adherents, who have proposed it partly for the sake of differentiating enharmonic pairs of notes, but chiefly because its triads are more consonant than those of equal temperament. Yasser holds that the harmony of Scriabin and the

[18]See Chapter III for further discussion of the various equivalents of the cyclic multiple systems.

[19]Institutioni armoniche, p. 140.

[20]Joseph Yasser, A Theory of Evolving Tonality (New York, 1932).

tone-rows of Schönberg show an intuitive striving toward the 19-division, since a scale as used should contain unequal divisions, being a selection from an equal division of more parts. Thus the Siamese scale of 7 equal parts is suitable for pentatonic melodies; the ordinary 12-note chromatic scale, for heptatonic melodies; and the 19-division for melodies built upon the 12-note scale. Yasser's attempt to give a historical foundation is so defective that his case emerges considerably weaker than if he had presented his system simply from the speculative point of view.

There does not seem to be much chance of the 19-division coming into use in our day. Its thirds and fifths have been discussed in Chapter III. To modern ears, accustomed to the sharp major thirds of equal temperament, the thirds of 379 cents, 1/3 comma flat, would sound insipid in the extreme. There would seem to be a better chance for the acceptance of a system that does not differ so markedly in its intervals from our own.

The 22-division belongs next in our study of equal divisions. It was not discussed by Sauveur, Romieu, or Drobisch. In fact, Bosanquet did not even mention it in his comprehensive book on temperament, although Opelt had treated it carefully twenty-five years before.[21] But the following year Bosanquet contributed an article to the Royal Society, "On the Hindoo Division of the Octave." In it he referred to S. M. Tagore's Hindu Music and an article in Fétis' Histoire générale. There the Hindoo scale was said to consist of 22 small intervals called "S'rutis." If these are considered equal, a new system arises with "practically perfect" major thirds (actually, being 381.5 cents, they are almost 5 cents flat) and very sharp fifths (709 cents, or 7 cents sharp). Riemann later was to include the 22-division in his discussion of various systems, and it is frequently mentioned today. Unfortunately, the Hindoo theory does not make the S'rutis all equal, but that does not prevent the division from finding an honored place among these others.

The thirds of the 22-division are better than those of the 19-division, and its fifths are no worse. However, it is not so good

[21]F. W. Opelt, Allgemeine Theorie der Musik, Chap. IV.

a system for the performance of European music. The difficulty lies in the formation of the major third. The fifth is taken as 13/22 octave, whence the tone has 4 parts and the ditone, 8. But 8/22 octave is 436 cents, an impossibly high value. Hence the major third must be only 7 parts, or 381.5 cents. This means that D# is taken as the major third above C, and Fb (or Cx) as the third above B. This is an awkward feature, but one that we shall run into with most of these equal divisions. It is not ordinarily possible to retain our ideas of tone relations while making a division of the octave that will provide good fifths and thirds.

The 24-division has the same good fifths and sharp thirds as the 12-division, and the deviations for the 29-division are very similar, but with plus and minus signs reversed. Both the 25- and the 28-divisions have good thirds and quite poor fifths. So none of these four divisions is of great import. The 24-division does have its place, as a possible realization of Aristoxenus' theory that the enharmonic diesis is a true quarter tone, the half of the equal semitone. Kircher[22] presented it as such, together with a geometrical method of obtaining the quarter tones on the monochord. Rossi[23] later gave the string-lengths for equal quarter tones, and Neidhardt offered a similar table many years afterwards.[24] The 29-division has its place as a member in the series that contains the 17-division, but that fact does not improve the quality of its thirds.

The next system of importance is the 31-division. It is the most ancient of them all and well worth the attention that has been given to it. Observe that 31 logically follows 19 in the Fibonacci series: 5, 7, 12, 19, 31, 50, 81, ... This system was first described by Vicentino[25] in 1555, as the method of tuning his Archicembalo. In theory this was constructed in an attempt to reconcile the ideas of the ancient Greeks with those of sixteenth century practice. In reality it was a clever method for extending the usual meantone temperament of 1/4 comma until

[22]Musurgia universalis, I, p. 208.

[23]Sistema musico, p. 102.

[24]J. G. Neidhardt, Sectio canonis harmonici, p. 31.

[25]L'antica musica, Book 5, Chaps. 3-5.

117

it formed practically a closed system.

The Archicembalo contained six ranks of keys, of which the first two represented the ordinary harpsichord keyboard with 7 natural keys, 3 sharps, and 2 flats. The third "order" contained 4 more sharps and 3 flats. The fourth order continued the flat succession with 7 more keys, and the fifth added 5 more sharps. (The sixth order is in tune with the first.) Thus all the notes would lie in a succession of fifths from G^{bb} to Ax, and the circle would be completed by taking Ex as equivalent to G^{bb} or C^{bb} to Ax. (Vicentino himself gave a second tuning to the fourth order that showed that he considered the above to be equivalent pitches.)

Vicentino specified that the first three orders of the Archicembalo should be tuned "justly with the temperament of the flattened fifth, according to the usage and tuning common to all the keyboard instruments, as organs, cembali, clavichords, and the like." But the other three orders may be tuned "with the perfect fifth" to the first three orders. For example, the G of the fourth order (that is, A^{bb}) is to be a perfect fifth above the C of the first order. It must be admitted that this part of Vicentino's scheme does not seem to make sense.

If we ignore this puzzling doctrine of the perfect fifth, we have a logical system, formed by a complete sequence of 31 tempered fifths. The amount of tempering is not specified, but was to be the same as that of common practice. The common practice was the ordinary meantone temperament, in which major thirds are perfect. This is undoubtedly what Vicentino used.

By logarithms Christian Huyghens[26] showed that the 31-division does not differ perceptibly from the 1/4-comma temperament. More specifically he said: "The fifth of our division is no more than 1/110 comma higher than the tempered fifths, which difference is entirely imperceptible; but which would render that consonance so much the more perfect." Riemann[27] was confused by this remark, not realizing that Huyghens meant that this fifth was 1/110 comma higher than a fifth tempered by 1/4 comma.

[26]"Novus cyclus harmonicus," Opera varia (Leyden, 1724), pp. 747-754.
[27]Geschichte der Musiktheorie, p. 359.

The difference between the logarithm of the meantone fifth, .174725011, and that of $2^{18/31}$, .1757916100, is .0000491089, which is quite close to 1/110 of the logarithm of the syntonic comma, .0053951317. Tanaka[28] and Riemann have described Gonzaga's harpsichord in the Museo Civico in Bologna, dated 1606. Essentially the same as Vicentino's instrument, its arrangement of notes is somewhat different, the second row, for example, consisting solely of sharped notes, instead of 3 sharps and 2 flats. Father Scipione Stella's eight-manual harpsichord also resembled Vicentino's, but had a couple of manuals duplicated to facilitate the execution.[29]

An improved version of Vicentino's Archicembalo was Colonna's 6-manual Sambuca Lincea.[30] The difficulty with Vicentino's system was the unsystematic arrangement of the second and third orders. Both $C^{\#}$ and E^{b}, for example, were in the second order, while D^{b} and $D^{\#}$ were in the third. If the instrument was to be considered merely an extension of an ordinary cembalo with twelve notes in the octave, such an arrangement was no doubt good enough. But, for its complete possibilities to be available, any such instrument needs what Bosanquet called a "generalized keyboard."

Colonna came close to supplying this lack. Each of his orders contained seven notes, and was 1/5 tone above the preceding order. In our notation, the notes between C in the first order and D in the sixth would be D^{bb}, $C^{\#}$, D^{b}, and Cx. Colonna's notation for them was Cx, $C^{\#}$, D^{b}, and $C^{\natural}$, respectively. This is very clumsy; but his idea of the division was entirely correct, as can be seen from the scales he listed as examples of the capabilities of the instrument. He included such remote major keys as C^{b}, $A^{\#}$, E^{bb}, and $G^{\#}$ — all of course with his peculiar notation.

[28]Shohé Tanaka, in Vierteljahrsschrift für Musikwissenschaft, VI (1890), pp. 74 f.

[29]Fabio Colonna, La sambuca lincea (Naples, 1618), p. 6.

[30]Ibid., passim.

The germ of the 31-division lay in the contention of Marchettus of Padua that a tone could be divided into five parts. After Vicentino, Salinas and Mersenne discussed the system without realizing its value. Hizler[31] referred to a 31-note octave, but used in practice only 13 notes, having both a D# and an Eb. Rossi[32] anticipated Huyghens in obtaining by logarithms the string-lengths for the 31-division, but did not call attention to the fact that its pitches were so close to those of the meantone temperament which he also presented. (With A at 41472, his meantone E was 27734, the 31-division E, 27730.) Gallimard[33] was to follow Huyghen's lead in comparing the logarithms of the two temperaments. Van Blankenburg[34] was to use the 31-division as a sort of tuning measure, much as Sauveur used the 43-division and Mercator the 53-division. According to van Blankenburg, Neidhardt's equal temperament was full of "young wolves, each 1/3 of the large wolf," because the major third of equal temperament contains 10 1/3 parts instead of the 10 parts of the 31-division.

The string-lengths for the 31-division were also given by Ambrose Warren,[35] for the octave 8000.0 to 4000.0. Warren showed how this temperament could be applied to the fingerboard of the violin, for a string 13 inches long.

For obtaining the 31-division mechanically, Rossi recommended the mesolabium. Salinas, Zarlino, and Philander have stated that the mesolabium could be used for finding an unlimited number of geometrical means between two lines, provided the number of parallelograms was increased correspondingly. Perhaps so, but Rossi[36] was undoubtedly correct in saying that "in dividing the octave into 31 parts you will experience greater dif-

[31]Daniel Hizler, Extract aus der neuen Musica oder Singkunst (Nürnberg, 1623), p. 31.

[32]Sistema musico, pp. 86, 64.

[33]J. E. Gallimard, L'arithmétique des musiciens (Paris, 1754), Table XVI, p. 25.

[34]Elementa musica, p. 115.

[35]The Tonometer (London, 1725), table at end of book.

[36]Sistema musico, p. 111.

ficulty because of the great number of rectangles," and Mersenne[37] said flatly that it "is of no use except for finding two means between two given lines."
Romieu[38] included the 31-division among those for which he had obtained correspondences, calling it a temperament of 2/9 comma. This is not very close, for 1/4 - 1/110 = 53/220. (Drobisch's 74-division is the real 2/9-comma temperament.) It is possible that writers before Romieu had this tuning in mind when they wrote about the 2/9-comma temperament. Printz[39] for example, spoke of a "still earlier" temperament that took 2/9 comma from each fifth. Earlier, perhaps, than Zarlino's 2/7 comma, which he had been discussing previously. But Lemme Rossi, who gave a detailed treatment to the 2/9-comma tuning, did not identify it with the 31-division.

The 34-division is a positive system, like the 22-division. That is, its fifth of 706 cents is larger than the perfect fifth, being the same size as for the 17-division. Its third is about 2 cents sharp. Thus it provides slightly greater consonance than the 31-division. But, like the 22-division, it has remained one of the stepchildren of multiple division, largely because it is in a series for which ordinary notation cannot be used. There is a surprising mention of the 34-division by Cyriac Schneegass in 1591 (see Chapter III), but his own monochord came closer to the 2/9-comma division. Bosanquet had indicated the relation between the 22- and 34-divisions, and had praised the 56- and 87-divisions also as similar systems. Opelt, too, has included it in his fairly short list.

The 36-division has little to recommend it, although its stringlengths were worked out by Berlin,[40] and Appun and Oettingen both found it worth describing.[41]

The 41-division has excellent fifths (702.4 cents), but thirds

---

[37]Harmonie universelle, p. 224.

[38]In Mémoires de l'académie royale des sciences, 1758, p. 837.

[39]Phrynis Mytilenaeus oder der satyrische Componist, p. 88.

[40]Johann Daniel Berlin, Anleitung zur Tonometrie (Copenhagen and Leipzig, 1767), pp. 26-27.

[41]Hugo Riemann, Populäre Darstellung der Akustik (Berlin, 1896), p. 138.

(380.5) that are almost six cents flat, being in this latter respect inferior to the 31- and 34-divisions. It occurs in a worthy series: 12, 17, 29, 41, 53, ... This system was not singled out by any of the earlier writers, but received considerable attention from such nineteenth century theorists as Delezenne, Drobisch, and Bosanquet. Paul von Janko[42] set himself the task of ascertaining the best system between 12 and 53 divisions, and chose the 41-division. Rather naïvely, he concluded he had discovered this system, since Riemann had not mentioned it!

The 43-division is associated with the name of Sauveur,[43] who used its intervals (Merides) as a unit of musical measure. The Merides were divided into seven parts called Eptamerides. For more subtle distinctions, Sauveur suggested using Decamerides, 10 of which comprised one Eptameride. But he did not use the Decamerides in practice. Thus there were 43 x 7 = 301 Eptamerides in the octave, or 3010 Decamerides. Since .30103 is the common logarithm of 2, it is possible to convert directly from logarithms to Eptamerides by dropping the decimal point and all but the first three digits of the logarithm.

The 43-division is a closed system approximating the 1/5-comma variety of meantone temperament, which, as we saw in Chapter III, had been mentioned by Verheijen and Rossi. Its thirds and fifths have an equal and opposite error of slightly over four cents, thus making it somewhat inferior to the 34-division, although the equality of the error may have some weight in ranking the two systems. Since 43 is a number occurring in a useful series for multiple division -- 12, 19, 31, 43, 55, ... — this division was treated by Romieu, Opelt, Drobisch, and Bosanquet.

The 50-division need not detain us long. It may be thought of as an octave composed of ditonic commas, since 1200 ÷ 24 = 50. It was advocated by Henfling in 1710 and criticized by Sauveur[44] the following year. A century later Opelt was to mention it.

[42]"Über mehr als zwölfstufige gleichschwebende Temperaturen," Beiträge zur Akustik und Musikwissenschaft, 1901, pp. 6-12.

[43]Joseph Sauveur, in Mémoires de l'académie royale des sciences, 1701, pp. 403-498.

[44]Joseph Sauveur, "Table générale des systèmes tempérés de musique," Mémoires de l'académie royale des sciences, 1711, p. 406 f.

Bosanquet has included it as a member of the series: 12, 19, 31, 50, ... This division shows no improvement over the 31-division. Its fifths have about the same value as those of the latter, and its thirds are flatter than the latter's were sharp. Kornerup[45] has waxed lyrical in its praise, as a closed system corresponding to Zarlino's 2/7-comma meantone temperament. He showed that the value for Zarlino's chromatic semitone (70.6724 cents) came very close to the mean of the chromatic semitones for the 19- and 31-divisions (70.2886), and might have added that this similarity extends throughout, since all three are regular systems. He found that the greatest deviation of the 2/7-comma tuning from the 50-division is a little over three cents, and is much less for most notes. We shall have more to say later about the special part of Kornerup's theory that has caused him to overvalue this system.

The most important system after the 31- is the 53-division. In theory it is also the most ancient. According to Boethius,[46] Pythagoras' disciple Philolaus held that, since the tone is divisible into minor semitones and a comma, and since the semitone is divisible into two diaschismata, the tone is then divisible into four diaschismata plus a comma. If, now, the diaschisma is taken as two commas exactly, the tone is divided into nine commas. (Note what was said about the ditonic comma in connection with the 50-division.)

This dictum about the number of commas in a tone was one of the most persistent parts of the Pythagorean system. Writers in the early sixteenth century sometimes mentioned the fact that there are nine commas in a tone, without giving any other tuning lore. They probably included, however, the statement that the diatonic semitone contains four commas, the chromatic semitone, five. Amusingly enough, after just intonation became the ideal, writers continued to talk about commas; but now it was the chromatic semitone that contained four commas, the diatonic semitone, five.

Since the Pythagorean diatonic semitone contains 90 cents,

---

[45]Thorvald Kornerup, Das Tonsystem des Italieners Zarlino (Copenhagen, 1930).

[46]A. M. S. Boethius, De institutione musica, Book 3, Chap. 8.

and the chromatic, 114, their ratio is 3 3/4:4 3/4, or approximately 4:5. Similarly, if we choose the larger just chromatic semitone of 92 cents and the smaller just diatonic semitone of 112 cents, the ratio will be 4 1/2:5 1/2, or, again, 4:5. But the ratio might be taken as 5:6, giving rise to the 67-division discussed below. The comma, taken as 1/9 Pythagorean tone, would have a mean value of 22.7 cents, lying between the syntonic and the ditonic commas.

If there are 9 commas in a tone, the octave contains 5 x 9 + 2 x 4 = 53 commas — provided we are thinking in terms of the Pythagorean tuning. If we are thinking in terms of just intonation, with a large diatonic semitone, there will be 5 x 9 + 2 x 5 = 55 commas. Thus the 55-division has received attention also.

There are several advantages to the 53-division. Its fifths are practically perfect (.1 cent flat), so that it is unnecessary to use a monochord for tuning. Its thirds are very slightly flat (1.4 cents). However, since it is a positive system, with fifths sharper than those of equal temperament, the pure major third above C is F^b, with 17 parts, whereas C-E represents the Pythagorean third, with 18 parts. This would be confusing to the performer.

After the time of the Greeks, the history of the 53-division takes us to China, where the Pythagorean tuning had been known for many centuries, probably since the invasion of Alexander the Great. In 1713 it was confirmed as the official scale, however widely instrumental tunings may have differed from it in practice.

One of the most remarkable of the early Chinese theorists was King Fâng, who, according to Courant,[47] "calculated exactly the proportional numbers to 60 lü," that is, he extended the Pythagorean system to 60 notes. These results were published by Seū-mà Pyeoū, who died in 306 A. D. King Fâng observed that the 54th note was almost identical with the first note. Courant's figures are 177,147 for the first; 176,777 for the 54th.

Seventeenth century European theorists who referred definitely to this system include Mersenne and Kircher. Tanaka

---

[47]Maurice Courant, "Chine et Corée," Encyclopédie de la musique et dictionnaire du conservatoire (Paris, 1913), Part I, Vol. I, p. 88.

mentioned Kircher's name in this connection, thus differing from the majority of his contemporaries, who ascribed the system to Mercator. According to Holder,[48] Nicholas Mercator had "deduced an ingenious Invention of finding and applying a least Common Measure to all Harmonic Intervals, not precisely perfect, but very near it." This was the division into 53 commas. There is no evidence, in Holder's account, that Mercator intended this system to be used on an instrument. It was to be merely a "Common Measure."

Of 25 systems that Sauveur discussed, only two, the 17- and 53-divisions, were positive. He was unable to appreciate the splendid value of the thirds of the latter, since, according to his theory, its thirds would have to be as large as Pythagorean thirds. Romieu did not even mention this system. Drobisch, too, did not at first (1853) appreciate the 53-division, discarding it because of its sharp thirds. But two years later he re-evaluated both the 41- and the 53-divisions, showing that a just major scale could be obtained with them by using C D F^b G B^{bb} C^b C.[49]

The stage was thus set for Bosanquet's detailed study of multiple division, which culminated in his invention of the "generalized keyboard" for regular systems. In his article in the Royal Society's Proceedings, 1874-75, Bosanquet gave a clear and comprehensive treatment of regular systems, both positive and negative, with a possible notation for them. He showed how various systems could be applied to his keyboard, especially the 53- and 118-divisions. In his symmetrical arrangement, 84 keys were needed for the 53 different notes in the octave. Obviously, then, Bosanquet's name should be singled out for especial mention, since he applied the system to an enharmonic harmonium and did not simply discuss it as his predecessors had done.

As has been noted above, the 55-division is the negative counterpart of the 53-division, thus having the advantage that ordinary notation can be used. That is its only advantage, for its fifths (698.2 cents) are no better than those of the 43-division,

[48]William Holder, Treatise...of Harmony, p. 79.

[49]M. W. Drobisch, "Über musikalische Tonbestimmung und Temperatur," Abhandlungen der mathematisch-physischen Classe der königlich sächsischen Gesellschaft der Wissenschaften, IV (1855), 82-86.

and its thirds (392.7 cents) are inferior to the latter's. Sauveur devoted considerable space to this system, saying it was "followed by the musicians." This is a reasonable statement, for this system corresponds closely to the 1/6-comma variety of meantone temperament favored by Silbermann. Thus we have confirmation from France of the spread of this method.

Romieu showed the correspondence between the 55-division and the 1/6-comma tuning, and adopted the latter for his "tempérament anacratique."[50] He referred to Sauveur, and also to Ramarin's system as given in Kircher. Mattheson[51] presented this division from Johann Beer's Schola phonologica, saying that it required "that an octave should have 55 commas, but no major or minor tones."

Sorge, after disapproving of the ordinary 1/4-comma meantone, continued: "I am better pleased by the famous Capellmeister Telemann's system of intervals, in which the octave is divided into 55 geometrical parts (commas), that grow smaller from step to step."[52] Sorge explained that in its complete state it could not be used on the clavier; but it might be applied to the violin and to certain wind instruments, and was easiest for singers.

---

[50]Correspondences between multiple divisions and temperaments by fractional parts of the syntonic comma can be worked out by continued fractions. When the temperament of the fifth is 1/2 comma, the octave contains 26 parts. If d is the denominator of the fractional part of the comma (21.5 cents), the following formula gives the parts in the octave for $2 < d < 11$:
$$Sd = 7 + 12 \left[\frac{114d - 150.5}{12(21.5 - 2d)}\right],$$ where the expression in brackets is to be taken to the nearest integer. The list of correspondences is: 1/3 comma, 19 parts; 1/4 comma, 31 parts; 1/5 comma, 43 parts; 1/6 comma, 55 parts; 1/7 comma, 91 parts; 1/8 comma, 139 parts; 1/9 comma, 247 parts; 1/10 comma, 499 parts. Temperaments in which the numerator of the fraction is 2 are formed as follows: $\frac{1+1}{2+3} = \frac{2}{5}$ comma, 26 + 19 = 45 parts; $\frac{1+1}{3+4} = \frac{2}{7}$ comma, 19 + 31 = 50 parts; $\frac{1+1}{4+5} = \frac{2}{9}$ comma, 31 + 43 = 74 parts; $\frac{1+1}{5+6} = \frac{2}{11}$ comma, 43 + 55 = 98 parts, etc.

[51]J. Mattheson, Critica musica (Hamburg, 1722-25), II, 73 f.

[52]Georg Andreas Sorge, Gesprach zwischen einem Musico theoretico und einem Studioso musices, pp. 51 f.

William Jackson[53] found that the octave consists of 55 10/12 syntonic commas, or 670 units of 1/12 comma. He might well have assumed the octave to contain 56 commas precisely, since this is a fairly good division. A half century after Jackson, an anonymous work printed in Holland[54] stated that the ratio 81:80 is contained 56 times in the octave, but did not advocate this as a system of multiple division. Bosanquet mentioned the 56-division. It has excellent thirds, being 1 cent flat, as in the 28-division. Its fifths are 5 cents sharp.

The 58-division is also positive, its fifths being 2 cents sharp, as in the 29-division, and its thirds being 7 cents sharp. This is the division that is at the base of Dom Bedos' temperament,[55] although he chose the pitches for his monochord somewhat irregularly from it.

There are only a few other systems that should be mentioned. The 65-division has splendid fifths (.5 cent flat) and slightly sharp thirds (1.4 cents sharp). The 84-division, on the other hand, has only average fifths (2 cents flat), but excellent thirds (.6 cent flat). The 87-division has slightly sharp fifths (1.4 cents sharp), and practically perfect thirds (.1 cent flat). The 118-division has both fifths and thirds that are superlative (.5 cent flat and .2 sharp respectively).

The above four systems excel all others with more than 53 parts in the octave. But the specialists in multiple division have not always appreciated them. Sauveur, for example, discussed the 67-, 74-, 98-, 105-, 112-, and 117-divisions, as well as others that are no better than they, but did not mention any of the four systems in the previous paragraph. Romieu did not discuss any systems beyond the 55-division, but would have approved the 67-, 79-, and 91-divisions. Drobisch particularly favored the 74-division among systems that formed the major third regularly, as

---

[53]A Scheme Demonstrating the Perfection and Harmony of Sounds (London, 1726 [?]), chart.

[54]Exposition de quelques nouvelles vues mathématiques dans la theorie de la musique (Amsterdam, 1760), p. 28.

[55]Dom François Bedos de Celles, L'art du facteur d'orgues, 2nd Part (Paris, 1770); facsimile ed. (Kassel, 1935), p. 430.

C-E; among those that used C-F^b as a major third, he mentioned the 65-, 70-, 77-, 89-, and 94-divisions, and found the 53- and 118-divisions best of all. Bosanquet, praising most highly the 53- and 118-divisions, had kind words for the 56-, 65-, and 87-divisions also.

Theory of Multiple Division

The reason for the divergent results obtained by these theorists is that each had a different theory regarding acceptable divisions of the octave. Sauveur, although he did list two positive systems, had no real understanding of divisions in which C-F^b could be a major third. To him, the diatonic semitone was the larger: the problem of temperament was to decide upon a definite ratio between the diatonic and chromatic semitones, and that would automatically give a particular division of the octave. If, for example, the ratio is 3:2, there are $5 \times 7 + 2 \times 4 = 43$ parts; if 5:4, there are $5 \times 9 + 2 \times 5 = 55$ parts. We have pointed out above that only the first of these divisions is at all satisfactory. Let us see what the limit of the value of the fifth would be if the $(n + 1):n$ series were extended indefinitely. The fifth is $(7n + 4)/(12n + 7)$ octave, and its limit, as $n \longrightarrow \infty$, is 7/12 octave; that is, the fifth of equal temperament. The third, similarly, approaches 1/3 octave. Therefore, the farther the series goes, the better become its fifths, the poorer its thirds. This would seem, then, to be an inferior theory.

In other divisions listed by Sauveur the difference between the two sizes of semitone was two, three, or even four parts. Here, again, the fifth eventually comes close to 7/12 octave and the third to 3/12 octave. Romieu followed Sauveur's theory. To an extent so did Bosanquet. But the latter added the theory of positive systems. The primary positive system is 17, 29, 41, 53, 65, 77, 89, ... Here the fifth can be expressed as $(7n + 3)/(12n + 5)$ octave. Just as in the negative systems above, the limit of this ratio is 7/12 octave. For the 53- and 65-divisions the fifths are practically perfect; the thirds of these divisions have approximately equal, but opposite, deviations. This suggests a secondary positive system, the mean between the former two: 118, with both fifths and thirds well-nigh perfect. But there is nothing in these series themselves to facilitate choosing the best division or the two best. That had to be ascertained by comparing the intervals in the various divisions after they had been chosen. Again it would seem as if there were an arbitrary factor present. We have already spoken of Kornerup and his fondness for the 50-division.[56] His "golden" system of music was suggested by a study made by P. S. Wedell and N. P. J. Bertelsen in 1915. By the method of least squares they obtained the following octave series in which both the major third (5:4) and the augmented sixth (that is, the minor seventh, 7:4) approach their pure values: 3, 5, 7, 12, 19, ·31, 50, 81, 131, 212, 343, ... These of course are "golden" numbers, the law of the series being $S_n = S_{n-1} + S_{n-2}$. As $n \longrightarrow \infty$, $\dfrac{S_n}{S_{n+1}} \longrightarrow \dfrac{\sqrt{5}-1}{2} = .61803398$, a ratio which Kornerup called ω. It is this ratio which is used in the golden section of a line, where $(1 - \omega)/\omega = \omega$, and which Kornerup used as the basis of his tuning system. By rather simple arithmetic we find that the golden fifth is $(15 - \sqrt{5})/22$ octave, or 696.2144738 cents. The golden third is 384.8579 cents, only a fair approximation, since the pure third is 386.3137 cents. Therefore, even if the series is continued indefinitely, the fifth will never be less than about 6 cents, nor the third than 1.5 cents flat. Since we have already observed several systems with better thirds and fifths than this, it would seem as if the golden system is an ignis fatuus.

Drobisch[57] gave an interesting formula which combined Bosanquet's primary and secondary positive systems. The fifth of these systems will be: $(7n - 1)/2(6n - 1)$. For odd values of n, the octave contains 6n - 1 parts; for even values, twice as many.

[56]See Thorvald Kornerup, Das goldene Tonsystem als Fundament des theoretischen Akustik (Copenhagen, 1935).

[57]In Abhandlungen der mathematisch-physischen Classe der königlich sächsischen Gesellschaft der Wissenschaften, IV (1855), 79 f.

Hence he obtained the series (with n ranging from 4 through 15) :
46, 29, 70, 41, 94, 53, 118, 65, 142, 77, 166, 89.

Somewhat more general was Drobisch's attempt to find a division of the octave that would insure a good value for the fifth. He expressed the ratio of the fifth (log 3/2) to the octave (log 2) as a decimal, .5849625, or as a fraction, 46797/80000. From this ratio, by binary continued fractions, he obtained the series 2, 5, 12, 41, 53, 306, 665, [15601] ,.... Next he found all the powers of 3/2 from the 13th to the 53rd, in order to ascertain which approach a pure octave. This should have checked closely with his previous list, to which 17 and 29 would be semi-convergents. This, however, is his complete list: 17, 19, 22, 29, 31, 41, 43, 46, 51, 53. Having eliminated all positive divisions (those with raised fifths), he still had 19, 31, and 43 to add to his previous list.

Although the 50-division did not appear on either list, Drobisch anticipated Kornerup by showing that its fifth lies almost exactly between the fifths of the 19- and 31-divisions.* After these promising beginnings, he went off at a tangent by trying to find, by least squares, the value of the fifth that would produce the best values for five different intervals. Then, again using continued fractions, he found that successive approximations to this value (.5810541) form the series: 2, 5, 7, 12, 31, 74,.... This is why the 74-division had an especial appeal for him.

Drobisch's continued fractions were the first really scientific method of dividing the octave with regard to the principal consonances, the thirds and the fifths. The difficulty with it is that there are three magnitudes to be compared (third, fifth, and octave), but only one ratio (third to octave, fifth to octave, possibly third to fifth) can be approximated by binary continued fractions. If we must choose a single ratio, it is better to use that of the fifth to the octave, as Drobisch did, since the third may be expressed in terms of the fifth. But the usual formula, T = 4F - 2O, is valid only through O = 12. We have already noted that as fine a musical theorist as Sauveur failed to appreciate the 53-division, since he used the above formula and obtained a third that was one part large. Since the syntonic comma is about 1/56 octave, this formula will fail to give a correct number of parts for the third for any octave division greater than 28. Thus if O = 41, and F = 24, the formula makes T = 4 x 24 - 2 x 41 = 14, whereas the correct value is 13. If O = 665, and F = 389, T = 4 x 389 - 2 x 665 = 226, instead of 214. Knowing the value of the comma, we can correct our formula to read: $T = 4F - 2O - \left[\dfrac{O}{56}\right]$. But even this would only by accident give a value for the third with as small a deviation as that for the fifth in the same division. What is needed is a method that will approach the just values for third and fifth simultaneously.

The desired solution can be obtained only by ternary continued fractions, which are a means by which the ratios of three numbers may be approximated simultaneously, just as the ratios of two numbers may be approximated by binary continued fractions. When the ordinary or Jacobi ternary continued fractions are applied to the logarithms of the major third (5:4), perfect fifth (3:2), and octave (2:1), the octave divisions will be: 3, 25, 28, 31, 87, 817,....

There are two serious faults in these results. In the first place, the expansion converges too rapidly, and we are interested chiefly in small values, those for which the octave has fewer than 100 parts. In the second place, the first few terms are foreign to every other proposed solution, such as those by Sauveur and Drobisch on previous pages.

To insure slow convergence, a mixed expansion was evolved, which yields the following excellent series of octave divisions: 3, 5, 7, 12, 19, 31, 34, 53, 87, 118, 559, 612,....[58] The only serious omission is the Hindoo division, with 22 parts in the octave. The last term shown above (612) was said by Bosanquet to have been considered very good by Captain J. Herschel.

There is no record that Captain Herschel ever constructed an experimental instrument with 612 separate pitches in the octave. Even if he had done so, it would have been a mechanical monster, incapable of producing genuine music at the hands of a

[58]J. Murray Barbour, "Music and Ternary Continued Fractions," American Mathematical Monthly, LV (1948), 545-555.

performer. With the possible exception of the 19- and 22-divisions, the same can be said of all these attempts at multiple division. Bosanquet's 53-division apparently was a success on the harmonium he constructed with the "generalized keyboard." But it, too, was cumbersome to play, and would have been very expensive if applied to a pipe organ or piano. Thus the mathematical theory, worked out laboriously by ternary continued fractions, remains theory and nothing more. The practice for the past five hundred years has favored almost exclusively systems with only twelve different pitches in the octave. There seems no immediate prospect of that practice being discarded in favor of any system of multiple division.

If we accept Bosanquet's definition that a "regular" tuning system is one in which every fifth, or every fifth save one, has the same value, this would include the Pythagorean tuning, equal temperament, and the several varieties of the meantone temperament, as well as equal divisions with more than twelve notes in the octave. With the addition of just intonation, it would seem as if this covered the ground pretty thoroughly. There are, however, a great many tuning systems that do not fall into any of the above-mentioned classes. At first glance these irregular systems present a bewildering variety. But some of them have been offered by their sponsors as modifications of existing tuning systems, and others, although not so designated, are also closely related to regular systems. In fact, it is possible, by making the bounds sufficiently elastic, to fit every one of these irregular systems into one or another of certain subclasses. So that, unless we retain Bosanquet's strict definition, there is no such thing as an irregular system — one that is wholly a law unto itself!

Our first group of irregular temperaments consists of modifications of the meantone temperament. The meantone wolf fifth is 35 cents sharp. The simplest modification of this temperament is to divide this excess equally between the fifths $C^{\#}$-$G^{\#}$ and $G^{\#}(A^{b})$-E^{b} (see Table 110). This is the modification gener-

Table 110. Meantone Temperament with Two Sharp Fifths

Names	C	$C^{\#}$	D	E^{b}	E	F	$F^{\#}$	G	$G^{\#}$	A	B^{b}	B	C
Cents	0	76	193	310	386	503	579	697	793	890	1007	1083	1200

M D. 17.2; S.D. 18.5

ally, but erroneously, ascribed to Schlick, and, according to Ellis, still in use in England in the early nineteenth century. The $G^{\#}$ is now almost a comma sharper than in the pure 1/4-comma

---

[1]For a condensed version of the material in this chapter, see J. Murray Barbour, "Irregular Systems of Temperament," Journal of the American Musicological Society, I (1948), 20-26.

temperament. The mean deviation is noticeably lower, but the standard deviation is affected less.

Mersenne has included a discussion of the meantone temperament with all his other tuning information. His account differs slightly in the different works where it occurs. In the Harmonie universelle (pp. 364 f.) he had made the fifths E^b-B^b-F perfect. In the Cogitata physico-mathematica (p. 338) he asked the reader to correct the "obvious errors" in the previous description. Here he indicated simply that the wolf fifth will be $G^\#$-E^b. Perhaps his real intent is to be found in Harmonicorum libri XII (p. 60), where these two fifths are to be sharp, but not so sharp as the wolf fifth, which is still unusable. Mersenne said that the meantone fifth is tempered "1/136, which is about 1/4 comma." This is a gross misstatement, for the ratio given is larger than 1/2 comma. He probably meant 1/316, which is a reasonably close value.

Mersenne's improvements upon the regular meantone temperament are worth showing, even if the second will be only an approximation to what he had in mind. In the first temperament (Table 111) the fifths E^b-B^b and B^b-F are pure. For the second (Table 112), note that the excess of the minor third $G^\#(A^b)$-F over the third of equal temperament is 30 cents. Let us divide this excess so that $G^\#$-E^b bears only half of it, the other two fifths one-quarter each.

Table 111. Mersenne's Improved Meantone Temperament, No. 1

Names	C	C$^\#$	D	E^b	E	F	F$^\#$	G	G$^\#$	A	B^b	B	C
Cents	0	76	193	299	386	503	579	697	773	890	1001	1083	1200

M.D. 17.2; S.D. 17.7

Table 112. Mersenne's Improved Meantone Temperament, No. 2

Names	C	C$^\#$	D	E^b	E	F	F$^\#$	G	G$^\#$	A	B^b	B	C
Cents	0	76	193	288	386	503	579	697	773	890	996	1083	1200

M.D. 15.3; S.D. 16.9

In Mersenne's first improved meantone system, the mean deviation is no lower than for the temperament previously shown; but the standard deviation is lower because more notes are involved in the change. Mersenne's second improvement was the pattern for a modification recommended by Rameau. Now Rameau is noted chiefly in tuning history for his advocacy of equal temperament. But he vacillated sufficiently in his adherence to it to follow Huyghens in acclaiming as "the most perfect of all" temperaments that in which "the fifth is diminished by the 1/4 part of a comma."[2] But he was aware of the pitfalls of the meantone temperament; for he showed that, if the tuning is begun on C, G# will be a "minor comma," 2025/2048 too flat. The remaining fifths, therefore, should be tuned "more just," "to regain the minor comma that has been lost." It would be even better to begin with C#, in order to spread the discrepancy over more notes.

This account sounds as if the excess should be divided equally among the last five fifths. But, in a later paragraph, Rameau declared that "the excess of the last two fifths and of the last four or five major thirds is tolerable, not only because it is almost insensible, but also because it is found in modulations little used." Apparently the first three of the five fifths are not to be so sharp as the final two fifths. Still later he recommended that "the division begin on B♭, and only those fifths that follow B-F# should be a little more just."

These directions are as vague as Mersenne's. In Table 113 the division is begun on B♭ as Rameau suggested. The fifths from B to G# have been made pure, and the excess has been divided equally between G#-D# and E♭-B♭.

Before considering a final, complicated modification of the 1/4-comma temperament, let us look at William Hawkes' im-

Table 113. Rameau's Modified Meantone Temperament

Names	C	C#	D	D#	E	F	F#	G	G#	A	B♭	B	C
Cents	0	87	193	298	386	503	585	697	789	890	1007	1083	1200

M.D. 12.5; S.D. 14.0

[2] J. P. Rameau, Nouveau système de musique théorique (Paris, 1726), pp. 107 ff.

provement upon the 1/5-comma temperament. This resembles Mersenne's first modification. In it, according to John Farey,[3] "each ascending fifth is flattened by one-fifth of a comma as the instrument is tuned, except that the fifth above E^b and the fifth below $G^{\#}$ are directed to be tuned perfect." Farey continued: "...but why these anomalies in the system are introduced I am at a loss to guess, especially as $G^{\#}$ is thereby made 1/5 comma the worse by it." Hawkes' reason is perfectly valid — to diminish the wolf fifth by 2/5 comma, although it will still be 16 cents sharp. The alteration results in a somewhat smaller deviation than for the pure 1/5-comma temperament.

The most involved of all these temperaments was that of J. E. Gallimard,[4] who brought a knowledge of logarithms to bear upon the problem, in order to obtain a subtly modified meantone temperament. He expressed intervals for all the principal tuning systems in Sauveur's Decamerides — four-place logarithms without the decimal point. The first of his original temperaments used the values of the 1/4-comma temperament for the eight notes from B^b to B. If Gallimard had continued in this fashion until the entire octave had been tuned, the final fifth $(D^{\#}\text{-}B^b)$ would have borne the usual wolf, amounting to 103 Deca. He split up this error by adding an ever-increasing amount to each logarithm for the five fifths from B to $A^{\#}$. Thus there would be a total of $1 + 2 + 3 + 4 + 5 = 15$ parts to be divided into 103 Deca., or about 7 Deca. for each part. In cents, this means that the first seven fifths have a value of 696 or 697 cents each, the others 699, 702, 705, 708, 710 cents respectively. Gallimard has pure thirds in all the principal triads of the keys of F and C, and the poorest thirds in the key of G^b. The third on G^b itself has 425 cents, practically a diesis sharp!

In Gallimard's second temperament, the first eight notes were tuned as in the previous temperament. But he distributed the error among the other five fifths, proportional to the series 1, 3, 6, 10, 15; that is, to the series $n(n-1)/2$. The cents values for

[3]"On Music," Philosophical Magazine, XXVI (1806), 171-176.

[4]L'arithmétique des musiciens, p. 26.

these altered fifths are 698, 700, 704, 708, and 714. Here the worst fifths are worse than in his first temperament, and this error is reflected in a slightly higher deviation. His worst third, G^b-B^b, is still a diesis sharp.

The deviations are still large for Gallimard's modification. Had he been willing to use a modification of the 1/6-comma temperament, with slightly sharp diatonic thirds, his system would have been better. Modifications of the latter temperament are to be found later in this chapter, by Young and Mercadier.

Arnold Schlick's temperament[5] deserves special honor, for apparently he was the first writer in any country to describe a temperament for each note of the chromatic octave. Shohé Tanaka and Hugo Riemann have broadcast the erroneous idea that Schlick founded the meantone system. The former spoke of the "exact instructions" that Schlick had given, and added, "In exact language this will mean that each fifth is to be flattened by 1/4 comma."[6] This reads well, but is utter nonsense with relation to what Schlick actually said. In place of "exact instructions" he gave very indefinite rules that create a problem for us.

Beginning with F on the organ manual, the fifth F-C is to be somewhat flat. This same rule is to be followed in tuning the other "claves naturales" by fifths, making the octaves perfect. As to the major thirds, Schlick said that "although they will all be too high, it is necessary to make the three thirds C-E, F-A, and G-B better, ... as much as the said thirds are better, so much will $G^\#$ be worse to E and B."

The tuning of the black keys is to be made similarly, tuning upward by flat fifths from B to obtain $F^\#$ and $C^\#$, and tuning downward from F to obtain B^b and E^b. The semitone between G and A received special attention. As $G^\#$ it was needed as the third above E; as A^b it was also needed as the third below C. So Schlick suggested a mean value for this note, directing that the fifth A^b-E^b is to be somewhat larger than a perfect fifth.

Whatever Schlick's system, it could not have been the mean-

---

[5]*Spiegel der Orgelmacher und Organisten*, in <u>Monatshefte für Musikge-schichte</u>, 1869, pp. 41 f.

[6]Shohé Tanaka, in <u>Vierteljahrsschrift für Musikwissenschaft</u>, VI (1890), 62.

tone system as described so carefully by Tanaka; for it lacks pure thirds. Schlick said definitely that "all will be too high." Not even the diatonic thirds are to be pure, only made "better than the rest."

What, then, was Schlick's tuning method? All that can be said with assurance is that it was an irregular system, lying somewhere between meantone and equal temperament. We cannot hope to reconstruct it exactly; but it will be worth while to give some idea, at least, of what it was like. Let us assume that Schlick used the same size of tempered fifth for each of the six diatonic fifths; a somewhat larger, but still flat, fifth for the four chromatic fifths; and a sharp fifth for the two fifths A^b-E^b and $C^{\#}$-$G^{\#}$. Call these temperaments x, y, and -z respectively. Then, since the ditonic comma must be absorbed in the course of the tuning,

$$6x + 4y - 2z = 24 \text{ cents.}$$

Now x is larger than y; let us assume that x = 2y. Since Schlick said that most of his fifths were to be "somewhat" flat and the other two fifths "somewhat" sharp, let us assume that x = z. Then

$$12y + 4y - 4y = 24 \text{ cents, } y = 2 \text{ cents, } x = z = 4 \text{ cents.}$$

Thus Schlick's diatonic fifths, of 698 cents, will be tempered by 1/6 comma; his chromatic fifths, of 700 cents, will be the same size as those in equal temperament; his two sharp fifths will be of 706 cents. His diatonic thirds will be six cents sharp; his chromatic thirds, 8 or 10 cents; the thirds E-$G^{\#}$ and A^b-C, 18 cents (not unbearable); and the "foreign" thirds, B-$D^{\#}$, $F^{\#}$-$A^{\#}$, and D^b-F, 26 cents, slightly more than a comma.

The deviations for Schlick's hypothetical temperament are less than half as large as those for the modified meantone temperament that Tanaka wrongly ascribed to him — the first temperament in this chapter. His is a good system, holding its own in comparison with systems that were proposed two or three centuries later. Of the irregular systems discussed in the first

section of this chapter, Schlick's is superior to Mersenne's, Rameau's, Hawkes', and Gallimard's.
Even so, Schlick's system is not so good as that of Grammateus, next to be discussed. Therefore we must not assume that the present reconstruction has erred on the side of Schlick. As a temperament, it has far greater significance for us than if it had been the meantone temperament, with two sharp fifths. It is an indication that in the early sixteenth century organ temperament was nearer to equal temperament than it generally was for centuries after this time. Schlick's directions have the added weight that they represent the practice of an actual organist, unconcerned with mathematics or the theories of the ancient Greeks.

Modifications of Regular Temperaments

In the next main group of irregular temperaments the diatonic notes are tuned according to one of the well-known regular temperaments and then each tone is divided equally to form the chromatic notes. The oldest and best of them was that of Henricus Grammateus,[7] or Heinrich Schreyber of Erfurt. Grammateus tuned the diatonic notes of his monochord according to the Pythagorean ratios. But when it came to the black keys, the "minor semitones," he followed a different procedure. These were formed by dividing each tone into two equal semitones by the Euclidean method for finding a geometric mean proportional. Grammateus had a figure to illustrate the construction. Perhaps he obtained this method of halving intervals directly from Euclid. But he may have owed it to Faber Stapulensis[8] (Jacques le Febvre), who had shown that it was impossible to divide a tone numerically into two equal parts, but that the halving of any interval could be accomplished by geometry. At any rate, Bermudo, whose one tuning method was identical with Grammateus', did depend upon Faber for the method of constructing the mean proportionals. Faber exerted great influence upon later writers

[7]"Arithmetica applicirt oder gezogen auff die edel Kunst musica," an appendix to his Ayn new kunstlich Buech (Nürnberg, 1518).

[8]Elementa musicalia (Paris, 1496).

Table 114. Hawkes' Modified 1/5-Comma Temperament

Names	C^0	$C^{\#-\frac{3}{5}}$	$D^{-\frac{2}{5}}$	$Eb^{+\frac{2}{5}}$	$E^{-\frac{4}{5}}$	$F^{+\frac{1}{5}}$	$F^{\#\frac{6}{5}}$	$G^{-\frac{1}{5}}$	$G^{\#-\frac{7}{5}}$	$A^{-\frac{3}{5}}$	$Bb^{+\frac{2}{5}}$	B^{-1}	C^0
Cents	0	83	195	303	390	502	586	698	785	893	1005	1088	1200

M.D. 12.7; S.D. 13.0

Table 115. Gallimard's Modified Meantone Temperament, No. 1

Names	C	$C^\#$	D	$D^\#$	E	F	$F^\#$	G	$G^\#$	A	Bb	B	C
Deca.	0	212	484	744	969	1263	1461	1747	1980	2232	2526	2716	3010
Cents	0	84	193	297	386	504	582	696	789	890	1007	1083	1200

M.D. 13.3; S.D. 14.9

Table 116. Gallimard's Modified Meantone Temperament, No. 2

Names	C	$C^\#$	D	$D^\#$	E	F	$F^\#$	G	$G^\#$	A	Bb	B	C
Deca.	0	204	484	734	969	1263	1457	1747	1969	2232	2526	2716	3010
Cents	0	81	193	293	386	504	581	696	785	890	1007	1083	1200

M.D. 14.0; S.D. 15.6

Table 117. Schlick's Temperament (Hypothetical)

Names	C^0	$C^{\#-1}$	$D^{-\frac{1}{3}}$	$Eb^{+\frac{1}{3}}$	$E^{-\frac{2}{3}}$	$F^{+\frac{1}{6}}$	$F^{\#-\frac{11}{12}}$	$G^{-\frac{1}{6}}$	$G^{\#\frac{5}{6}}$	$A^{-\frac{1}{2}}$	$Bb^{+\frac{1}{3}}$	$B^{-\frac{5}{6}}$	C^0
Cents	0	90	196	302	392	502	590	698	796	894	1002	1090	1200

M.D. 8.0; S.D. 8.6

Table 118. Grammateus' Monochord (Pythagorean with Mean Semitones)

Names	C^0	$C^{\#-\frac{1}{2}}$	D^0	$D^{\#-\frac{1}{2}}$	$(Eb^{+\frac{1}{2}})$	E^0	F^0	$F^{\#-\frac{1}{2}}$	G^0	$G^{\#-\frac{1}{2}}A^0$	$Bb^{+\frac{1}{2}}$	B^0	C^0
Cents	0	102	204	306		408	498	600	702	804 906	1008	1110	1200

M.D. 3.3; S.D. 4.5

140

who attempted to solve the tuning problem. Especially among mathematical writers who dabbled in this field, Faber's name was held in something of the same esteem as that of Boethius.

This monochord division of Grammateus is seen to be of a subtle and theoretical nature. It is equivalent to dividing the Pythagorean comma equally between the fifths B-F$^{\#}$ and B^{b}-F. As such, it is identical with Marpurg's tuning K. This tuning may have been used in practice, but hardly by anyone who was accustomed, like Schlick, to tune by ear. Note that it was presented as a method not for fretted instruments, but for organs. Grammateus said in his introduction: "There follows herewith an amusing reckoning which serves the art of song called music, and from such reckoning springs the division of the monochord, from which will then be taken the proportionate length and width of the organ pipes after the opinion of Pythagoras."

So far as we know, Grammateus was the earliest writer with a method for finding equal semitones as applied to a tuning system. Of course only ten semitones will be equal, the other two being twelve cents smaller. Probably many men who later spoke about equal semitones on the lute may have had in mind some such division, perhaps made by dividing the tones arithmetically instead of geometrically.

Ganassi[9] had a method for obtaining equal semitones on the lute and viol by linear divisions, using the ratios of just intonation for his basic scale. Although he described his procedure in more complicated terms, his monochord might have been tuned as follows: with A the fundamental, form the minor third C with the ratio 6:5; form F and G as perfect fourth and fifth to C with the respective ratios 4:3 and 3:2; divide the space between A and C into three equal parts for B^{b} and B; divide the space between C and F into five equal parts for C$^{\#}$, D, E^{b}, and E; F$^{\#}$ will be half way between F and G, and G$^{\#}$ half way between G and the octave A. The construction will be even easier if we start with C: form F and G as perfect fourth and fifth to C; divide the space between C and F into five equal parts, between F and G into two equal parts, and between G and the octave C into five equal parts.

---

[9]Sylvestro Ganassi, Regola Rubertina. Lettione seconda (1543); ed. Max Schneider (Leipzig, 1924), Chap. IV.

In the monochord shown in Table 119, the lengths and ratios have been added according to Ganassi's directions.

Actually, the above monochord does not quite represent Ganassi's ideas. His lute had only eight frets, so that the position of the notes above F is rather conjectural. However, he placed a dot where G, the tenth fret, would naturally fall, and it is reasonable to suppose that he would have made a linear division for the semitones on either side of G. A greater departure from his ideas lies in ignoring the tempering of the first and second frets: the second fret is to be placed higher than 8/9 by the width of the fret, and the first fret higher than 17/18 by half the width of the fret. Similarly the sixth fret is to be placed lower than 17/24 by the width of the fret. His drawing for the monochord is made with unusual care (see Figure H). It appears as if the width of the fret were about 1/2 of 1 percent of the length of the string. This tempering would make B^b and B sharper by about half a comma, and E^b flatter by the same amount. The first two changes would not affect the tuning greatly, but the change in the position of the sixth fret would be harmful. Since Ganassi was not specific as to the relative length and breadth of the string, we merely indicate here that he advocated these three tempered values.

.Fig. H. Ganassi's Method for Placing Frets on the Lute and Viol
Reproduced by courtesy of the Library of Congress

Table 119. Ganassi's Monochord (Just with Mean Semitones)

Lengths	120		114		108		102		96		90		85
Ratios		19/20		18/19		17/18		16/17		15/16		17/18		16/17
Names	C^0		x		D^{-1}		x		E^{-1}		F^0		x
Cents	0		88		182		281		386		498		597

Lengths	80		76		72		68		64		60
Ratios		19/20		18/19		17/18		16/17		15/16	
Names	G^0		x		A^{-1}		x		B^{-1}		C^0
Cents	702		790		884		983		1088		1200

M.D. 6.5; S.D. 7.8

Table 120. Reinhard's Monochord (Variant of Ganassi's)

Lengths	60		56 2/3		53 1/3		50 2/3		48	45		42 1/2		40		38
Names	C^0		x		D^0		x		E^{-1}	F^0		x		G^0		x
Cents	0		99		204		292		386	498		597		702		790

Lengths	36	34		32		30
Names	A^{-1}	x		B^{-1}		C^0
Cents	884	983		1088		1200

M.D. 6.5; S.D. 7.8

Table 121. Malcolm's Monochord (Variant of Ganassi's)

Ratios		16/17		17/18		18/19		19/20		15/16		16/17		17/18
Names	C^0			x		D^0		x		E^{-1}		F^0		x
Cents	0			105		204		298		386		498		603

Ratios		18/19		19/20		16/17		17/18		15/16
Names	G^0			x		A^{-1}		x		B^{-1}		C^0
Cents	702			796		884		989		1088		1200

M.D. 6.5; S.D. 7.8

Except for the arithmetical divisions, Ganassi's tuning resembles Grammateus' treatment of the Pythagorean tuning, the difference being that the basic scale here is just intonation. It also resembles Artusi's treatment of the meantone temperament, shortly to be described. But even if Ganassi had used the Euclidean method to divide his tones, his monochord (M.D. 6.0; S.D. 7.3) would have been inferior to either of the other two, since the diatonic just scale varies more greatly from equal temperament than either the Pythagorean or meantone does. But this is a good division, and has the tremendous advantage that it is the easiest of all chromatic monochords to form.

Ganassi's method was discovered independently by Andreas Reinhard,[10] who described the syntonic tuning, and then gave a table in which the space of each tone, whether major or minor, is halved to obtain the chromatic note. His table gave string-lengths only, beginning with 45 for F. Since he used D^0 instead of D^{-1}, his intervals are in a slightly different order from Ganassi's.

Ten years after Reinhard, his tuning method was taken over by Abraham Bartolus,[11] the sole difference being that the latter began with E (48) instead of F (45). Bartolus gave Reinhard as his source. At first he advocated the method for keyboard instruments, and later prescribed it also for fretted instruments and bells. This general application of a tuning method is something that is found in very few theorists of Bartolus' period, most of whom continued to say with Vicentino that fretted instruments used equal temperament, and keyboard instruments, the meantone temperament.

In one of the curious dialogs of Printz's Phrynis Mytilenaeus[12] this same temperament is mentioned. "Charis" describes it and gives the string-lengths for the C octave, 360 to 180, thus avoiding the fractions that Reinhard had encountered. Very likely Printz intended this for Reinhard's tuning, but his perplexing use

---

[10]Monochordum (Leipzig, 1604).

[11]Musica mathematica: the 2nd part of Heinrich Zeising's Theatri machinarum (Altenburg, 1614), pp. 151 f, 165 ff.

[12]Part 3, Chap. 6.

of anagrams effectively conceals Reinhard's name, if it is indeed hidden there.

Alexander Malcolm[13] had a division very similar to those of Ganassi and Reinhard. In fact, it is the inversion of Ganassi's, with semitones paired in contrary motion. Although Malcolm said that the tones were to be divided arithmetically, as 16:17:18, his table of string-lengths (lengths of chords) represents a very unlikely division, difficult to make. Marpurg, who called the system ugly, has represented it by a series of increasing numbers, as C, C#, D are 48, 51, 54. This would mean that Malcolm's ratios are to be taken as vibration numbers, improbable in view of his own terminology for them.

Since Malcolm's scale contains the same ratios for semitones as Ganassi's and Reinhard's, although in a different order, the deviation for the three scales will be the same. But his chromatic notes are all five or six cents higher than Reinhard's. It is very probable that Malcolm intended the same division as Reinhard. Malcolm stated that Thomas Salmon had written about this scale. But it is often referred to by Malcolm's name alone. Certainly these well-nigh equal semitones of Ganassi, Reinhard, Bartolus, Salmon, and Malcolm represent a long-lived (almost two centuries) and very good way to divide the octave with ease.

Levens' "Sisteme"[14] also had linear divisions only, but was far less successful than those just described. His monochord had integer numbers starting with 48 for C. Ganassi's system had only five consecutive semitones formed by equal divisions of a larger interval, but Levens' had seven, from 42 for D to 28 for A. Thus Levens' consecutive semitones vary in size from 85 to 119 cents. Furthermore, his semitone A-B^b is very small (63 cents), with the Archytas ratio, 28:27; whereas his semitone B^b-C^b, with the ratio 27:25, is more than twice as large (133 cents). Levens' deviations are as great as for some varieties of just intonation.

---

[13] A Treatise of Musick (Edinburgh, 1721), p. 304.

[14] Abrégé des regles de l'harmonie (Bordeaux, 1743), p. 87.

145

Since C is 48 in Levens' tuning, the monochord could easily be constructed with a foot rule. But it would not be so easy to construct a monochord of indefinite length for this tuning. A slight change in the values of A and B would greatly simplify the construction of the monochord, and at the same time would almost cut the deviation in half. It would then be formed thus: Divide the entire string into 8 parts, putting D at the first point of division, F at the second, and A^b at the third. Divide the space between C and D into two parts for $C^#$. Divide the space between D and F into three parts, for E^b and E, and apply EF twice from F toward A^b, for $F^#$ and G. Divide the space from A^b to the higher C (midpoint of the string) into four equal parts, for A, B^b, and B.

The third distinct method of forming equal semitones upon the lute stems from Giovanni Maria Artusi.[15] But, as with Grammateus' division, only ten of the semitones would be equal. In pointing out the "errors of certain modern composers," Artusi gave two examples of "intervals false for singing, but good for playing on the lute." Thus the diminished seventh, $C^#$-B^b, in the beginning of Marenzio's madrigal "False Faith," is "false for voices and for modulation, but not false on the lute and the chitarone."

On the lute, he continued, "the tone is divided into two equal semitones." So far Artusi had been speaking very much as had his predecessors. But he then stated that the tone in question is not the 9:8 tone, but the mean tone used on the lute and other instruments. Later he called the tempered semitone "the just half of the mean tone." For constructing this temperament he mentioned the mesolabium and the Euclidean construction for a mean proportional, with references to Zarlino and Faber. The mesolabium would have been useless for this purpose, unless Artusi had desired complete equal temperament. But Euclid's method would have served for constructing meantones from just major thirds, and then for constructing mean semitones from mean tones.

Since Artusi did not give a detailed account of how his temperament was to be formed, we can only surmise that all the di-

---

[15]Seconda parte dell' Artusi overo della imperfettioni della moderna musica (Venice, 1603), pp. 30 ff.

Table 122. Levens' Monochord (Linear Divisions)

Lengths	48	45	42	40	38	36	34	32	30	28	27	25	24
Names	C^0	D^{b+1}	D	E^{b+1}	E	F^0	x	G^0	A^{b+1}	A	B^{b0}	C^{b+2}	C^0
Cents	0	112	231	316	404	498	597	702	814	933	996	1129	1200

M.D. 16.7; S.D. 19.9

Table 123. Levens' Monochord (Altered Form)

Lengths	48	45	42	40	38	36	34	32	30	28 1/2	27	25 1/2	24
Names	C^0	D^{b+1}	D	E^{b+1}	E	F^0	x	G^0	A^{b+1}	A	B^{b0}	B	C^0
Cents	0	112	231	316	404	498	597	702	814	902	996	1095	1200

M.D. 8.8; S.D. 10.3

Table 124. Artusi's Monochord (Meantone with Mean Semitones)
(Bonded Clavichord Tuning, No. 1)

Names	C^0	x	$D^{-\frac{1}{2}}$	x	E^{-1}	$F^{\pm\frac{1}{6}}$	x	$G^{-\frac{1}{4}}$	x	$A^{-\frac{3}{4}}$	x	$B^{-\frac{5}{4}}$	C^0
Cents	0	97	193	290	386	503	600	697	794	890	987	1083	1200

M.D. 5.7; S.D. 7.6

Table 125. Bonded Clavichord Tuning, No. 2

Names	C^0	x	$D^{-\frac{1}{3}}$	x	$E^{-\frac{2}{3}}$	$F^{+\frac{1}{6}}$	x	$G^{-\frac{1}{6}}$	x	$A^{-\frac{1}{2}}$	x	$B^{-\frac{5}{6}}$	C^0
Cents	0	97	197	294	394	502	599	698	795	895	992	1092	1200

M.D. 2.6; S.D. 3.8

atonic notes were to be tuned as in the ordinary meantone temperament and the chromatic notes by dividing each of the tones
in half. This is the "semi-meantone temperament" mentioned
by Ellis,[16] "in which the natural notes C, D, E, F, G, A, B were
tuned in meantone temperament, and the chromatics were inter-
polated at intervals of half a meantone." According to Ellis, it
had been in use on "the old fretted or bonded clavichords." Unfortunately, Ellis did not give the source of this information.

If these bonded clavichords had had their notes paired CC#
DD# E FF# GG# AA# B C, a fixed ratio could have existed between the notes in each pair, so that C#, for example, would always
be 96.5 cents higher than C. Of course, the two diatonic semitones, E-F and B-C, would be about a comma larger, at 117
cents each.

Some writers have said that the bonded clavichords necessarily used the meantone temperament. But nothing would have
prevented the performer from tuning his diatonic tones sharper
than mean tones. Suppose, for example, it had become the fashion
to diminish the fifth by 1/6 comma, as in Bach's day. Then the
bonded clavichord would have had the scale shown in Table 125.

In this tuning the standard deviation is fairly large because
the semitones E-F and B-C have a deviation of eight cents. If E
and B are made four cents sharper, the mean deviation is unchanged, but the standard deviation is reduced to 3.0. This much
can be done without changing the ratio of C to C#. But a bonded
clavichord that was constructed at the time Douwes was writing
(1699; see Chapter III) would have had the ratio of this pair of
notes fixed according to the temperament then in use, perhaps
the 1/6-comma meantone system, and the mean-semitone tuning
would then have been even better than in Table 125.

Furthermore, there is no valid reason why the ratio of the
semitones on a single string could not have been $\sqrt[12]{2}$, if the bonded
clavichord had been constructed at a time when equal temperament was widely accepted. The only difficulty is that the free
clavichords were more common then. But it is nonsense to think

[16]Alexander Ellis, "On the History of Musical Pitch," Journal of the Society
of Arts, XXVIII (1880), 295.

---

that there was any connection between free clavichords and equal temperament, except where an old clavichord had retained semitonal ratios that belonged to a type of tuning that had been superseded. Even then, as we have shown, the open strings could have been tuned so that the instrument as a whole would have varied only slightly from equal temperament.

The only troublesome situation would occur when the bonded clavichord had its ratios fixed so that, for example, the semitone between C^0 and $D^{-\frac{1}{2}}$ was not a mean semitone, but $C^{\#-\frac{7}{4}}$. Remember that Artusi was writing about equal semitones on the lute, not on the clavichord. And other theorists, advocating meantone temperament for keyboard instruments, made no distinction between the clavichord, on one hand, and the organ ·and harpsichord, on the other. Let us see, in Table 126, what could be done when the fixed chromatic semitone has only 76 cents, the diatonic semitone, 117 cents.

Here we assume that $C-C^{\#}$, $F-F^{\#}$, and $G-G^{\#}$ are each 76 cents, and that $D-E^b$ and $A-B^b$ are each 117 cents. The other seven semitones are free. If we make them all equal, each will have 105.4 cents. That means that D and A are flatter than in the regular meantone temperament; E, F, G, and B sharper. After this somewhat eccentric tuning of the diatonic notes, the deviation is almost half that of the regular meantone temperament, but is still not quite so good as that of the old Pythagorean tuning, untempered. Therefore on a bonded clavichord that was built for the complete meantone temperament, even the most scientific tuning of the free strings would not make a very acceptable temperament. And such clavichords would certainly have delayed the acceptance of equal temperament.

A corroboration of Artusi's method of forming equal semitones on the lute came from Ercole Bottrigari.[17] He had classified instruments by their tuning, as Zarlino had done. He went on to show that the lute cannot play in tune with the cembalo. If the E string of the lute is tuned in unison with the E of the cem-

---

[17] *Il desiderio, ovvero de' concerti di varii stromenti musicali* (Venice, 1594); new ed. by Kathi Meyer (Berlin, 1924).

Table 126. Bonded Clavichord Tuning, No. 3

Names	C	C#	D	Eb	E	F	F#	G	G#	A	Bb	B	C
Cents	0	76	181	298	403	509	585	691	767	872	989	1094	1200

M.D. 12.0; S.D. 13.7

balo, the F's will be out of tune, the G's will again be in tune, and the G#'s out of tune. He explained that, since on the lute the tone was divided into two equal semitones, and on the cembalo into two unequal semitones, then the diatonic semitone E-F, with the ratio of 16:15 tempered, would be higher on the cembalo than on the lute; but the chromatic semitone G-G# (25:24 tempered) would be higher on the lute.

This explanation would be true, even if the lute were in equal temperament. But the interesting question is why the G's were in tune if the E's were, and vice versa. If the lute were in equal temperament, it would have no pitches in unison with the cembalo save the one that was tuned to a unison to begin with. Now, Bottrigari was referring to a tuning in which the order of strings was D, G, C, E, A, D. Of these the E string was called the "mezanina," the middle string. On either D string or on the A string, the 2nd, 3rd, and 5th frets formed a diatonic sequence — A, B, C, D or D, E, F, G.

Since the position of the frets was the same on all the strings, the succession on the E string would have been E, F#, G, A. Therefore, if the diatonic notes on the D and A strings were tuned in unison with those on the cembalo, as in Artusi's tuning, the notes E, F#, G, and A on the E string will also be in unison. But E-F on the lute will be half a mean tone and so will G-G#, whereas the E-F of the cembalo will be a tempered major semitone and the G-G# a tempered minor semitone. (F#-G, about which Bottrigari said nothing, will be the ordinary major semitone of the meantone temperament on both instruments, and will be almost a comma larger than these other semitones on the lute.) This is the only reasonable explanation of Bottrigari's statement, and, since it was made only nine years earlier than Artusi's account, we may surmise that this method of tuning was in common use about 1600. We should be careful, therefore, not to assume that every statement about the use of equal semitones on the lute necessarily meant equal temperament, with the ratio of $^{12}\sqrt{2}$ for the semitone.

Temperaments Largely Pythagorean

A great many irregular temperaments are largely Pythagorean, that is, they contain many pure fifths. This is reasonable enough, since pure fifths are easy to tune and do not depart greatly from the fifths of equal temperament. As we shall see, many of these are typical "paper" temperaments, ill adapted either to tuning by ear or to setting upon a monochord. But first we shall examine several that used linear divisions only.

Martin Agricola,[18] who was responsible for a good version of just intonation, showed a monochord for the lute in which the diatonic notes, like those of Grammateus, were joined by pure fifths. To divide the tones into diatonic and chromatic semitones, Agricola applied the old doctrine that the tone is divisible into 9 commas, 5 for the chromatic semitone and 4 for the diatonic. He tuned a G string, marking off $G^{\#}$ as 5/9 the distance from G to A. That means that $G:G^{\#}:A$ as 81:76:72. Thus the diatonic semitone $G^{\#}$-A had the ratio 19:18, or almost 94 cents, instead of 256:243 or 90 cents, and the chromatic semitone 110 cents instead of 114.

Agricola formed his $A^{\#}$ and $C^{\#}$ like the $G^{\#}$. As there were only seven frets on this string, he did not give values for $D^{\#}$, F, and $F^{\#}$. But F is of course a major tone below G, and he had previously shown E^{b} (although he called it "dis") to be a tone below F. But there B^{b} had been shown to be a tone lower than C, 20 cents flatter than the $A^{\#}$ on the other string. These inconsistencies are bound to arise when any unequal tuning is used on a fretted instrument, as Galilei pointed out. For the sake of a logical construction, let us assume (see Table 127) that each of the five tones in the octave is divided into 5 + 4 commas. This may be slightly better than Agricola's tuning would have been if

---

[18]Musica instrumentalis deudsch (4th ed.; Wittenberg, 1545). Reprinted as Band 20 of Publikation älterer praktischer und theoretischer Musikwerke, 1896. The reference here is to page 227 of the latter.

151

Table 127. Agricola's Pythagorean-Type Monochord

Names	C^0	$C^{\#-\frac{1}{6}}$	D^0	$D^{\#-\frac{1}{6}}$	E^0	F^0	$F^{\#-\frac{1}{6}}$	G^0	$G^{\#-\frac{1}{6}}$	A^0	$A^{\#-\frac{1}{6}}$	B^0	C^0
Cents	0	110	204	314	408	498	608	702	812	906	1016	1110	1200

M.D. 8.3; S.D. 8.6

Table 128 Wắng Phŏ's Pythagorean-Type Monochord

Lengths	900	844	800	751	713	668	633	600	563	534	501	475	450
Names	C	$C^\#$	D	$D^\#$	E	$E^\#$	$F^\#$	G	$G^\#$	A	$A^\#$	B	C
Cents	0	111	204	313	403	516	609	702	812	904	1014	1107	1200

M.D. 8.9; S.D. 9.0

he had applied it to an entire octave.

This system, if we can call it a system, is appreciably better than the ordinary Pythagorean tuning. It contains ten pure fifths; the fifth B-F$^\#$ is four cents flat (1/6 comma), and A$^\#$-F is twenty cents flat. But none of the credit belongs to the inventor. Agricola, like many another good man, confused geometrical with arithmetical proportion. The old statement about the sizes of semitones is very nearly correct when geometrical magnitudes are in question, but is less accurate when applied to linear divisions. Furthermore, it was a happy accident that led him to make his chromatic notes sharps. If he had divided the tone G-A into G-A^b-A in this same manner, his diatonic semitone would have contained 88 cents, the chromatic, 116, thus diverging more widely from equality than the Pythagorean semitones do. An accidental improvement is the best we can say for this tuning of Agricola.

Agricola's approximation for the Pythagorean tuning suggests the monochord of an early Chinese theorist, Wắng Phŏ, who lived toward the end of the tenth century.[19] Perhaps he was familiar with the excellent temperament of Hô Tchheng-thyēn, but, if so, was too timid to follow his example. Starting with the Pythagorean tuning for the octave 900-450, he has retained the purity

---

[19]Maurice Courant, in Encyclopedie de la musique et dictionnaire du conservatoire, Part 1, Vol. I, p. 90.

of G and D. He lowered the pitches of all the other notes by adding two units for $C^\#$, $D^\#$, E, and $E^\#$, and one unit for $F^\#$, $G^\#$, A, $A^\#$, and B. This was too small a correction for most of the notes, as can be seen from Table 128, which is comparable to that of Agricola.

John Dowland is another writer whose tuning system, like those of Ramis, Grammateus, Agricola, and others, had a strong Pythagorean cast. In his account of "fretting the lute," C, D, F, G, and A have Pythagorean tuning.[20] The chromatic semitone from C to $C^\#$ is 33:31, or 108 cents, not far from the Pythagorean of 114 cents. The diatonic semitone from D to E^b is 22:21, or 80 cents, considerably flatter than the Pythagorean of 90 cents. $G^\#$ and B^b form pure fifths to $C^\#$ and E^b respectively. An unusual feature of the tuning is $F^\#$ taken as the arithmetical mean between F and G, and E (!) as the mean between E^b and F. The value for E thus obtained, 264:211, is 388 cents, almost a pure third above C, instead of the expected Pythagorean third. The third D-$F^\#$, of 393 cents, is likewise an improvement. Thus the deviation is somewhat less than that for the Pythagorean tuning, being almost the same as that of Agricola's system. There is no B on this string, but we have made B a pure fifth above E.

The trend of Dowland's tuning resembles that of Ornithoparchus, whose Micrologus was translated into English by Dowland. Ornithoparchus' division of the monochord was entirely Pythagorean, a ten-note system extending from A^b to B by pure fifths. It was natural for Ornithoparchus to advocate the Pythagorean tuning, since most of his contemporaries had not yet departed from it. But a century later, the Pythagorean tuning was becoming somewhat rare. And yet Dowland's fellow countryman Thomas Morley, whose precepts have been quoted by everyone who writes about Elizabethan music, gave only a Pythagorean monochord.

Unusual ratios are a feature of Colonna's tunings also, although he definitely included some ratios that belong to just intonation as well.[21] He is noted in the field of multiple division

---

[20] Robert Dowland, Variety of Lute-Lessons (London, 1610). "Of Fretting the Lute" comes under "Other Necessary Observations to Lute-playing by John Dowland, Bachelor of Music."

[21] Fabio Colonna, La sambuca lincea, p. 22.

for having described an instrument, the Sambuca Lincea, similar to Vicentino's Archicembalo, upon which the division of the octave into 31 parts could be accomplished. His mathematical theory of intervals is very ingenious, including superparticular proportions, but also more subtle fractions. He began with certain well-known consonant ratios: 1:1 (unison), 6:5 (minor third), 5:4 (major third), 4:3 (fourth), 3:2 (fifth), and 5:3 (major sixth). Then if a string of the monochord is divided to produce a certain interval, the sounding part of the string should produce with the other part (the Residuo) either one of the above intervals or a higher octave of it. This means that if any of the above ratios is called b:a, intervals derived from it have ratios of the form $(2^k b + a):2^k b$. For example, from 1:1 comes 17:16; from 6:5 comes 11:6; from 3:2 comes 25:24. Colonna's two chromatic monochords are shown in Tables 130 and 131. Each contains seven pure fifths and several pure thirds. The worst feature of both monochords is the 55:54 chromatic semitone of 30 cents (as G-G$^\#$ or B^b-B) — not much larger than a comma. Almost as bad is the 12:11 diatonic semitone of 152 cents, as G$^\#$-A or B-C.[22] The 27:25 diatonic semitone of 134 cents, as F$^{\#-2}$-G^0 or C$^{\#-2}$-D^0, is not good either, but is a blemish found also in ordinary just intonation. A redeeming feature of the first monochord is the division of the 9:8 tone into 17:16 and 18:17 semitones.

Colonna's division of the 10:9 tone into 12:11 and 55:54 "semitones" is reminiscent of the superparticular division of the 10:9 tone that Ptolemy used for his soft chromatic tetrachord, 5/6 x 14/15 x 27/28, and of the common division of just intonation derived from Didymus' chromatic, 5/6 x 24/25 x 15/16.[23] Other

[22]Henri Louis Choquel used a 12:11 semitone between A and B^b and a 33:32 semitone between B^b and B, in what was otherwise a monochord in ordinary just intonation. La musique rendue sensible par la méchanique (New ed., Paris, 1762).

[23]A. M. Awraamoff in 1920 devised a tuning for the chromatic octave that outdoes Colonna's. The natural seventh, 8:7, is exploited in this tuning, and such superparticular near-commatic intervals occur in it as 49:48 (36 cents) and 64:63 (27 cents)! "Jenseits von Temperierung und Tonalität," Melos, Vol. I (1920).

Table 129. Dowland's Lute Tuning

Ratios	1	33:31	9:8	33:28	264:211	4:3	24:17	3:2	99:62
Names	C	C$^{\#}$	D	E^{b}	x	F	x	G	G$^{\#}$
Cents	0	108	204	284	388	498	597	702	810

Ratios	27:16	99:56	[396:211]	2:1
Names	A	B^{b}	x	C
Cents	906	986	1090	1200

M.D. 8.2; S.D. 10.1

Table 130. Colonna's Irregular Just Intonation, No. 1

Lengths	50		48		45		[42 6/17]		40		37 1/2		36
Ratios		24/25		15/16		16/17		17/18		15/16		24/25	25/27
Names	C^{o}		C$^{\#-2}$		D^{-1}		[E^{b}]		E$^{\dashv}$		F^{o}		F$^{\#-2}$
Cents	0		70		182		287		386		498		568

Lengths	33 1/3		32 8/11		30		28 4/17		26 2/3		25
Ratios		54/55		11/12		16/17		17/18		15/16	
Names	G^{o}		G$^{\#}$		A^{-1}		B^{b}		B^{-1}		C^{o}
Cents	702		732		884		989		1088		1200

M.D. 22.0; S.D. 30.3

Table 131. Colonna's Irregular Just Intonation, No. 2

Lengths	1920		2000		2160		2304		2400		2560		2688
Ratios		24/25		25/27		15/16		24/25		15/16		20/21	14/15
Names	C^{o}		C$^{\#-2}$		D^{o}		E^{b+1}		E^{-1}		F^{o}		F$^{\#}$
Cents	0		70		204		316		386		498		618

Lengths	2880		3072		3200		3456		3520		3842
Ratios		15/16		24/25		25/27		54/55		11/12	
Names	G^{o}		A^{b+1}		A^{-1}		B^{b+1}		B		C^{o}
Cents	702		814		884		1018		1048		1200

M.D. 29.3; S.D. 33.8

possible divisions of the 10:9 tone are 13:12 and 40:39, which is somewhat better than Colonna's division, and the linear division 19:18 and 20:19, as in Ganassi. Divisions of the 9:8 tone include 17:16 and 18:17, as well as 15:14 and 21:20, both of which Colonna used. Other possible superparticular divisions of the 9:8 tone are 13:12 and 27:26; 12:11 and 33:32; 11:10 and 45:44; and 10:9 and 81:80, this last, of course, being the minor tone and comma.

Divisions of the Ditonic Comma

The Pythagorean-type temperaments in our second group are more difficult to construct, in that they contain unusual divisions of the ditonic comma. By ear, these temperaments would have been almost impossible in many cases, because there are no pure intervals to check by as in some varieties of the meantone temperament, nor are there even fairly definite tempered intervals, such as the C E G$^\#$ C of equal temperament, which also provide a good check. For the division of the monochord, these temperaments could have been set down readily with the aid of logarithms, and they can be expressed in our modern cents with the greatest of ease. Computers who did not use logarithms were able to achieve comparable results by a linear division of the comma, but had less success if they ignored the schisma which separates the syntonic from the ditonic comma. In most of our tables we shall assume, for the sake of convenience, that the ditonic comma has been given a correct geometric division, and shall assign cents values to the intervals accordingly.

The leading exponents of this sophisticated sort of comma-juggling were Werckmeister, Neidhardt, and Marpurg.[24] Each has expressed the alteration of his fifths and thirds in the 12th part of a comma, which, strictly, should be the ditonic comma.

[24]See Johann George Neidhardt, Gäntzlich erschöpfte, mathematische Abtheilungen des diatonisch-chromatischen, temperirten Canonis Monochordi (Königsberg and Leipzig, 1732), pp. 29 (the Fifth-Circles) and 38 (Third-Circles). See also F. W. Marpurg, Versuch über die musikalische Temperatur, p. 158, for the lettered temperaments A through L. All other references will be indicated in footnotes.

Since the ditonic comma is approximately 24 cents, this means that 2 cents will be taken as the unit of tempering. Thus the octave would contain 600 parts, or thereabouts. This is an interesting forerunner of the cents representation.

In evaluating this group of temperaments, it should be pointed out that there are two opposing points of view. Since we are likely to regard most highly those irregular systems that come closest to equal temperament, there will be in each subclass a temperament by Marpurg or Neidhardt that wins the award because in it the altered fifths are symmetrically arranged among the entire 12 fifths of the temperament. In these temperaments all keys are pretty much alike, whether nearer to C major or F# major.

But the whole intent of having a "circulating" temperament, of having the octave "well tempered," was to have greater consonance in the keys most used than in those more remote. This is made very clear in the writings of Werckmeister and Neidhardt. We should fail in our duty, therefore, did we not refer at the end of this chapter to temperaments we have discussed that satisfy this ideal of graduated dissonance. Both Werckmeister and Neidhardt had a proper respect for equal temperament also, but a fanatic like Tempelhof,[25] writing fifty to seventy-five years later, could say that equal temperament was the worst possible temperament because one scale <u>must</u> differ from another in its tuning!

The simplest alteration of the Pythagorean tuning is to divide the comma into two equal parts. If the altered fifths are consecutive, there will be a temperament somewhat like the modification of the meantone temperament shown at the beginning of this chapter. This is Kirnberger's tuning,[26] except that he has divided the <u>syntonic</u> comma <u>arithmetically</u> between the fifths D-A and A-E, thus getting a slightly smaller deviation than if he had divided the ditonic comma (see Table 132).

---

[25]Georg Friedrich Tempelhof, <u>Gedanken über die Temperatur des Herrn Kirnberger</u> (Berlin and Leipzig, 1775), pp. 10, 18.

[26]J. P. Kirnberger, <u>Die Kunst des reinen Satzes in der Musik</u>, Part I, p. 13.

Table 132. Kirnberger's Temperament (1/2-Comma)

Ratios	1	256:243	9:8	32:27	5:4	4:3	45:32	3:2	128:81
Names	C^0	D^{b0}	D^0	E^{b0}	E^{-1}	F^0	$F^{\#-1}$	G^0	A^{b0}
Cents	0	90	204	294	386	498	590	702	792

Ratios	270:161	16:9	15:8	2:1
Names	$A^{\left[-\frac{1}{2}\right]}$	B^{b0}	B^{-1}	C^0
Cents	895	996	1088	1200

M.D. 9.0; S.D. 9.7

Baron von Wiese's second tuning was exactly the same as Kirnberger's. He was so confirmed a Pythagorean that he called E^{-1}, $F^{\#-1}$, and B^{-1} by the respective names F^{b0}, G^{b0}, and C^{b0}, each of which would have been 2 cents (the schisma) flatter than the corresponding syntonic value. However, von Wiese's first temperament[27] actually did divide the ditonic comma, making his $F^\#$ the mean between D^b and B^0 (Table 133). His ratio for $F^\#$, 5760:4073, is an excellent approximation for the square root of one-half.

Von Wiese's other three temperaments are respectable enough, for in them the tempered fifths are separated by a minor or major third. Since the deviation is the same for all three, we show No. 3 only (Table 134). Von Wiese has indicated it as extending from B^b to $D^\#$; but from the construction it extends from G^b to B, with the fifths E^b-B^b and B-G^b each tempered by half the ditonic comma. The best arrangement of the tempered fifths is for them to be separated by a semitone or a tritone. The lat-

Table 133. Von Wiese's Temperament, No. 1 (1/2-Comma)

Names	C^0	D^{b0}	D^0	E^{b0}	E^0	F^0	$F^{\#-\frac{1}{2}}$	G^0	A^{b0}	A^0	B^{b0}	B^0	C^0
Cents	0	90	204	294	408	498	600	702	792	906	996	1110	1200

M.D. 10.0; S.D. 10.8

[27]Christian Ludwig Gustav, Baron von Wiese, Klangeintheilungs-, Stimmungs- und Temperatur-Lehre (Dresden, 1793), p. 9 (No. 1) and p. 12 (No. 3).

Table 134. Von Wiese's Temperament, No. 3 (1/2-Comma)

Names	C^0	$D^{b+\frac{1}{2}}$	D^0	$E^{b+\frac{1}{2}}$	E^0	F^0	$G^{b+\frac{1}{2}}$	G^0	$A^{b+\frac{1}{2}}$	A^0	B^{b0}	B^0	C^0
Cents	0	102	204	306	408	498	600	702	804	906	996	1110	1200

M.D. 5.0; S.D. 6.6

ter arrangement occurs in Grammateus' temperament, shown earlier in this chapter, which is identical with Marpurg's K. Note that von Wiese's No. 3 is the same as Grammateus' except for B^b.

Next in order would be temperaments in which the ditonic comma is divided among three thirds. Charles, Earl Stanhope[28] advocated such a division, but indicated that the syntonic comma should be divided among the fifths G-D, D-A, and A-E. This left the schisma, 2 cents, to be divided among the four fifths from B^b to G^b, the other five fifths being pure. Thus the four black keys are only one cent sharper than if the tuning were purely Pythagorean. He might better have divided the ditonic comma among his first three fifths, and not have had the approximate fifths to worry over. With the ditonic comma divided among three consecutive fifths, the mean deviation is 9.0, the standard deviation 9.7. Stanhope's own temperament (Table 135) is slightly better than this, just as Kirnberger's was better than von Wiese's No. 1, because the former divided the syntonic comma.

Werckmeister[29] has shown a temperament in which the comma is divided into three parts. It is, however, even less satisfactory than Stanhope's, because it contains five fifths flat by 1/3 comma, two fifths sharp by 1/3 comma, and only five perfect fifths (see Table 136). This is the poorest of the three temperaments Werckmeister called "correct."

Bendeler has used the 1/3-comma tempering in two of his

---

[28] "Principles of the Science of Tuning Instruments with Fixed Tones," Philosophical Magazine, XXV (1806), 291-312.

[29] Andreas Werckmeister, Musicalische Temperatur (Frankfort and Leipzig, 1691), Plate.

Table 135. Stanhope's Temperament (1/3-Comma)

Lengths	120	113.84	107.1	101.19	96	90	85.38
Names	C^0	D^{b0}	$D^{-\frac{1}{3}}$	E^{b0}	E^{-1}	F^0	G^{b0}
Cents	0	91	197	295	386	498	589
Lengths	80	75.89	71.7	67.5	64	60	
Names	G^0	A^{b0}	$A^{-\frac{2}{3}}$	B^{b0}	B^{-1}	C^0	
Cents	702	793	892	996	1088	1200	

M.D. 7.8; S.D. 8.7

three organ temperaments.[30] In the first, the tempering is shared by the fifths C-G, G-D, and B-F$^{\#}$ (Table 137). Since these are not all consecutive fifths in the circle of fifths, his deviation is considerably less than Stanhope's.

In Bendeler's second temperament (Table 138), the comma is divided among the three fifths C-G, D-A, and F$^{\#}$-C$^{\#}$. Since the

Table 136. Werckmeister's Correct Temperament, No. 2 (1/3-Comma)

Names	C^0	$C^{\#-\frac{4}{3}}$	$D^{-\frac{1}{3}}$	E^{b0}	$E^{-\frac{2}{3}}$	F^0	$F^{\#-1}$	$G^{-\frac{1}{3}}$	$G^{\#-\frac{4}{3}}$	$A^{-\frac{2}{3}}$	$B^{b+\frac{1}{3}}$	B^{-1}	C^0
Cents	0	82	196	294	392	498	588	694	786	890	1004	1086	1200

M.D. 9.2; S.D. 10.7

Table 137. Bendeler's Temperament, No. 1 (1/3-Comma)

Names	C^0	$C^{\#-1}$	$D^{-\frac{2}{3}}$	E^{b0}	$E^{-\frac{2}{3}}$	F^0	$F^{\#-1}$	$G^{-\frac{1}{3}}$	$G^{\#-1}$	$A^{-\frac{2}{3}}$	B^{b0}	$B^{-\frac{2}{3}}$	C^0
Cents	0	90	188	294	392	498	588	694	792	890	996	1094	1200

M.D. 5.0; S.D. 5.8

Table 138. Bendeler's Temperament, No. 2 (1/3-Comma)

Names	C^0	$C^{\#-1}$	$D^{-\frac{1}{3}}$	E^{b0}	$E^{-\frac{2}{3}}$	F^0	$F^{\#-\frac{2}{3}}$	$G^{-\frac{1}{3}}$	$G^{\#-1}$	$A^{-\frac{2}{3}}$	B^{b0}	$B^{-\frac{2}{3}}$	C^0
Cents	0	90	196	294	392	498	596	694	792	890	996	1094	1200

M.D. 4.0; S.D. 4.8

[30]J. P. Bendeler, Organopoeia (2nd ed.; Frankfurt and Leipzig, 1739), p. 40 (No. 1) and p. 42 (No. 2).

160

fifths are more widely separated than before, the deviation is less than for No. 1.

The best arrangement of the three tempered fifths is to have them separated by major thirds, as in Marpurg's I, where E and $G^{\#}$ are the same pitches as in equal temperament (see Table 139).

The most famous of Werckmeister's irregular divisions has the comma divided equally among the four fifths C-G, G-D, D-A, and B-F$^{\#}$.[31] Since three of these fifths are consecutive, the deviation is comparatively large (see Table 140). This is the only temperament that Sorge has ascribed to Werckmeister. The same division was accepted by Marpurg, and a modern acoustician, Karl Erich Schumann,[32] has followed suit, without mentioning any secondary source.

In Werckmeister's third "correct" temperament (Table 141), five fifths (D-A, A-E, F$^{\#}$-C$^{\#}$, C$^{\#}$-G$^{\#}$, and F-C) are flattened by 1/4 comma, and one fifth, G$^{\#}$-D$^{\#}$, is raised by the same amount. Thanks, however, to the more nearly symmetrical arrangement of the tempered fifths, the deviation is slightly less than for his first temperament.

In his third temperament, Bendeler,[33] unhampered by a sharp fifth and with a fairly symmetrical arrangement of the four flattened fifths (C-G, G-D, E-B, G$^{\#}$-D$^{\#}$), succeeded in achieving a very good division (Table 142).

But, as usual, the best temperament for a particular division of the comma is completely symmetrical, and so Neidhardt, in his fourth Fifth-Circle (Table 143), gave E^{b}, F$^{\#}$, and A the same pitches they would have in equal temperament. (Marpurg's H is identical with this.)

When the comma is divided into five parts and the tempered fifths are arranged as symmetrically as possible, the deviation begins to approach the vanishing point. (Paradoxically, this deviation is lower than for a wholly symmetrical arrangement of six fifths tempered by 1/6 comma, shown in the next section.) In

[31]Werckmeister (see Table 140), loc. cit.

[32]Akustik (Breslau, 1925), p. 31.

[33]Organopoeia, p. 42.

Table 139. Marpurg's Temperament I (1/3-Comma)

Names C^0 $C^{\#-\frac13}D^0$ $E^{\flat+\frac13}$ $E^{-\frac13}$ $F^{+\frac13}$ $F^{\#-\frac13}G^0$ $G^{\#-\frac23}A^0$ $B^{\flat+\frac13}$ $B^{-\frac13}$ C^0

Cents 0 106 204 302 400 506 604 702 800 906 1004 1102 1200

M.D. 3.0; S.D. 3.5

Table 140. Werckmeister's Correct Temperament, No. 1 (1/4-Comma)

Names C^0 $C^{\#-1}D^{-\frac12}$ $E^{\flat o}$ $E^{-\frac34}$ F^0 $F^{\#-1}$ $G^{-\frac14}$ $G^{\#-1}$ $A^{-\frac34}$ $B^{\flat o}$ $B^{-\frac34}$ C^0

Cents 0 90 192 294 390 498 588 696 792 888 996 1092 1200

M.D. 6.0; S.D. 7.5

Table 141. Werckmeister's Correct Temperament, No. 3 (1/4-Comma)

Names C^0 $C^{\#-\frac34}D^0$ $E^{\flat+\frac14}$ $E^{-\frac12}$ $F^{+\frac14}$ $F^{\#-\frac12}G^0$ $G^{\#-1}$ $A^{-\frac14}$ $B^{\flat+\frac14}$ $B^{-\frac12}$ C^0

Cents 0 96 204 300 396 504 600 702 792 900 1002 1098 1200

M.D. 5.0; S.D. 5.7

Table 142. Bendeler's Temperament, No. 3 (1/4-Comma)

Names C^0 $C^{\#-\frac34}D^{-\frac12}$ $E^{\flat o}$ $E^{-\frac12}$ F^0 $F^{\#-\frac34}$ $G^{-\frac14}$ $G^{\#-\frac34}$ $A^{-\frac12}$ $B^{\flat o}$ $B^{-\frac34}$ C^0

Cents 0 96 192 294 396 498 594 696 798 894 996 1092 1200

M.D. 3.3; S.D. 3.7

Table 143. Neidhardt's Fifth-Circle, No. 4 (1/4-Comma)

Names C^0 $C^{\#-\frac34}D^{-\frac14}$ $E^{\flat+\frac14}$ $E^{-\frac12}$ F^0 $F^{\#-\frac12}$ $G^{-\frac14}$ $G^{\#-\frac34}$ $A^{-\frac14}$ $B^{\flat o}$ $B^{-\frac12}$ C^0

Cents 0 96 198 300 396 498 600 696 798 900 996 1098 1200

M.D. 2.7; S.D. 2.8

Table 144. Marpurg's Temperament G (1/5-Comma)

Names C^0 $C^{\#-\frac35}D^{-\frac15}$ $E^{\flat+\frac15}$ $E^{-\frac25}$ F^0 $F^{\#-\frac25}G^0$ $G^{\#-\frac35}$ $A^{-\frac15}$ $B^{\flat+\frac15}$ $B^{-\frac25}$ C^0

Cents 0 100 199 299 398 498 602 702 802 901 1001 1100 1200

M.D. .7; S.D. 1.3

Marpurg's G (Table 144) this near-symmetrical division is made. Marpurg called the amount of tempering $2\frac{1}{2}/12 = 5/24$ comma, which would be 5 cents, slightly larger than 1/5 comma or 4.8 cents. Although the difference between the two is wholly negligible, the latter amount of tempering has been used in making the table, with the values rounded off to even cents.

The 1/6-comma temperament is recommended by Thomas Young,[34] as a simpler method than the irregular temperament described later in this chapter. In his own words, "In practice, nearly the same effect may be very simply produced, by tuning C to F, B^b, E^b, $G^{\#}$, $C^{\#}$, $F^{\#}$ six perfect fourths; and C, G, D, A, E, B, $F^{\#}$ six equally imperfect fifths." In other words, he had six consecutive fifths tempered by 1/6 ditonic comma (see Table 145). As a practical tuning method, this would not be difficult,

Table 145. Young's Temperament No. 2 (1/6-Comma)

Names	C^0	D^{b0}	$D^{-\frac{1}{3}}$	E^{b0}	$E^{-\frac{2}{3}}$	F^0	G^{b0}	$G^{-\frac{1}{6}}$	A^{b0}	$A^{-\frac{1}{2}}$	B^{b0}	$B^{-\frac{5}{6}}$	C^0
Cents	0	90	196	294	392	498	588	698	792	894	996	1090	1200

M.D. 6.0; S.D. 6.8

and it certainly does differentiate between near and remote keys. This is the tuning of the Out-Of-Tune Piano, the sort of tuning into which a piano originally in equal temperament might fall if played upon by a beginner.[35] Young's key of G is the best, that of D^b the worst. If he had commenced his set of tempered fifths with F instead of C, the key of C would have been best.

In Neidhardt's second Fifth-Circle (Table 146), all the fifths

Table 146. Neidhardt's Fifth-Circle, No. 2 (1/6-Comma)

Names	C^0	$C^{\#-\frac{1}{2}}D^0$	$E^{b+\frac{1}{6}}$	$E^{-\frac{1}{3}}$	$F^{+\frac{1}{6}}$	$F^{\#-\frac{1}{3}}G^{-\frac{1}{6}}$	$G^{\#-\frac{2}{3}}A^{-\frac{1}{6}}$	$B^{b+\frac{1}{3}}$	$B^{-\frac{1}{2}}$	C^0
Cents	0	102 204	298	400	502	604 698	800 902	1004	1098	1200

M.D. 3.0; S.D. 3.4

---

[34] "Outlines of Experiments and Inquiries Respecting Sound and Light," Philosophical Transactions, XC (1800), 145.

[35] J. Murray Barbour, "Bach and The Art of Temperament," Musical Quarterly, XXXIII (1947), 66 f, 89.

are altered by 1/6 comma, nine being lowered and three raised. Since the arrangement is completely symmetrical, the deviation is low.

Of course, a symmetrical arrangement of fifths alternately pure and lowered by 1/6 comma comes closest to equal temperament. Both Neidhardt (Third Fifth-Circle) and Marpurg (F) have presented this temperament (Table 147). Observe that in it the consecutive notes are alternately the same as in equal temperament and 2 cents higher, so that the mean deviation and standard deviation both are equal to 2.0. More elaborate patterns of semitones either 2 cents higher or lower than in equal temperament could be obtained by having two pure fifths alternate

Table 147. Neidhardt's Fifth-Circle, No. 3 (1/6-Comma)

Names	C^0	$C^{\#-\frac{1}{2}}$	$D^{-\frac{1}{6}}$	$E^{b+\frac{1}{3}}$	$E^{-\frac{1}{3}}$	$F^{+\frac{1}{6}}$	$F^{\#-\frac{1}{2}}$	G^0	$G^{\#-\frac{2}{3}}$	$A^{-\frac{1}{6}}$	$B^{b+\frac{1}{6}}$	$B^{-\frac{1}{3}}$	C^0
Cents	0	102	200	302	400	502	600	702	800	902	1000	1102	1200

M.D. 2.0; S.D. 2.0

with two tempered fifths, or by having three pure fifths similarly alternate with three tempered ones.

Bermudo,[36] who had also formed equal semitones on the lute by the method of Grammateus, made a real contribution to tuning theory in a chapter "concerning the seven-stringed vihuela upon which all the semitones can be played." This was a method intended for experienced players. His account of the division is necessarily lengthy and need not be given as a whole. G is the fundamental, and there are 10 frets, thus making no provision for $F^\#$ on this string. The notes from E^b to G inclusive are formed by a succession of pure fifths. The thirds G-B and A-$C^\#$ are each 2/3 syntonic comma sharper than pure thirds. The tone G-A is 1/6 comma less than a major tone. Then D and E form pure fourths with A and B, respectively, and $G^\#$ is a fourth below $C^\#$.

The geometry, which consists of linear divisions only, is easy to follow, especially with the aid of Bermudo's monochord dia-

---

[36]J. Bermudo, Declaracion de instrumentos musicales (Ossuna, 1555), Book 4, Chap. 86.

gram (see Figure I). In ratios, as will be seen in Table 148, it becomes quite complicated, and, if these ratios were to be rep-

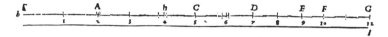

Fig. I. Bermudo's Method for Placing Frets on the Vihuela
Reproduced by courtesy of the Library of Congress

Table 148. Bermudo's Vihuela Temperament (1/6-,1/2-Comma)

Names	G^0	$G^{\#-\frac{1}{2}}$	$A^{-\frac{1}{6}}$	B^{b0}	$B^{-\frac{1}{3}}$	C^0
Ratios	1	492075:463684	540:481	32:27	1215:964	4:3
Cents	0	102.9	200.3	294.2	400.6	498.0

Names	$C^{\#-\frac{1}{2}}$	$D^{-\frac{1}{6}}$	E^{b0}	$E^{-\frac{1}{3}}$	F^0	$\left[F^{\#-\frac{1}{2}}\right]$	G^0
Ratios	164025:115921	720:481	128:81	405:241	16:9	[218700:115921]	2:1
Cents	600.9	698.3	792.1	898.6	996.1	[1098.9]	1200

M.D. 3.9; S.D. 4.2

resented by least integers, as was done in many of these systems, the fundamental note G would have to be 62,985,600! Let us assume that $F^\#$, the unused 11th fret, is a pure fourth above $C^\#$.

The reason Bermudo's system is presented in connection with the use of fifths tempered by 1/6 comma is that that is precisely what he has. If the temperament of successive fifths is examined, it will be seen that the fifths on G, A, and B are each tempered by 1/6 comma, eight fifths are pure, and the usual wolf fifth, $G^\#$-E^b, is 1/2 comma flat. (It really should not be called a wolf fifth, since it is flat, not sharp, and the usual poor thirds of the meantone temperaments, on B through $G^\#$, are the best of all!)

This is the first time, so far as is known, that any writer had suggested the formation of notes used in equal temperament by the proper division of the comma for those notes. Of course he was making an arithmetical division of the syntonic comma, and thus had small errors. But so did the late seventeenth and most of the eighteenth century comma-splitters from Werckmeister to Kirnberger and Stanhope. Bermudo's three tempered fifths

165

are as symmetrically arranged as in the Neidhardt-Marpurg system shown before this. It is too bad he did not continue his process by tempering $D^\#$ by 2/3 comma and $E^\#$ by 5/6 comma. Then he would not have had the half-comma error concentrated on a single fifth, nor a Pythagorean third on E^b. But this method of Bermudo is worthy of our respect as a very early approach to equal temperament, somewhat difficult, but not impracticable for a skilled performer to use.

Werckmeister is the only later writer to temper his fifths by the 7th part of a comma, perhaps following the example of Zarlino's 2/7-comma variety of meantone temperament.[37] But his Septenarium temperament is a rather eccentric thing. In it the fifths C-G, B^b-F, and B-$F^\#$ are 1/7 comma flat; $F^\#$-$C^\#$ is 2/7 comma flat; G-D is 4/7 comma flat; D-A and $G^\#$-$D^\#$ are 1/7 comma sharp; the remaining five fifths are pure. (The cents

Table 149. Werckmeister's Septenarium Temperament (1/7-Comma)

Lengths	196	186	176	165	156	147	139	131	124	117	110	104	98
Names	C^0	$C^{\#-1}$	$D^{-\frac{5}{7}}$	$E^{b+\frac{1}{7}}$	$E^{-\frac{4}{7}}$	F^0	$F^{\#-\frac{5}{7}}$	$G^{-\frac{1}{7}}$	$G^{\#-1}$	$A^{-\frac{4}{7}}$	$B^{b+\frac{1}{7}}$	$B^{-\frac{4}{7}}$	C^0
Cents	0	91	186	298	395	498	595	698	793	893	1000	1097	1200

M.D. 4.7; S.D. 5.6

Table 150. Symmetric Septenarium Temperament (1/7-Comma)

Names	C^0	$C^{\#-\frac{4}{7}}$	$D^{-\frac{1}{7}}$	$E^{b+\frac{2}{7}}$	$E^{-\frac{2}{7}}$	$F^{+\frac{1}{7}}$	$F^{\#-\frac{4}{7}}$	$G^{-\frac{1}{7}}$	$G^{\#-\frac{5}{7}}$	$A^{-\frac{2}{7}}$	$B^{b+\frac{1}{7}}$	$B^{-\frac{3}{7}}$	C^0
Cents	0	100	201	301	401	501	598	699	799	899	999	1100	1200

M.D. 0.5; S.D. 1.0

values have been worked out from Werckmeister's string-lengths, and are slightly inaccurate.)

For the sake of a comparison with Werckmeister's temperament, a symmetric version of the 1/7-comma temperament is shown in Table 150. It is even nearer equal temperament than Marpurg's G, which had a symmetric distribution of the fifth part of the comma.

[37]A. Werckmeister, Musicalische Temperatur, Plate.

166

Next we have a large group of temperaments in which some fifths are tempered by 1/6 comma and others by 1/12 comma, while the remaining fifths are pure. Since 1/12 comma is the temperament of the fifth of equal temperament, there will be as many pure fifths as there are fifths tempered by 1/6 comma. This group of temperaments might be considered, therefore, as variants of the previously described temperaments in which there are six pure fifths and six fifths tempered by 1/6 comma.

Neidhardt was the great inventor of temperaments in which the comma was divided into both 6 parts and 12 parts.[38] All three "circulating" temperaments fall into this group. They happen to be among the poorest of this type that he or the other theorists have evolved — that is, when compared with equal temperament. But we shall see that they do satisfy Neidhardt's purpose in creating them. The first circulating temperament (Table 151) has four fifths in each group — pure, tempered by 1/12 comma, and by 1/6 comma. Since four consecutive fifths in it are tempered by 1/6 comma, it may be considered a variant of the 1/6-comma meantone temperament.

The first of Thomas Young's pair of temperaments is very like the Neidhardt temperament shown in Table 151.[39] Young said, "It appears to me, that every purpose may be answered, by making C:E too sharp by a quarter of a comma, which will not offend the nicest ear; E:G$^\#$ and A^b:C equal; F$^\#$:A$^\#$ too sharp by a comma; and the major thirds of all the intermediate keys more or less perfect as they approach more or less to C in the order of modulation."

Table 151. Neidhardt's Circulating Temperament, No. 1
(1/12-, 1/6-Comma)

Names	C^0	C$^{\#-\frac{5}{6}}$	D$^{-\frac{1}{3}}$	E^{b0}	E$^{-\frac{2}{3}}$	F^0	F$^{\#-\frac{5}{6}}$	G$^{-\frac{1}{6}}$	G$^{\#-\frac{5}{6}}$	A$^{-\frac{1}{2}}$	B^{b0}	B$^{-\frac{3}{4}}$	C^0
Cents	0	94	196	296	392	498	592	698	796	894	996	1092	1200

M.D. 4.0; S.D. 4.6

[38] J. G. Neidhardt, Sectio canonis harmonici, pp. 16-18.

[39] Thomas Young, in Philosophical Transactions, XC (1800), 145 f.

Young accomplished the first result by tempering the fifths on C, G, D, and A by 3/16 syntonic comma, and the other results by tempering the fifths on F, B^b, E, and B by approximately 1/12 syntonic comma, and leaving the other four fifths pure. The total amount of tempering would be 13/12 syntonic comma, this being sufficiently close to the ratio of the ditonic to the syntonic comma. Young has given numbers for his monochord, and they agree well with his theory. He has made a mistake, however, in calculating the length for E^b (83810), which was intended as a pure fourth below G$^{\#}$. The corrected length is given in Table 152.

Table 152. Young's Temperament, No. 1 (1/12-, 3/16-Comma)

Lengths	100000	94723	89304	84197	79752	74921	71041
Names	C^0	C$^{\#-\frac{11}{12}}$	D$^{-\frac{3}{8}}$	E$^{b+\frac{1}{6}}$	E$^{-\frac{3}{4}}$	F$^{+\frac{1}{12}}$	F$^{\#-\frac{11}{12}}$
Cents	0	94	196	298	392	500	592
Lengths	66822	63148	59676	56131	53224	50000	
Names	G$^{-\frac{3}{16}}$	G$^{\#-\frac{11}{12}}$	A$^{-\frac{9}{16}}$	B$^{b+\frac{1}{6}}$	B$^{-\frac{5}{6}}$	C^0	
Cents	698	796	894	1000	1092	1200	

M.D. 5.3; S.D. 5.9

Now 3/16 syntonic comma is an awkward interval to deal with. If, instead, we take 1/6 ditonic comma as the temperament of Young's four diatonic fifths, and 1/12 ditonic comma for his second group of fifths, his monochord will be precisely of the Neidhardt type. The differences from the monochord he did give are so small that the cents values do not differ. The arrangement of his second group of fifths is slightly different from Neidhardt's, and this accounts for the difference in deviation.

Mercadier's temperament (Table 153) closely resembles Young's, even to the total amount of tempering — 13/12 syntonic comma.[40] He directed that the fifths from C to E should be flat by 1/6 syntonic comma, and those from E to G$^{\#}$ flat by 1/12 comma. Then G$^{\#}$ is taken as A^b, the next three fifths are to be just, and the fifth F-C then turns out to be about 1/12 comma flat.

[40]Antoine Suremain-Missery, Théorie acoustico-musicale (Paris, 1793), p. 256.

Table 153. Mercadier's Temperament (1/12-, 1/6-Comma)

Names	C^0	$C^{\#-\frac{11}{12}}$	$D^{-\frac{1}{3}}$	$E^{b-\frac{1}{12}}$	$E^{-\frac{2}{3}}$	$F^{-\frac{1}{12}}$	$F^{\#-\frac{5}{6}}$	$G^{-\frac{1}{6}}$	$G^{\#-1}$	$A^{-\frac{1}{2}}$	$B^{b-\frac{1}{12}}$	$B^{-\frac{3}{4}}$	C^0
Cents	0	94	197	296	394	500	594	698	794	895	998	1094	1200

M.D. 4.1; S.D. 4.5

Table 154. Marpurg's Temperament D (1/12-, 1/6-Comma)

Names	C^0	$C^{\#-\frac{2}{3}}$	$D^{-\frac{1}{4}}$	$E^{b+\frac{1}{4}}$	$E^{-\frac{5}{12}}$	F^0	$F^{\#-\frac{1}{2}}$	$G^{-\frac{1}{6}}$	$G^{\#-\frac{3}{4}}$	$A^{-\frac{1}{4}}$	$B^{b+\frac{1}{2}}$	$B^{-\frac{1}{2}}$	C^0
Cents	0	98	198	300	398	498	600	698	798	900	998	1098	1200

M.D. 1.3; S.D. 1.6

Table 155. Neidhardt's Circulating Temperament, No. 2
(1/12-, 1/6-Comma)

Names	C^0	$C^{\#-\frac{3}{4}}$	$D^{-\frac{1}{3}}$	$E^{b+\frac{1}{6}}$	$E^{-\frac{1}{12}}$	$F^{+\frac{1}{12}}$	$F^{\#-\frac{2}{3}}$	$G^{-\frac{1}{6}}$	$G^{\#-\frac{5}{6}}$	$A^{-\frac{1}{2}}$	$B^{b+\frac{1}{6}}$	$B^{-\frac{7}{12}}$	C^0
Cents	0	96	196	298	394	500	596	698	796	894	1000	1096	1200

M.D. 3.3; S.D. 3.7

Table 156. Neidhardt's Circulating Temperament, No. 3
(1/12-, 1/6-Comma)

Names	C^0	$C^{\#-\frac{3}{4}}$	$D^{-\frac{1}{3}}$	$E^{b+\frac{1}{6}}$	$E^{-\frac{7}{12}}$	F^0	$F^{\#-\frac{2}{3}}$	$G^{-\frac{1}{4}}$	$G^{\#-\frac{5}{6}}$	$A^{-\frac{1}{2}}$	$B^{b+\frac{1}{12}}$	$B^{-\frac{7}{12}}$	C^0
Cents	0	96	196	298	394	498	596	696	796	894	998	1096	1200

M.D. 2.7; S.D. 2.9

Table 157. Neidhardt's Third-Circle, No. 4 (1/12-, 1/6-Comma)

Names	C^0	$C^{\#-\frac{3}{4}}$	$D^{-\frac{1}{3}}$	E^{b0}	$E^{-\frac{1}{2}}$	F^0	$F^{\#-\frac{2}{3}}$	$G^{-\frac{1}{6}}$	$G^{\#-\frac{5}{6}}$	$A^{-\frac{1}{2}}$	$B^{b+\frac{1}{6}}$	$B^{-\frac{2}{3}}$	C^0
Cents	0	96	196	296	396	498	596	698	796	894	1000	1094	1200.

M.D. 2.7; S.D. 3.4

As usual, Marpurg has presented the symmetric version (Table 154) of the above temperaments. It has negligible deviations.

In the second and third of Neidhardt's "circulating" temperaments, six fifths are tempered by 1/12 comma, and three each are pure or are tempered by 1/6 comma. These two temperaments (Tables 155 and 156) are quite similar, both containing three consecutive fifths tempered by 1/6 comma. Thus they possibly represent the extreme case of modification of the 1/6-comma meantone temperament. Number 3 has a shade greater symmetry and hence smaller deviation.

Temperaments 4 and 3 of Neidhardt's Third-Circle have deviations very similar to those of the temperaments shown in Tables 155 and 156. In fact, their mean deviations are equal respectively to those of No. 2 and No. 3 in these tables, but their standard deviations are higher because they contain some sharp fifths. In No. 4 (Table 157), there are three fifths tempered by 1/12 comma and five by 1/6 comma; three fifths are pure, and one is 1/12 comma sharp. In No. 3 (Table 158), four fifths are 1/12 comma flat, six are 1/6 comma flat, and two are 1/6 comma sharp. (The same tempered fifths as in No. 3 appear in our hypothetical version of Schlick's temperament, but differently arranged.)

Once again Marpurg has given the symmetric version of Neidhardt's temperaments, specifically of the second and third "circulating" temperaments.

Logically we show next two temperaments (Tables 160 and 161) in which eight fifths are flat by 1/12 comma and two by 1/6 comma, while two are pure. Such a temperament is the fifth of Neidhardt's Third-Circle.

The temperament shown in Table 160 comes so close to equal temperament that in practice it could not be improved upon. But the canny Marpurg has halved its deviation by using greater symmetry (see Table 161).

Another temperament of Neidhardt has the same deviations as those of his fifth Third-Circle (Table 160). This is the fifth temperament in his Fifth-Circle (Table 162), in which six fifths are

IRREGULAR SYSTEMS

Table 158. Neidhardt's Third-Circle, No. 3 (1/12-, 1/6-Comma)

Names C^0 $C^{-\frac{3}{4}}$ $D^{-\frac{1}{3}}$ $E^{\flat\flat}$ $E^{-\frac{7}{12}}$ $F^{+\frac{1}{12}}$ $F^{\#-\frac{7}{12}}$ $G^{-\frac{1}{6}}$ $G^{\#-\frac{5}{6}}$ $A^{-\frac{5}{12}}$ $B^{\flat+\frac{1}{4}}$ $B^{-\frac{3}{4}}$ C^0

Cents 0 96 196 296 394 500 598 698 796 896 1002 1092 1200

M.D. 3.3; S.D. 4.7

Table 159. Marpurg's Temperament C (1/12-, 1/6-Comma)

Names C^0 $C^{\#-\frac{2}{3}}D^{-\frac{1}{6}}$ $E^{\flat+\frac{1}{4}}$ $E^{-\frac{1}{3}}$ F^0 $F^{\#-\frac{1}{2}}G^{-\frac{1}{12}}$ $G^{\#-\frac{2}{3}}A^{-\frac{1}{3}}$ $B^{\flat+\frac{1}{6}}$ $B^{-\frac{5}{12}}$ C^0

Cents 0 98 200 300 400 498 600 700 800 898 1000 1100 1200

M.D. 1.0; S.D. 1.4

Table 160. Neidhardt's Third-Circle, No. 5 (1/12-, 1/6-Comma)

Names C^0 $C^{\#-\frac{7}{12}}D^{-\frac{1}{6}}$ $E^{\flat+\frac{1}{4}}$ $E^{-\frac{5}{12}}F^{+\frac{1}{6}}$ $F^{\#-\frac{7}{12}}G^{-\frac{1}{12}}G^{\#-\frac{2}{3}}A^{-\frac{1}{4}}$ $B^{\flat+\frac{1}{6}}$ $B^{-\frac{1}{2}}$ C^0

Cents 0 100 200 300 398 502 598 700 800 900 1000 1098 1200

M.D. 1.3; S.D. 2.0

Table 161. Marpurg's Temperament B (1/12-, 1/6-Comma)

Names C^0 $C^{\#-\frac{2}{3}}D^{-\frac{1}{4}}$ $E^{\flat+\frac{1}{4}}E^{-\frac{1}{3}}$ $F^{+\frac{1}{12}}$ $F^{\#-\frac{1}{2}}G^{-\frac{1}{6}}$ $G^{\#-\frac{3}{4}}A^{-\frac{1}{3}}$ $B^{\flat+\frac{1}{6}}$ $B^{-\frac{5}{12}}$ C^0

Cents 0 98 198 298 400 500 600 698 798 898 1000 1100 1200

M.D. .7; S.D. 1.1

Table 162. Neidhardt's Fifth-Circle, No. 5 (1/12-, 1/6-Comma)

Names C^0 $C^{\#-\frac{7}{12}}D^{-\frac{1}{6}}$ $E^{\flat+\frac{1}{6}}E^{-\frac{1}{4}}$ $F^{+\frac{1}{6}}$ $F^{\#-\frac{1}{2}}G^{-\frac{1}{12}}G^{\#-\frac{2}{3}}A^{-\frac{1}{3}}$ $B^{\flat+\frac{1}{4}}$ $B^{-\frac{1}{3}}$ C^0

Cents 0 100 200 298 402 502 600 700 800 898 1002 1102 1200

M.D. 1.3; S.D. 2.0

flat by 1/12 comma and four by 1/6 comma, while two are sharp by 1/12 comma.

The remaining temperaments in this group come from Marpurg. The first (Table 163) of his temperaments in which some fifths are sharp contains six fifths flat by 1/6 comma, and three fifths each flat or sharp by 1/12 comma.[41] Obviously, this is a variant upon the temperament in which six fifths are flat by 1/6 comma, the other six pure. The mean deviation, 2.0, is the same, but, as expected, the standard deviation is higher here. Other possible variants would contain, in addition to the six fifths tempered by 1/6 comma, two fifths each flat or sharp by 1/12 comma or pure; or four pure fifths and one each flat or sharp by 1/12 comma.

The second temperament (Table 164) in this other set by Marpurg has fifths that do not differ greatly from those in the previous temperament. Here the six fifths are tempered by the unusual amount of 5/24 comma (shown as the same fraction that did duty as 1/5 in his Temperament G, but really 5/24 this time), and three each are pure or 1/12 comma sharp.

In Marpurg's Temperament A (Table 165), ten fifths are flat by 1/12 comma, and one each is pure or 1/6 comma flat. This is as far as one can go in this direction, for the next step would be to have twelve fifths flat by 1/12 comma — that is, equal temperament.

The other limit for this sequence of temperaments by Marpurg is his own Temperament F, already shown as Neidhardt's Fifth-Circle, No. 3 (Table 147). In it there are no fifths tempered by 1/12 comma, and six fifths each pure or flat by 1/6 comma. Just before it in the set comes Temperament E (Table 166), which has two fifths flat by 1/12 comma, and five fifths each pure or flat by 1/6 comma.

Marpurg's Temperament E, shown in Table 166, has the least deviation of the five temperaments in the set. Note the deviations again: A, 1.7, 1.8; B, 0.7, 1.1; C, 1.0, 1.4; D, 1.3, 1.6; E, 0.3, 0.8. From the table for E it is easy to see why its deviation is low: there are seven consecutive notes with cents values end-

---

[41]Marpurg, <u>Versuch über die musikalische Temperatur</u>, p. 163.

Table 163. Marpurg's Temperament, No. 1 (1/12-, 1/6-Comma)

Names	C⁰	C$^{\#-\frac{1}{2}}$	D$^{-\frac{1}{12}}$	E$^{b+\frac{5}{12}}$	E$^{-\frac{1}{3}}$	F$^{+\frac{1}{6}}$	F$^{\#-\frac{5}{12}}$	G$^{+\frac{1}{12}}$	G$^{\#-\frac{2}{3}}$	A$^{-\frac{1}{6}}$	B$^{b+\frac{1}{4}}$	B$^{-\frac{1}{4}}$	C⁰
Cents	0	102	202	304	400	502	602	704	800	902	1002	1104	1200

M.D. 2.0; S.D. 2.4

Table 164. Marpurg's Temperament, No. 2 (1/12-, 5/24-Comma)

Names	C⁰	C$^{\#-\frac{3}{4}}$	D$^{-\frac{5}{12}}$	E$^{b+\frac{1}{8}}$	E$^{-\frac{1}{3}}$	F$^{-\frac{1}{12}}$	F$^{\#-\frac{3}{4}}$	G$^{-\frac{5}{24}}$	G$^{\#-\frac{2}{3}}$	A$^{-\frac{5}{12}}$	B$^{b-\frac{1}{12}}$	B$^{-\frac{13}{24}}$	C⁰
Cents	0	96	194	297	400	496	594	697	800	896	994	1097	1200

M.D. 3.0; S.D. 3.1

Table 165. Marpurg's Temperament A (1/12-, 1/6-Comma)

Names	C⁰	C$^{\#-\frac{1}{2}}$	D$^{-\frac{1}{6}}$	E$^{b+\frac{1}{4}}$	E$^{-\frac{1}{4}}$	F$^{+\frac{1}{12}}$	F$^{\#-\frac{5}{12}}$	G$^{-\frac{1}{12}}$	G$^{\#-\frac{7}{12}}$	A$^{-\frac{1}{6}}$	B$^{b+\frac{1}{6}}$	B$^{-\frac{1}{3}}$	C⁰
Cents	0	102	200	300	402	500	602	700	802	902	1000	1102	1200

M.D. 1.7; S.D. 1.8

Table 166. Marpurg's Temperament E (1/12-, 1/6-Comma)

Names	C⁰	C$^{\#-\frac{7}{12}}$	D$^{-\frac{1}{12}}$	E$^{b+\frac{1}{3}}$	E$^{-\frac{1}{4}}$	F$^{+\frac{1}{6}}$	F$^{\#-\frac{5}{12}}$	G$^{-\frac{1}{12}}$	G$^{\#-\frac{2}{3}}$	A$^{-\frac{1}{4}}$	B$^{b+\frac{1}{6}}$	B$^{-\frac{5}{12}}$	C⁰
Cents	0	100	202	302	402	502	602	700	800	900	1000	1100	1200

M.D. 0.3; S.D 0.8

Table 167. Neidhardt's Fifth-Circle, No. 6 (1/12-, 1/4-Comma)

Names	C⁰	C$^{\#-\frac{7}{12}}$	D$^{-\frac{1}{3}}$	E$^{b+\frac{1}{4}}$	E$^{-\frac{1}{3}}$	F$^{-\frac{1}{12}}$	F$^{\#-\frac{1}{2}}$	G$^{-\frac{1}{12}}$	G$^{\#-\frac{5}{6}}$	A$^{+\frac{1}{4}}$	B$^{b+\frac{1}{6}}$	B$^{-\frac{7}{12}}$	C⁰
Cents	0	100	196	300	400	496	600	700	796	900	1000	1096	1200

M.D. 2.7; S.D. 3.3

Table 168. Neidhardt's Fifth-Circle, No. 9 (1/12-, 1/4-Comma)

Names	C⁰	C$^{\#-\frac{2}{3}}$	D$^{-\frac{1}{3}}$	E$^{b+\frac{1}{4}}$	E$^{-\frac{1}{3}}$	F⁰	F$^{\#-\frac{2}{3}}$	G$^{-\frac{1}{12}}$	G$^{\#-\frac{2}{3}}$	A$^{-\frac{1}{3}}$	B^{b0}	B$^{-\frac{5}{12}}$	C⁰
Cents	0	98	196	300	400	498	596	700	800	898	996	1100	1200

M.D. 2.0; S.D. 2.4

ing in 00, and five ending in 02. Therefore the total deviation will be only 4 cents, or a mean deviation of 0.3. In the other temperaments of the set, some values end in 00 and others in 98 or 02. But in no other temperament do all the 00's come together as they do in E. Therefore the deviation is higher in the other temperaments. But it need not have been higher. If in A the pure fifth is followed directly by the fifth flat by 1/6 comma, there will be only one note with an 02 ending, and eleven notes with 00. The fifths in B, C, and D can be so arranged that there will be respectively 2, 3, and 4 consecutive notes with an 02 (or 98) ending, the other endings being 00. Thus the minimum deviation (M.D. 0.3; S.D. 0.8) will be the same for all five temperaments, but this will not always involve the most symmetrical version of the fifths.

The remaining nine temperaments are all by Neidhardt, and each contains some fifths tempered by 1/4 comma. His Fifth-Circle, No. 6 (Table 167) has four fifths each flat by 1/4 comma or flat or sharp by 1/12 comma. His arrangement is symmetric.

In Temperament No. 9 of this same set (Table 168), Neidhardt has three fifths flat by 1/4 comma, three flat by 1/12 comma, and six pure. Again the arrangement is symmetric. The deviation is lower than for the previous temperament.

In Temperaments 7 and 10 (Table 169 and 170), Neidhardt divides the comma into 4 or 6 parts. No. 7 is especially complicated, having eight fifths flat by 1/6 comma and two sharp by 1/6 comma, and one each flat or sharp by 1/4 comma. It would be difficult to construct a symmetric arrangement from such an array, and Neidhardt has not attempted to do so.

Table 169. Neidhardt's Fifth-Circle, No. 7 (1/6-, 1/4-Comma)

Names	C^0	$C^{\#-\frac{5}{6}}$	$D^{-\frac{5}{12}}$	$E^{b+\frac{1}{6}}$	$E^{-\frac{1}{3}}$	$F^{-\frac{1}{6}}$	$F^{\#-\frac{2}{3}}$	$G^{-\frac{1}{4}}$	$G^{\#-\frac{2}{3}}$	$A^{-\frac{7}{12}}$	B^{b0}	$B^{-\frac{1}{2}}$	C^0
Cents	0	94	194	298	400	494	596	696	800	892	996	1098	1200

M.D. 3.3; S.D. 4.1

Table 170. Neidhardt's Fifth-Circle, No. 10 (1/6-, 1/4-Comma)

Names	C^0	$C^{\#-\frac{5}{6}}$	$D^{-\frac{1}{4}}$	$E^{b+\frac{1}{6}}$	$E^{-\frac{2}{3}}$	F^0	$F^{\#-\frac{2}{3}}$	$G^{-\frac{1}{4}}$	$G^{\#-\frac{5}{6}}$	$A^{-\frac{1}{2}}$	B^{b0}	$B^{-\frac{2}{3}}$	C^0
Cents	0	94	198	298	392	498	596	696	796	894	996	1094	1200

M.D. 3.0; S.D. 3.8

Table 171. Neidhardt's Fifth-Circle, No. 10, Idealized

Names	C^0	$C^{\#-\frac{5}{6}}$	$D^{-\frac{1}{4}}$	$E^{b+\frac{1}{6}}$	$E^{-\frac{5}{12}}$	F^0	$F^{\#-\frac{7}{12}}$	$G^{-\frac{1}{4}}$	$G^{\#-\frac{5}{6}}$	$A^{-\frac{5}{12}}$	B^{b0}	$B^{-\frac{7}{12}}$	C^0
Cents	0	94	198	298	398	498	598	696	796	896	996	1096	1200

M.D. 1.3; S.D. 2.4

Table 172. Neidhardt's Sample Temperament, No. 2
(1/12-, 1/6-, 1/4-Comma)

Names	C^0	$C^{\#-1}$	$D^{-\frac{5}{12}}$	E^{b0}	$E^{-\frac{11}{12}}$	$F^{-\frac{1}{12}}$	$F^{\#-\frac{11}{12}}$	$G^{-\frac{1}{6}}$	$G^{\#-1}$	$A^{-\frac{2}{3}}$	$B^{b-\frac{1}{12}}$	$B^{-\frac{11}{12}}$	C^0
Cents	0	90	194	294	386	496	590	698	792	890	994	1088	1200

M.D. 6.3; S.D. 7.2

Temperament 10 (Table 170) is considerably simpler, with two fifths flat by 1/4 comma, three by 1/6 comma, and the remaining seven pure. The deviation is slightly lower than for No. 7.

But in No. 10 also the arrangement is far from symmetric. Let us see what would result from an approach to symmetry. Although the deviation is about halved in Table 171, it is possible that, as in the alphabetically named temperaments by Marpurg, the least deviation for all four of these Neidhardt temperaments will not occur with the most nearly symmetric arrangement of the fifths.

In the remaining five temperaments in this group, Neidhardt has tempered his fifths by 1/4, 1/6, and 1/12 comma. His second and third "sample" temperaments (the first was just intonation) have relatively high deviations.[42] No. 2 (Table 172) has three fifths flat by 1/4 comma, one by 1/6, two by 1/12, five pure, and one 1/12 comma sharp.

---

[42] J. G. Neidhardt, Gäntzlich erschöpfte mathematische Abtheilung, p. 34.

Neidhardt's No. 3 (Table 173) is somewhat less erratic than No. 2, with six pure fifths, and two each flat by 1/4, 1/6, or 1/12 comma. It also has a lower deviation than No. 2.

Rather similar to the above sample temperaments is his Third-Circle, No. 1 (Table 174), in which five fifths are pure, two flat by 1/4 comma, one by 1/6, and four by 1/2.

Two temperaments from the Fifth-Circle are considerably better than the three just mentioned. In No. 11 (Table 175) there are no pure fifths; two fifths are flat by 1/4 comma, two by 1/6, five by 1/12, while three are 1/12 comma sharp.

Table 173. Neidhardt's Sample Temperament, No. 3
(1/12-, 1/6-, 1/4-Comma)

Names	C^0	$C^{\#-\frac{11}{12}}$	$D^{-\frac{1}{3}}$	$E^{b+\frac{1}{12}}$	$E^{-\frac{5}{6}}$	F^0	$F^{\#-\frac{5}{6}}$	$G^{-\frac{1}{6}}$	$G^{\#-\frac{11}{12}}$	$A^{-\frac{7}{12}}$	B^{b0}	$B^{-\frac{5}{6}}$	C^0
Cents	0	92	196	296	388	498	592	698	794	892	996	1090	1200

M.D. 5.7; S.D. 6.4

Table 174. Neidhardt's Third-Circle, No. 1 (1/12-, 1/6-, 1/4-Comma)

Names	C^0	$C^{\#-\frac{5}{6}}$	$D^{-\frac{1}{4}}$	$E^{b+\frac{1}{12}}$	$E^{-\frac{3}{4}}$	F^0	$F^{\#-\frac{5}{6}}$	$G^{-\frac{1}{12}}$	$G^{\#-\frac{11}{12}}$	$A^{-\frac{1}{2}}$	$B^{b+\frac{1}{12}}$	$B^{-\frac{3}{4}}$	C^0
Cents	0	94	198	296	390	498	592	700	794	894	998	1092	1200

M.D. 5.3; S.D. 5.9

Table 175. Neidhardt's Fifth-Circle, No. 11 (1/12-, 1/6-, 1/4-Comma)

Names	C^0	$C^{\#-\frac{3}{4}}$	$D^{-\frac{1}{4}}$	$E^{b+\frac{1}{12}}$	$E^{-\frac{7}{12}}$	$F^{+\frac{1}{12}}$	$F^{\#-\frac{7}{12}}$	$G^{-\frac{1}{12}}$	$G^{\#-\frac{2}{3}}$	$A^{-\frac{1}{2}}$	B^{b0}	$B^{-\frac{1}{2}}$	C^0
Cents	0	96	198	296	394	500	598	700	800	894	996	1098	1200

M.D. 2.7; S.D. 3.2

Table 176. Neidhardt's Fifth-Circle, No. 12 (1/12-, 1/6-, 1/4-Comma)

Names	C^0	$C^{\#-\frac{7}{12}}$	$D^{-\frac{1}{4}}$	$E^{b+\frac{1}{4}}$	$E^{-\frac{1}{2}}$	F^0	$F^{\#-\frac{1}{2}}$	$G^{-\frac{1}{12}}$	$G^{\#-\frac{3}{4}}$	$A^{-\frac{1}{4}}$	B^{b0}	$B^{-\frac{1}{2}}$	C^0
Cents	0	100	198	300	396	498	600	700	798	900	996	1098	1200

M.D. 2.0; S.D. 2.3

176

In No. 12 (Table 176) there are six pure fifths, and two each flat by 1/4, 1/6, or 1/12 comma. This has precisely the same number of each size of fifth as the third sample temperament, in which the deviation was almost three times as great. The reason, of course, is to be found in the symmetry of No. 12.

Metius' System

At the beginning of this chapter it was said that "by making the bounds sufficiently elastic" all irregular systems could be classified. That statement is severely tested by the final tuning method listed in this part of the chapter, one presented by Adrian Metius. It was not possible to see Metius' own description, and Nierop, who gave the monochord, seemed to have been puzzled by it himself.[43] Nierop has shown this monochord in two forms, one from 1000 to 500 and the other from 11520 to 5760, with E the fundamental. It is evident from the context that the second monochord was given simply to show how its lengths have been increased or diminished by arithmetic divisions of the syntonic comma, and that only the first table comes from Metius directly.

By using Metius' lengths, it is possible to reconstruct the tempering, indicated by the exponents. Apparently there is only one pure fifth, C-G. The fifths on B^b and A are 1/12 comma flat, those on F and E 1/6 comma flat, on B and $C^\#$ 1/2 comma flat, and on G 3/4 comma flat! The fifths on D and $F^\#$ are 1/6 comma sharp, that on $D^\#$ 1/3 comma sharp, and on $G^\#$ 1/2 comma sharp.

Metius' system does not seem to follow any known system of temperament or modification thereof. Specifically, it does not resemble the meantone temperament, for only the thirds on B^b and E are pure, the other thirds varying in size up to 417 cents for G^b-B^b and 419 cents for A^b-C. But there is no pattern apparent in the alterations, no planned shift from good to poor keys. The fifth G-D, 3/4 comma flat, is almost as unsatisfactory as this same fifth would be in just intonation. There is no good reason for both of the fifths B-$F^\#$ and $C^\#$-$G^\#$ to be half a comma flat

[43]D. R. van Nierop, Wis-konstige Musyka (Amsterdam, 1650). The reference here is to page 60 of the 2nd edition (1659).

and then to have the fifth G$^{\#}$-D$^{\#}$ half a comma sharp. All in all, Metius has been just about as erratic as he could be.

And yet the system, despite its irregularities, is much better than the ordinary 1/4-comma meantone temperament and is slightly better than the Pythagorean or the 1/6-comma meantone. That much we must grudgingly admit. Metius' temperament contains eight different sizes of fifth. But that is not much less regular than many of the fairly good temperaments we have shown that had four sizes of fifth, while Werckmeister's Septenarium and Neidhardt's second sample temperament had five different sizes. And so let us label it highly irregular, but not really unworkable.

"Good" Temperaments

With Metius' enigmatic temperament we have described the last of our irregular tuning systems, and are in a position to try to formulate a judgment upon them. It is easy to see how the modifications of the Pythagorean, just, or meantone system by the halving of tones, as in the systems of Grammateus, Ganassi, or Artusi, would make these systems much more like equal temperament. But it is more difficult to see what Werckmeister, Neidhardt, and Marpurg were driving at in their multifarious attempts to distribute the comma unequally among the twelve fifths.

If, as was pointed out at the beginning of an earlier section of this chapter, our ideal is equal temperament, we shall praise highly some of the beautifully symmetric systems of Marpurg and Neidhardt. But the trouble is that they are too good! The deviations for most of them are lower than for a piano allegedly tuned in equal temperament by the most skillful tuner. In some cases these temperaments might have been successfully transferred from paper to practice by calculating the number of beats for each of the beating fifths. Since most of the fifths were to be tuned pure, such a method might have been easier than that pursued today. These same temperaments might have been reduced to distances on a monochord with slightly greater ease than equal temperament could be, although it must be remembered that usually even the most innocent set of cents values needs logarithmic computation before yielding figures for a monochord. But it will be safe to dismiss most of these oversubtle systems as useless, even for the age when they were devised.

What do we have left? It will be of interest to consider which of his twenty systems Neidhardt considered the best. In the Sectio canonis he had said, "In my opinion, the first [of the circulating temperaments] is, for the most part, suitable for a village, the second for a town, the third for a city, and the fourth for the court." The fourth was equal temperament; the mean deviations of the other temperaments had been 4.0, 3.3, and 2.7 cents, respectively.

In the much later Mathematische Abtheilungen Neidhardt presented eighteen different irregular temperaments, together with just intonation and equal temperament. He then attempted to choose the best of these twenty tunings. He chose equal temperament, of course, and the two temperaments (Third-Circle, No. 2, and Fifth-Circle, No. 8) that were identical with the first and second circulating temperaments above. Now half of the rejected temperaments had deviations lower than that of the second circulating temperament (3.3), and a couple of others were just about as good. But none of these was considered worthy in the final appraisal. Neidhardt had, incidentally, changed his ideas somewhat as to the relative position of the best temperaments: the Circulating Temperament, No. 2 (Fifth-Circle, No. 8) is now considered best for a large city; No. 1 (Third-Circle, No. 2) for a small city; and Third-Circle, No. 1, not included before, for a village.

If we examine the deviations of the major thirds in the three temperaments Neidhardt himself considered superior, we quickly find why he liked them. In the second circulating temperament (Table 155) the thirds on C and F are 8 cents sharper than a pure third, and the sharpness gradually increases in both directions around the circle of fifths until the three worst thirds are 18 cents sharp. In the first circulating temperament (Table 151) the third on C is only 6 cents sharp, and there is the same gradual increase until the five poorest thirds are all 18 cents sharp. In the Third-Circle, No. 1 (Table 174), the third on C is 4 cents sharp, and the six poorest thirds are either 18 or 20 cents sharp.

179

Werckmeister's third temperament, the first of the three he has labeled "correct" (Table 140), is much like the Neidhardt temperament just mentioned. Its thirds on C and F are only 4 cents sharp, but the thirds of the principal triads in the key of D^b are all a syntonic comma, 22 cents, sharp. Werckmeister himself said that some people who advocated equal temperament held that "in the future ... it will be just the same to play an air in D^b as in C."[44] But he held consistently "that one should let the diatonic thirds be somewhat purer than the others that are seldom used."[45]

A good comparison can be made between two temperaments of Neidhardt, already mentioned as having fifths of four different sizes and the same number of each size, but with a different arrangement. The Fifth-Circle, No. 12 (Table 176) has a symmetric arrangement and a low mean deviation, 2.0. Its thirds show no trend whatever from near to far keys, but are sufficiently irregular to make this seem a poor attempt at equal temperament. Not so its companion, the third sample temperament (Table 173), in which the third on C is only 2 cents sharp, whereas four of the five poorest thirds are 20 cents sharp. To be sure, the deviation for this temperament, 5.7, is almost three times as great as for the other one, and there is a painful lack of symmetry. But the unsymmetric temperament is "circulating," and therefore deserves an honored place among the "good" temperaments.

Thomas Young's temperaments also deserve mention for their circulating nature. His first temperament (Table 152) is equivalent to a temperament with four pure fifths and four fifths each tempered by 1/6 or 1/12 comma. It is constructed with scientific accuracy so that the thirds range in sharpness from 6 cents for C-E to 22 cents, a syntonic comma, for $F^\#$-$A^\#$. Its mean deviation is 5.3. On the other hand, there is the symmetric form of this temperament, Marpurg's D (Table 154), with a mean deviation of 1.3. And the even better, nonsymmetric form, with a

[44]A. Werckmeister, Hypomnemata musica (Quedlinburg, 1697), p. 36.

[45]Werckmeister, Musicalische Paradoxal-Discourse (Quedlinburg, 1707), p. 113.

mean deviation of 0.3! But these last-mentioned temperaments are curiosities only, whereas Young's differentiated admirably between near and far keys.

However, Young's first temperament was too difficult to construct, as he had described it with fifths tempered by 3/16 and "approximately" 1/12 syntonic comma. Therefore he substituted his second method (Table 145), which was of the utmost simplicity, with six consecutive perfect fifths and six consecutive fifths tempered by 1/6 ditonic comma. Its mean deviation was 6.0. In it the thirds on C, G, and D are each 6 cents sharp, whereas those on F#, C#, and G# are each 22 cents sharp. Neidhardt's Fifth-Circle, No. 3 (Marpurg's F) is the symmetric version of this temperament (Table 147), with a mean deviation of 2.0. Again we may well say that Young's version is an excellent irregular temperament, while the symmetrical version represents having fun with figures.

So many versions of good circulating temperaments have appeared on these pages, each with its points of excellence, that we cannot resist the temptation to close this chapter with an irregular temperament to end irregular temperaments! Gallimard's modification of the ordinary meantone temperament, by a systematic variation in the size of the chromatic fifths, was good enough in principle, but could not have been too successful because of the large number of other fifths tempered by 1/4 comma.

What is really needed, in order to have a more orderly change in the size of the thirds, is to have the variable tempering applied to all the fifths, instead of to only five of them. Let the fifth D-A be the flattest, and let each succeeding fifth in both directions around the circle of fifths be a little sharper until the fifth on A♭ is the sharpest. Then the total parts to be added will be 1 + 2 + 3 + 4 + 5 + 6 + 5 + 4 + 3 + 2 + 1 = 36 parts. Since these parts are to be added to 12 fifths, it is evident that D-A, the flattest fifth, will be flatter than the fifth of equal temperament by three of these parts; the fifths B-F# and F-C will be precisely the size of the equal fifth; and the sharpest fifth, A♭-E♭, will be larger than the equal fifth by three parts. The thirds will vary as follows (the error being expressed as the number of parts below or above the third of equal temperament): C-E, -8; G-B, -8;

D-F$^{\#}$, -6; A-C$^{\#}$, -2; E-G$^{\#}$, 2; B-D$^{\#}$, 6; G^{b}-B^{b}, 8; D^{b}-F, 8; A^{b}-C, 6; E^{b}-G, 2; B^{b}-D, -2; F-A, -6.

We can choose the value for one part that will give the desired size of thirds. If the part is one cent, the fifth D-A is 697 cents, practically a meantone fifth, and the fifth A^{b}-E^{b} is 703, practically perfect; the best thirds, C-E and G-B, are 392, 1/4 comma sharp; the poorest thirds, G^{b}-B^{b} and D^{b}-F, are 408, precisely a Pythagorean third.

Table 178 should have satisfied the desire of Werckmeister and his contemporaries for a circulating temperament in which all the thirds are sharp, but none more than a comma, and all the fifths are flat or pure. As the size of the part is reduced, the tuning approaches equal temperament. When the part is increased to 1 3/4 cents, the best thirds are pure. But the poorest thirds are now 414 cents, about 5/4 comma sharp. Thus Table 178 probably represents the limit of a tolerable temperament in the extreme keys. Since the mean deviation for the entire series of temperaments formed in this manner is precisely proportional to the size of the part, it would be easy to devise a system with the deviation of any of the systems in this chapter, but with a more orderly distribution of the errors, as regards common keys and less-used keys.

The Temperament by Regularly Varied Fifths may be regarded as the ideal form of Werckmeister's "correct" temperaments and of Neidhardt's "circulating" temperaments and of all "good" temperaments that practical tuners have devised by rule of thumb. Let us see, therefore, how closely it is approached by these other temperaments. In Table 179, the deviations have been computed, not only from equal temperament, but also from our temperament with variable fifths. The table shows clearly that the temperaments with greatest symmetry do not fit so well into the desired pattern as do those that are much less regular in their construction. In general, the temperaments with lowest deviation from the one ideal temperament will have a high deviation from the other. Neidhardt's second circulating temperament has the unique position of ranking the same with regard to both.

182

Table 177. Metius' Irregular Temperament

Lengths	1000	940	896	837	800	749	704	668	628	596	563	530	500
Names	E^0	$F^{+\frac{5}{6}}$	$F^{\#-\frac{2}{3}}$	$G^{+\frac{2}{3}}$	$G^{\#-1}$	$A^{+\frac{1}{12}}$	$B^{b+\frac{1}{12}}B^{-\frac{1}{6}}$		$C^{+\frac{2}{3}}$	$C^{\#-\frac{1}{2}}$	$D^{-\frac{1}{12}}D^{\#-\frac{1}{2}}$		E^0

M.D. 9.5; S.D. 11.6

Table 178. Temperament by Regularly Varied Fifths

Names	C	x	D	x	E	·F	x	G	x	A	x	B	C
Cents	0	92	197	297	392	500	591	699	794	894	999	1091	1200

M.D. 5.8; S.D. 6.6

Table 179. Deviations of Certain Temperaments

	From Equal Temperament		From Varied Fifths	
	M.D.	S.D.	M.D.	S.D.
Neidhardt's Circulating, No. 1	4.0	4.6	2.1	2.3
No. 2	3.3	3.7	3.3	3.7
No. 3	2.7	2.9	4.2	4.7
Third-Circle, No. 1	5.3	5.9	1.2	1.5
Werckmeister's				
Correct, No. 1	6.0	7.5	1.9	2.3
No. 2	9.2	10.7	4.7	5.7
No. 3	5.0	5.7	3.8	4.2
Neidhardt's Fifth-Circle, No. 12	2.0	2.3	6.2	6.7
Sample, No. 3	5.7	6.4	1.5	1.8
Young's No. 1	5.3	5.9	1.7	1.9
Marpurg's Letter D	1.3	1.6	6.7	7.1
Young's No. 2	6.0	6.8	1.9	2.0
Neidhardt's Fifth-Circle, No. 3	2.0	2.0	5.0	5.8
Schlick's (Hypothetical)	8.0	8.6	2.7	3.1
Neidhardt's				
Third-Circle, No. 3	3.3	4.7	3.0	3.8

Our hypothetical reconstruction of Arnold Schlick's temperament had the same size of fifths as Neidhardt's Third-Circle, No.
3, but differently arranged, and with a fairly high deviation. Observe that, with this other standard of varied dissonance, Schlick's
temperament is even a little better than Neidhardt's. Of all the
temperaments shown in our table, Neidhardt's Third-Circle, No.

1 seems to be the best, with our new standard, although Neidhardt himself said it was best for a village! But it would have been difficult to tune, and therefore Thomas Young's Temperament, No. 2 probably cannot be surpassed from the practical point of view. Even so, the highest honor must be paid to old Arnold Schlick, writing so long before these other men, but stating as clearly as need be for his very practical purpose, "Although they will all be too high, it is necessary to make the three thirds C-E, F-A, and G-B better,...as much as the said thirds are better, so much will $G^\#$ be worse to E and B."

Table 180. Compass of the Lute

	G Tuning 0	1	2	3	4	5	6	7	8	A Tuning 0	1	2	3	4	5	6	7	8
1.	G	A^b	A	B^b	B	C	$D^b(C^\#)$	D	E^b	A	B^b	B	C	$C^\#(D^b)$	D	E^b	E	F
2.	D	E^b	E	F	$F^\#$ G	$A^b(G^\#)$	A	B^b		E	F	$F^\#$ G	$G^\#(A^b)$	A	B^b	B	C	
3.	A	B^b	B	C	$C^\#$ D	$E^b(D^\#)$	E	F		B	C	$C^\#$ D	$D^\#(E^b)$	E	F	$F^\#$ G		
4.	F	G^b	G	A^b	A	B^b	$C^b(B)$	C	D^b	G	A^b	A	B^b B	(C^b)	C	D^b	D	E^b
5.	C	D^b	D	E^b	E	F	$G^b(F^\#)$	G	A^b	D	E^b	E	F	$F^\#(G^b)$	G	A^b	A	B^b
6.	G	A^b	A	B^b	B	C	$D^b(C^\#)$	D	E^b	A	B^b	B	C	$C^\#(D^b)$	D	E^b	E	F

Chapter VIII. FROM THEORY TO PRACTICE

In our intensive study of scores of tuning systems we have failed
to note what may be learned from the music itself. Some of the
theorists who have written on tuning were able composers as well.
When they described with precision a particular division of the
monochord, their theory may well have coincided with fact. But
the tuning theories of the mere mathematicians do not carry so
much weight. Nor do the rules of thumb the musicians more
commonly presented. All of these theories may be put into neat
little pigeonholes, but one can be sure that the practice itself,
because of the limitations of the human ear, was even more varied than the extremely varied theories.

It is not to be expected that a study of the music will provide
a precise picture of tuning practice. It is to be used more by
way of corroborating what the theorists have said. Let us consider first the contention of Vicentino that the fretted instruments
were always in equal temperament. In general we can reach
certain conclusions concerning tuning by examining the range of
modulation. However, this is not definitive as regards the lutes
and viols. Körte listed $D^{\#}$'s in lute music from 1508, an $A^{\#}$ from
1523, and many D^{b}'s from 1529.[1] But the mere presence of
notes beyond the usual 12-note compass proves little, because
the lutes were not restricted to a total compass of 12 semitones.
As shown in Table 180, the normal compass with the G tuning
was C^{b} to $C^{\#}$ and for the A tuning from D^{b} to $D^{\#}$.

Ordinarily, lutes and viols had six strings, tuned by fourths,
with a major third in the middle. Thus the open strings might
be G C F A D G or A D G B E A. It is easy to see here the
prototype of Schönberg's chords built by fourths. Because of the
perfect fourths, the fretted instruments might have inclined toward the Pythagorean tuning, as the later violins have done.
Mersenne pointed out that the major third in the middle would

---

[1]Oskar Körte, "Laute und Lautenmusik bis zur Mitte des 16. Jahrhunderts,"
Internationale Musikgesellschaft, Beiheft 3 (1901).

then be sharp by a comma.

But the strings of lutes and viols were tuned by forming unisons, fifths, or octaves with the proper frets on other strings, thus making the tuning uniform throughout the instrument. Vincenzo Galilei[2] stated that if the tuning were not equal, semitones on the A string (mezzana) of the lute based on G would have the note names shown in Table 180. Since the frets were merely pieces of gut tied straight across the fingerboards at the correct places, the order of diatonic and chromatic semitones would have to be the same on all strings. Thus the chromatic compass of a lute with six strings and eight frets would be as shown in Table 180, if meantone temperament had been used.

There might be some question for the G tuning regarding notes produced by the 6th fret, since B would be a better choice than C♭ on the 4th string. But the remaining notes for the 6th fret agree somewhat better with other notes in the compass than the equivalent sharped notes would have done. Galilei pointed out that G♭ (4th string, 1st fret) was not a pure fifth to C♯ (3rd string, 4th fret), nor was D♭ (5th string, 1st fret) a pure octave to the C♯. He might have added that D♭ (1st string, 6th fret) was not a pure octave above the C♯ either.

It is easy to multiply examples of unsatisfactory intervals on the unequally tuned lute in G. (Read them a tone higher for the A tuning.) Try building major triads upon the notes of the 6th string, starting with B♭. C, D♭, and E♭ are satisfactory as roots also, but false triads are generated on B and D. On the 5th string, starting with D, the satisfactory triads are on E♭, F, and A♭; false triads on D, E, G♭, and G. On the 4th string, starting with G, the only unsatisfactory triad is on C♭. On the 3rd string, starting with C, the other satisfactory triads are on D, E♭, and F, with false triads on C♯ and E. Thus, of 26 major triads in close position, only 17, about 2/3, are available. Some of the triads, those on G, D, and A, unsatisfactory in the lower octave, can be played correctly in the higher octave. But the complete E and B major triads are unavailable anywhere, because there are no G♯ and D♯ — unless, of course, the 6th fret runs to sharps rather than to flats.

[2]Fronimo (Venice 1581; revised edition, 1584), pp. 103 f.

As illustrations of incongruous notes on particular frets, let us examine some of the Austrian lute music of the sixteenth century, as found in Volume 18 of the Austrian Denkmäler. The first collection represented is Hans Judenkünig's Ain schone kunstliche Underweisung (1523). His third Priamell is modal, but often suggests C minor. Like most of the German and Austrian composers, Judenkünig used the A tuning of the lute. In bar 3 the note a^b appears as the 4th fret on the 2nd string, indicating that this fret has a flat tuning (see Table 180). But in bar 4 there is a b and in bar 19 a c$^{\#''}$, both of which belong to the sharp tuning for this fret.

For Judenkünig's fourth Priamell the editor has put the signature of three sharps, as an indication of the prevailing sharpness. This even extends to the 6th fret, which would then include an e$^{\#'}$. Actually there is an e$^{\#'}$ in the music, and no f$'$. Therefore it would have been possible to play this piece with an unequal temperament, but not without changing the 6th fret from its normal flat tuning.

Simon Gintzler's fifth Recercar (1547) used the Italian G tuning. Here the 6th fret has a flat tuning, as shown by a$^{b'}$ and a very frequent e$^{b'}$. But in bar 10 there is a b instead of the c$^{b'}$ belonging to the flat tuning. In Gintzler's setting of Senfl's song "Vita in ligno moritur," the 6th fret is again flat, but in bar 15 both a$^{b'}$ and b occur.

The a$^{b'}$ and b also occur several times in Bakfark's Fantasias (1565). More interesting is his setting of "Veni in hortum meum, soror mea" (1573). In bar 50, d$^{\#''}$ occurs as the third of the B major triad, indicating a sharp tuning for the 6th fret. This means that f$'$ is not available on this fret; but f$'$ does occur in bar 56 and elsewhere. In bar 62 the complete C minor triad occurs: c$'$ e$^{b'}$ g$'$ c$''$, with the e$^{b'}$ the 4th fret on the 3rd string. But this fret must have had a sharp tuning, since the notes d$^{\#'}$, g$^{\#'}$, and c$^{\#''}$ occur on it with great frequency.

It would be easy to multiply examples, from the music of Italian, French, and Spanish composers. Those that have been given are sufficient to show that in the golden age of lute music the composers were indifferent to discords that would have arisen if an unequal temperament had been used. The example from Judenkünig occurs so early in the century (1523) that it seems very probable that lutes and viols did employ equal temperament from an early time, perhaps from the beginning of the sixteenth century.

We need not be too much concerned with what the equal temperament for the fretted instruments was really like. It might have been the Grammateus-Bermudo tuning — Pythagorean with mean semitones for the chromatic notes. It might have been the Ganassi-Reinhard mean semitones applied to just intonation, or Artusi's more subtle system of mean semitones in meantone temperament. Or the frets might have been placed according to Galilei's 18:17 ratio, or (correctly) according to Salinas' ratio of the 12th root of 2. In any case, it would have been a good, workable temperament.

Tuning of Keyboard Instruments

In the early sixteenth century Schlick and Grammateus described systems for keyboard instruments that came close to equal temperament, and the correct application of Lanfranco's tuning rules must have resulted in equal temperament itself. But these systems were anomalous for a day when few accidentals were written. Examples of organ music from the late fifteenth and the entire sixteenth century are found in numerous collections, such as Schering's Alte Meister aus der Frühzeit des Orgelspiels; Volume 1 of Bonnet's Historical Organ Recitals; Kinkeldey's Orgel und Clavier in der Musik des 16. Jahrhunderts; Volume 1 of Margaret Glyn's Early English Organ Music; Volume 3 of Torchi's L'arte musicale in Italia; Wasielewski's Geschichte der Instrumentalmusik im 16. Jahrhundert; Volume 6 of the Italian Classics series.

With the exception of the English composers, the compass used by all these composers was less than 12 notes — E^b-$F^{\#}$ or B^b-$C^{\#}$. Both Tallis and Redford had $D^{\#}$ in one piece and E^b in another, thus posing a problem with regard to the tuning. But except for them, there was no problem about performance: all of this organ music could have been played on an instrument in meantone temperament.

Even 12 of Schlick's 14 little pieces (Monatshefte für Musikgeschichte, 1869) lie within a compass of E^b-$C^\#$. One of the remaining pieces has an A^b; the other, $G^\#$. Since Schlick had directed that the wolf be divided equally between the fifths $C^\#$-$G^\#$ and A^b-E^b, these notes would have caused him no difficulty. Perhaps Tallis and Redford were dividing the error similarly.

Much the same can be said for the clavier music of this period. Merian's Der Tanz in den deutschen Tabulaturbüchern (Leipzig, 1927) contains about 200 tiny keyboard pieces, and Volume 2 of Böhme's Geschichte des Tanzes about 20 more. None exceeds the E^b-$G^\#$ compass. The famous English collection of virginal music, Parthenia, reveals nothing beyond the fact that Byrd preferred E^b, the younger composers Bull and Gibbons, $D^\#$. In Margaret Glyn's edition of Gibbons' Complete Keyboard Works, five of the 33 virginal pieces have a $D^\#$, but only two contain E^b's, one of these, a Pavan in G minor, having also an A^b. But that does not necessarily mean that Gibbons did not use the meantone temperament. The virginals could have been set for an A^b at one time and for a $D^\#$ at another — a point that will be discussed at some length later. More significant are the A^b and $D^\#$ that occur in a G minor Fancy for organ by Gibbons. Unless Gibbons' tuning was appreciably better than the meantone temperament, this Fancy would have had some very rough places. This same A^b-$D^\#$ was used in Tarquinio Merula's Sonata Cromatica, a work having a modern ring because of its chromaticism.[3]

Just a word about chromaticism. Other things being equal, a piece that contains many chromatic progressions is more likely to have an excessive tonal compass than one that is not chromatic. But, since there are 12 different pitch names in the meantone compass, E^b-$G^\#$, it is entirely possible for a chromatic piece to lie within it. A Toccata by Michelangelo Rossi, for example, published in 1657, is very chromatic, but carefully re-

[3]Luigi Torchi, L'arte musicale in Italia (Milan, post 1897), III, 345-352.

mains within the meantone bounds.[4]

The great English manuscript source of the early seventeenth century, the Fitzwilliam Virginal Book, is a monument to the boldness of the clavier composers of that time. Naylor[5] has given a fascinating and exhaustive account of the music in this collection, and has shown that many of the progressions containing accidentals resemble modulations to our major and minor keys more than they do modal cadences. Twenty-five of the 297 compositions contain D#'s, with Bull, Byrd, Farnaby, and Tomkins in the lead. Bull, Farnaby, Tisdall, and Oystermayre have A#'s also.

With one exception, the largest compass in the entire collection is that of Byrd's "Ut, re, mi, fa, sol, la," which extends from Ab to D#. That exception, of course, is John Bull's composition on the hexachord, with the same title as Byrd's. It overlaps the circle of fifths by six notes, with the compass Cb-A#. Bull states his Canto Fermo first on G and rises by tones through A, B, Db, Eb, and F. He then begins afresh with Ab, Bb, C, D, E, F#, and G. An enharmonic modulation occurs at the beginning of Section 4, where the chord of F# is quitted as Gb. The editors of the Fitzwilliam Virginal Book were so impressed with this passage that they correctly stated in a footnote, "This interesting experiment in enharmonic modulation is thus tentatively expressed in the MS.; the passage proves that some kind of 'equal temperament' must have been employed at this date."[6]

This remarkable composition is not a mere juggling with sounds, as Naylor has alleged. It has real musical interest, and because of its sustained style seems better adapted to the organ than to the clavier. But do not try to build up a theory of the use of equal temperament in England during Queen Elizabeth's reign on the basis of Dr. Bull's composition. Remember that it stands practically alone. It seems almost as if Bull had written a Fancy for four viols, and then, led by some mad whim, had transcribed

[4]Ibid., p. 309.

[5]An Elizabethan Virginal Book (London, 1905).

[6]J. A. Fuller-Maitland and W. Barclay Squire, The Fitzwilliam Virginal Book (Leipzig, 1899), I, 183.

it for virginals and tuned his instrument to suit.

One of the boldest of the keyboard composers of the early seventeenth century was Frescobaldi, an exact contemporary of Gibbons. Of his 31 works for organ and clavier,[7] three contain D^b, three a $D^\#$, and one an $A^\#$. One of the most interesting of these is the Partite sopra Passacagli for organ, with a compass of D^b-$G^\#$. The $G^\#$ is the third of the dominant triad of A minor, and the D^b the third of the subdominant triad of F minor. Hence the ordinary meantone temperament would be inadequate for Frescobaldi.

In decided contrast to Frescobaldi are Sweelinck (German Denkmäler, IV Band, 1. Folge) and Scheidt (German Denkmäler, I Band). Sweelinck's Fantasia Cromatica, with E^b-$D^\#$ compass, was the only one of 36 pieces examined to exceed 12 scale degrees, and Scheidt, although not averse to chromaticism and rather fond of $D^\#$'s, had no single composition, of 44 examined, with more than 12 degrees.

As we reach the middle of the seventeenth century, we shall have to differentiate more carefully between music for organ and for clavier. The organ had a fixed compass, usually E^b-$G^\#$, but perhaps B^b-$D^\#$ or A^b-$C^\#$. Even if the composer did not employ A^b and $D^\#$, for example, in the same composition, as Gibbons and Merula had done, the presence of these notes in separate compositions was an indication that he was using at least a modified version of the meantone temperament.[8]

Not so for clavier. A study of the accidentals in clavier music suggests that tuning practice must have accommodated itself to the music to be played. The performer would retune when changing from sharp to flat keys. Bach could tune his entire harpsichord in fifteen minutes; to change the pitches of only a couple of notes in each octave would have taken a much shorter time. Moreover, all the movements of the common dance suites

---

[7] I classici della musica italiana (Milan, 1919), Vol. XII; Torchi, op. cit., Vol. III.

[8] The course of the argument and most of the examples in the remaining part of this section have been taken freely from my article "Bach and The Art of Temperament," Musical Quarterly, XXXIII (1947), 64-89.

were in the same key, and this helped to restrict the compass to not more than twelve different pitch names, even if that compass was not the conventional E^b-$G^{\#}$.

The theorists give us little information about the variable tuning of claviers. Mersenne hinted at the practice. He had given two keyboards in just intonation, the first with sharps only (except for B^b) and the second with flats. Current practice, he said, was represented by either of these, but with tempered, not just, intervals. Some eighty-five years later Kuhnau wrote to Mattheson that the strings of his Pantalonisches Cimbal (a large keyed dulcimer) vibrated so long he could not use equal temperament upon it, but had to "correct one key or another" when turning from flats to sharps.

More valuable evidence of the variable tuning practice for clavier comes from the music itself. Of Froberger's 67 clavier compositions (<u>Austrian Denkmäler</u>, VI, 2. Theil, and X, 2. Theil), 6 use 14 scale degrees, 10 use 13, and the remaining 51 use 12 or fewer. But only half (26) of the 51 lie wholly within the usual meantone compass. His accidentals range altogether from G^b to $E^{\#}$.

Similarly, Johann Pachelbel's clavier music (<u>Bavarian Denkmäler</u>, 2. Jahrgang, 1. Band) suggests a variable tuning. Of 49 compositions examined, only 2 have more than 12 scale degrees. But of the remaining 47, only 21, or less than half, lie within the E^b-$G^{\#}$ compass, and the total range is from D^b to $B^{\#}$. An exception among Pachelbel's works, the Suite in A^b (Suite ex Gis), beginning with an Allemand in A^b minor, contains an enharmonic modulation at the point where the F^b major triad is treated as E major by resolving upon A minor, just before a cadence in E^b major! With a range from D^{bb} to B for this single movement, it seems evident that for the moment Pachelbel was as reckless as Bach.

Kuhnau's works (<u>German Denkmäler</u>, IV Band, 1. Folge) give musical evidence of variability to buttress what he wrote to Mattheson. Of his 28 clavier works, 3 of the 6 Biblical Sonatas have a compass of 14 scale degrees; the other 3 sonatas and 5 other works have 13. But of the remaining 17 works that have no more than 12 different pitches in the octave, only 2 lie wholly within the E^b-$G^\#$ tuning. Actually Kuhnau preferred equal temperament upon the clavier. But most of these works would have been passable in meantone temperament if he had "corrected" some of the notes, just as he did on the Pantalon.

Of François Couperin's 27 charming suites for clavecin, only 6 have no more than 12 different scale degrees. They are all in the minor key, and in each the flattest note is a semitone higher than the keynote, as No. 8 in B minor has the compass C-$E^\#$. Twenty of the remaining 21 suites exceed the circle of fifths by one or two notes. But here again it is characteristic to have the flattest note a semitone above the tonic. For example, all five suites in D major-minor have the precise compass E^b-$A^\#$. Couperin leaves a strong impression that the dissonance inevitable in the slightly extended compass was a coolly calculated risk, and that a variable meantone tuning was used for these suites also. The one exception is No. 25, in E^b major and C major-minor. The compass here is 15 scale degrees, from G^b to $D^\#$. This would, perhaps, be carrying piquancy too far.

There is ample evidence that in Italy during the first half of the eighteenth century equal temperament or its equivalent was being practiced. Three composers represented in the Italian Classics had, in a particular composition, a similar compass, 15 notes in the overlapping circle of fifths. They are Zipoli, D^b-$D^\#$, Vol. 36; Serini, C^b-$C^\#$, Vol. 29; and Durante, G^b-$G^\#$, Vol. 11. Of 70 of Domenico Scarlatti's delightful little "sonatas,"[9] 45, or more than half, overlap the circle. In one sonata he had a compass of 18 degrees, D^b-$B^\#$; in another, 17, G^b-$A^\#$. All of these men upon occasion wrote notes so remote from the tonal center that meantone temperament seems wholly out of the question. Both Serini and Durante used Fx, and Scarlatti, Cx.

At this time, in Germany, Telemann was advocating a form of multiple division with 55 notes in the octave, for a clavier with only 12 notes in the octave, which was practically the same as Silbermann's 1/6-comma variety of meantone temperament. We might expect, therefore, that his compositions for clavier

[9]Heinrich Barth, Klavierwerke von Domenico Scarlatti (4 vols.; Vienna, c. 1901).

would not exceed the bounds of the meantone temperament. However, Telemann's 36 Clavier Fantasies have a total range of G^b-$B^{\#}$, the same as for Couperin's suites. Only 8 of the fantasies overlap the circle, by one or two degrees. Of the remaining 28, only one lies within the ordinary meantone bounds, E^b-$G^{\#}$. The others swing to the sharp side or the flat side, depending upon the key. Thus Telemann undoubtedly used the meantone temperament, but with variable intonation.

It has been suggested in the preceding pages that composers such as Bull, Gibbons, Frescobaldi, and Domenico Scarlatti, whose works exceed the meantone bounds by several scale degrees, were not using the meantone temperament. Were they, then, using equal temperament? That question is difficult to answer, especially since there was a type of tuning that would have been fairly satisfactory in many of these cases. The title of Bach's great collection of preludes and fugues, Das wohltemperirte Clavier, has usually been taken to mean, as Parry called it, "The Clavichord Tuned in Equal Temperament." But even in Bach's day there was a good German phrase for equal temperament — "die gleichschwebende Temperatur," "the equally beating temperament." Bach's title might better be paraphrased, "The Well-Tuned Piano."

Now, "well-tuned" had been used in a somewhat technical sense by the Flemish mathematician Simon Stevin, over a century before the first volume of the "48" was compiled in 1722, and by Bach's great French contemporary Rameau also, with a meaning nearly the same as Parry has given to it. To German theorists, however, there was a distinction. Andreas Werckmeister has erroneously been hailed as the father of equal temperament because of the title of one of his works on tuning, Musicalische Temperatur, and because of Mattheson's eulogy. Mattheson had said, "And thus the fame previously divided between Werckmeister and Neidhardt remains ineradicable — that they brought temperament to the point where all keys could be played without offense to the ear."[10] (Underscoring is the present au-

[10]J. Mattheson. Critica musica. II, 162.

194

thor's.) Werckmeister himself has used the phrase "wohl temperirt" as follows: "But if we have a well-tuned clavier, we can play both the major and minor modes on every note and transpose them at will. To one who is familiar with the entire range of keys, this affords variety upon the clavier and falls upon the ear very pleasantly."

What did Werckmeister mean by these words? To use Neidhardt's phrase, he meant a "completely circulating genus," that is, a tuning in which one could circumnavigate the circle of fifths without <u>mal de son.</u> Both men, as we have seen in Chapter VII, presented a number of different monochords, with the "foreign" thirds beating as much as a comma. Werckmeister said of them, "It would be very easy to let the thirds D^b-F, G^b-B^b, A^b-C beat less than a full comma; but since thereby the other, more frequently used thirds obtain too much, it is better that the latter should remain purer, and the harshness be placed upon those that are used the least." Elsewhere Werckmeister described equal temperament with fair accuracy, but demurred, "I have hitherto not been able to approve this idea, because I would rather have the diatonic keys purer." And so to Werckmeister "well-tuned" meant "playable in all keys — but better in the keys more frequently used."

If, then, a composer exceeded twelve different pitch names rarely and then only by a few scale degrees, his works could have been played to good advantage on a "well-tuned clavier." Composers like Bull and Pachelbel and Scarlatti, however, who effected enharmonic modulations and used double sharps, would have been badly served even by Werckmeister's best-known "correct" temperament, in which the key of D^b had Pythagorean thirds for all its major triads. Equal temperament was needed for their works.

An equal temperament was needed for the keyboard works of Bach, both for clavier and for organ. It is generally agreed that Bach tuned the clavier equally. Actually he was opposed to equal temperament, in the sense that there must be strict mathematical ratios, which are first applied to the monochord and from there to the instrument to be tuned. Of course he was right. The best way to tune in equal temperament, as Ellis stated, is to count beats. Have you ever heard of a contemporary piano tuner who carried a monochord with him? And yet the underlying theory must be correct or the result will be unsatisfactory: Ellis could not have given his practical tuning rule with assurance had he not been able to calculate accurately how far its use would fall short of the perfection implied by the term "equal temperament."

The organ works of Bach show as great a range of modulation as his clavier works do. Except for a dozen chorale preludes in the Orgelbüchlein, there are only 3 organ works of 148 examined that do not overstep the compass of the conventionally tuned organ. The compass of individual organ pieces is very frequently 13, 14, and 15 scale degrees, and even 18, 19, and 21 degrees have been observed. The compass of Bach's organ works as a whole is E^{bb}-Cx, 25 degrees! In these works is a host of examples of triads in remote keys that would have been dreadfully dissonant in any sort of tuning except equal temperament. For corroboration, if corroboration be necessary, we need but note the advice that Sorge gave to the instrument-maker Silbermann, two years before Bach's death. Sorge, a proponent of equal temperament, said: "In a word — Silbermann's way of tempering cannot exist with modern practice. I call upon all impartial and experienced musicians — especially the world-famous Herr Bach in Leipzig — to witness that this is all the absolute truth. It is to be desired, therefore, that the excellent man [Silbermann] ... should alter his opinion regarding temperament...."[11]

Just Intonation in Choral Music

We have seen that just intonation exists in many different forms, and that the best version, if modulations are to be made to keys beyond B^b and A, comes near the Pythagorean tuning, as with Ramis. The contention has often been made that unaccompanied voices sing in just intonation. Zarlino[12] listed instru-

---

[11]Georg Andreas Sorge, Gespräch zwischen einem Musico theoretico und einem Studioso musices, p. 21.

[12]Sopplimenti musicali, Chaps. 33-37.

196

ments in three groups, each with a different tuning: keyboard instruments in meantone temperament; fretted instruments in equal temperament; voices, violins, and trombones in just intonation. His argument was that since intonation is free for these three last-named groups, they would use an intonation in which thirds and sixths are pure. Three hundred and forty-eight years later Lindsay Norden said, "As we shall show, no singer can sing a cappella in any temperament.... A cappella music, therefore, is always sung in just or untempered intonation."[13]

Let us see what is implied by these statements. In the first place, singers must be able to sing the thirds and sixths purely.[14] This may sound like a self-evident truth, too absurd to discuss. But scientific studies of intonation preferences show that the human ear has no predilection for just intervals, not even the pure major third.[15] Alexander Ellis declared that it was unreliable to tune the pure major thirds of meantone temperament directly, preferring results obtained by beating fifths. Hence the singers must be highly trained to be able to sing the primary triads of a key justly.

In the second place, the singers must be able to differentiate intervals differing by the syntonic comma, 1/9 tone. We have seen that in Ptolemy's version of the syntonic tuning the D minor triad, the supertonic triad of the key of C major, will be false. If, as Kornerup and others advocate, the Didymus tuning is used instead of Ptolemy's, the dominant triad will be false, which is a greater loss. But a singer trained to niceties of intonation would have to vary his pitch by a comma in such critical places, and thus save the situation. Very good. But studies at the Uni-

[13]N. Lindsay Norden, "A New Theory of Untempered Music," Musical Quarterly, XXII (1936), 218.

[14]Except for the reference to the Italian madrigalists, the remaining part of this section has been freely adapted from my article "Just Intonation Confuted," Music and Letters, XIX (1938), 48-60 by permission of the editor of Music and Letters, 18 Great Marlborough Street, London, W. 1.

[15]Paul C. Greene, "Violin Intonation," Journal of the Acoustical Society of America, IX (1937-38), 43-44; Arnold M. Small, "Present-Day Preferences for Certain Melodic Intervals...," Ibid., X (1938-39), 256; James F. Nickerson, "Intonation of Solo and Ensemble Performance...," Ibid.,XXI (1949), 593-95.

versity of Iowa[16] have shown that there is no such thing as stability of pitch among singers: scooping is found in almost half the attacks and averages a whole tone in extent; portamento is very common; the sustained part of the pitch varies from the true pitch by a comma or more in one-fourth of the notes analyzed. If we add to these errors the omnipresent vibrato, with an average extent of a semitone, it would seem that the ambitious and optimistic director of an unaccompanied choir has an impossible task.

Let us assume, for the moment, that it is possible for a choir to sing without these pitch fluctuations, that all its members can sing a note a comma higher or lower when necessary, and that the director has analyzed the music and marked the places where the comma shifts are to be made. What have we then? Strangely enough, if the harmony consists of simple diatonic progressions, typical of the seventeenth and eighteenth centuries, the pitch will probably fall. With modal progressions, as in Palestrina, it is more likely to remain stationary. According to Gustav Engel, if one were to consider possible comma shifts whenever a modulation occurs, most of the recitatives in Mozart's Don Giovanni would fall from one to four commas if sung unaccompanied, and the final pitch of the opera would be five or six semitones flatter than at the beginning, A or A^b instead of D!

If the music contains much chromaticism and remote modulations, even the best-trained choir would probably flounder. And yet there are choral compositions of the sixteenth and early seventeenth centuries that seem strikingly modern because of these very features. De Rore's madrigal "Calami sonum ferentes" for four basses (c. 1555) begins with an ascending chromatic scale passage treated in imitation. Later it has a remarkable faburden of inverted major triads a semitone apart — G F$^\#$ G A^b G. Caimo's madrigal "E ben raggion" (1585) contains a very smooth example of modulation in which the F$^\#$ major triad is heard, and, 24 bars later, its enharmonic equivalent, the G^b major triad. In just intonation the latter triad would be a large diesis (42 cents, or almost a quarter tone) higher than the former.

[16]Carl E. Seashore, The Vibrato (Iowa City, Iowa, 1932).

198

And what of Marenzio's madrigal "O voi che sospirate a miglior note," where there is a modulation around the circle of fifths from C to G^b, an enharmonic change from G^b to F$^\#$, and further modulation on the sharp side? According to Kroyer, from whom all these examples have been taken, this is the first time in music that the circle of fifths has been completed.[17] Could Marenzio's madrigal have been sung in just intonation?

Gesualdo has the respect of the moderns because of his harmonic freedom. The best known of his chromatic madrigals is the "Resta di darmi noia," in which he passes from G minor to E major, and then sequentially from A minor to F$^\#$ major. Listen to the recording of this madrigal by a group of unaccompanied singers in the album 2000 Years of Music and you will probably agree that the attempt to record it was a noble experiment and nothing more.

Of course the point that is missed by all these rabid exponents of just intonation in choral music is that this music was not ordinarily sung unaccompanied in the sixteenth century. A cappella meant simply the absence of independent accompaniment, not of all accompaniment. If a choir usually sang motets accompanied by an organ in meantone temperament, it would quickly adapt itself to the intonation of the organ. If this choir were in the habit of singing madrigals accompanied by lutes or viols in equal temperament, its thirds would be as sharp as the thirds are today. Kroyer thought the pronounced chromaticism of the Italian madrigalists showed the influence of keyboard instruments. On the contrary: it must have been the fretted instruments, already in equal temperament, that influenced composers like de Rore, Caimo, Marenzio, and Gesualdo to write passages in madrigals that could not have been sung in tune without accompaniment.

Present Practice

What is tuning like today? A generation ago, Anglas made some excellent observations about the intonation of the symphony

[17]Theodor Kroyer, "Die Anfänge der Chromatik im italienischen Madrigal des XVI. Jahrhunderts," Internationale Musikgesellschaft, Beiheft 4 (1902).

orchestra.[18] The pedals of the harp are constructed to produce the semitones of equal temperament; therefore, once the harp is put in tune with itself, it, and it alone of all the instruments, will be in equal temperament. The violins show a tendency toward the Pythagorean tuning, both because of the way they are strung and because of the players' tendency to play sharps higher than enharmonic flats. Furthermore, in a high register both the violins and the flutes are likely to play somewhat sharp for the sake of brilliance. He might have added that the brass instruments, making use of a more extended portion of the harmonic series than the woodwinds, have a natural inclination toward just intonation in certain keys. The result is "a very great lack of precision," with heterogeneous sounds that are a mixture of "just, Pythagorean, tempered, or simply false." Of course the ears of the audience, trained for years to endure such cacophony, actually are pleased by what seems to be a good performance.

Ll. S. Lloyd has written an article with the frightening title "The Myth of Equal Temperament."[19] It would be pretty discouraging for the present author to have done extended research upon the history of equal temperament only to learn at last that his subject matter was in the class with the story of Cupid and Psyche! But Lloyd has not actually consigned equal temperament to the category of the tale of George Washington and the cherry tree. His argument is against rigidity of intonation, the rigidity that is inherent in any fixed system of tuning. He holds that the players in a string quartet or the singers in a madrigal group are likely to be guided by the music itself as to what intonation to use, sometimes approaching Pythagorean intervals when melodic considerations are paramount or just intervals when the harmony demands it. And undoubtedly this freedom of intonation, plus a well-defined vibrato, does increase the charm of these more intimate chamber ensembles.

Not even the piano is exempt from the charge of inexactness. Three-quarters of a century ago Alexander Ellis showed that the

[18] J. P. L. Anglas, Précis d' acoustique physique, musical, physiologique (Paris, 1910), p. 206.

[19] Music and Letters, XXI (1940), 347-361.

best British tuners of his day failed to tune pianos in equal temperament within desirable limits of error. There is no reason to believe that modern British tuners, or American ones either, are doing a better job than was done then. Schuck and Young even show that, because of the inharmonicity of the upper partials of the piano, a tuner is bound to tune the upper octaves progressively sharper and the lowest octaves progressively flatter than those in the middle range.[20] Their theoretical findings agree with measurements Railsback had already made of pianos tuned in equal temperament. However, the psychologists tell us that "stretched" octaves at top and bottom are a concomitant of normal hearing. Therefore the sharpness and the flatness respectively would probably be heard as correct intonation.

Now all of this paints a dismal picture. Apparently nobody — not the pianist, nor the singer, nor the violinist, nor the windplayer — is able to perform in correct equal temperament. The harpist is left sitting alone, but no doubt he will be joined by the Hammond organist, whose instrument comes closest to the equal tuning.

This contemporary dispute about tuning is perhaps a tempest in a teapot. It is probably true that all the singers and players are singing and playing false most of the time. But their errors are errors from equal temperament. No well-informed person today would suggest that these errors consistently resemble departures from just intonation or from any other tuning system described in these pages. Equal temperament does remain the standard, however imperfect the actual accomplishment may be.

The trend of musical composition during the late nineteenth and the first half of the twentieth century has been to exploit the resources of equal temperament, of an octave divided into 12 equal parts, and hence also into 2, 3, 4, or 6 parts. To ascertain how far back this trend extends is not the purpose of this book. It would be foolish to deny that this modern trend is different in kind from the progressions of classic harmony, progressions that were almost as common in 1600 as in 1800. But it may be denied that these classic progressions were intimately connected

[20] O. H. Schuck and R. W. Young, "Observations on the Vibrations of Piano Strings," Journal of the Acoustical Society of America, XV (1943), 1-11.

with the meantone temperament, as has often been alleged; for we have seen that the original 1/4-comma meantone system did not even reign supreme in 1600, much less in 1700 or 1750. In 1600 there were half a dozen or more ways to tune the octave; in 1732 Neidhardt gave his readers a choice of twenty! Moreover, there is every reason to believe that in practice there were far greater departures from these extremely varied tuning methods of the seventeenth and eighteenth centuries than there are from equal temperament today.

In the very nature of things, equal temperament has undergone vicissitudes during the last four hundred years, and will continue to do so. Perhaps the philosophical Neidhardt should be allowed to have the last word on the subject: "Thus equal temperament carries with itself its comfort and discomfort, like the holy estate of matrimony."[21]

---

[21]Gäntzlich erschöpfte, mathematische Abtheilungen, p. 41.

LITERATURE CITED

Adlung, Jacob. Anleitung zu den musikalischen Gelahrtheit. Erfurt, 1758.
—— Musica mechanica organoedi. Berlin, 1768.
Agricola, Martin. Musica instrumentalis deudsch. 4th ed., Wittenberg, 1545. Reprinted as Band 20 of Publikation älterer praktischer und theoretischer Musikwerke, 1896.
—— Rudimenta musices. Wittenberg, 1539.
Amiot, Pere Joseph Maria. De la musique des Chinois. (Mémoires concernant l'histoire,...des Chinois, Vol. VI.) Paris, 1780.
Anglas, Jules Philippe Louis. Précis d'acoustique physique, musical, physiologique. Paris, 1910.
Ariel. Das Relativitätsprincip der musikalischen Harmonie, Band I. Leipzig, 1925.
Aristoxenus. See H. S. Macran, The Harmonics of Aristoxenus. Oxford, 1902.
Aron, Pietro. Toscanello in musica. Venice, 1523. Revised edition of 1529 was consulted.
Artusi, Giovanni Maria. Seconda parte dell' Artusi overo della imperfettioni della moderna musica. Venice, 1603.
Awraamoff, A. M. "Jenseits von Temperierung und Tonalität," Melos, I (1920), 131-134, 160-166, 184-188.
Bach, Johann Sebastian. For his keyboard works see particularly Vols. III, XIII, XIV, XV, XXV, and XXXVIII of the Bach-Gesellschaft Edition, Leipzig, 1851-1900; facsimile edition, Ann Arbor, 1947.
Bakfark, Valentin. (His lute music is reprinted in Denkmäler der Tonkunst in Österreich, Vol. XVIII.)
Barbour, J. Murray. "Bach and The Art of Temperament," Musical Quarterly, XXXIII (1947), 64-89.
—— "Irregular Systems of Temperament," Journal of the American Musicological Society, I (1948), 20-26.
—— "Just Intonation Confuted," Music and Letters, XIX (1938), 48-60.

—— "Music and Ternary Continued Fractions," American Mathematical Monthly, LV (1948), 545-555.

—— "Musical Logarithms," Scripta Mathematica, VII (1940), 21-31.

—— "Nierop's Hackebort," Musical Quarterly, XX (1934), 312-319.

—— "The Persistence of the Pythagorean Tuning System," Scripta Mathematica, I (1933), 286-304.

—— "A Sixteenth Century Approximation for π," American Mathematical Monthly, XL (1933), 68-73.

Barca, Alessandro. "Introduzione a una nuova teoria di musica, memoria prima," Accademia di scienze, lettere ed arti in Padova. Saggi scientifici e lettari (Padova, 1786), pp. 365-418.

Bartolus, Abraham. Musica mathematica: the 2nd part of Heinrich Zeising's Theatri machinarum. Altenburg, 1614.

Bedos (Dom François Bedos de Celles). L'art du facteur d'orgues, 2nd part. Paris, 1770. Facsimile ed., Kassel, 1935.

Beer, Johann. Schola phonologica: a manuscript work referred to in Mattheson's Critica musica.

Bendeler, Johann Philipp. Organopoeia. 2nd ed., Frankfurt and Leipzig, 1739.

Berlin, Johann Daniel. Anleitung zur Tonometrie. Copenhagen and Leipzig, 1767.

Bermudo, Juan. Declaracion de instrumentos musicales. Ossuna, 1555.

Blankenburg, Quirinus van. Elementa musica. The Hague, 1739.

Böhme, Franz Magnus. Geschichte des Tanzes in Deutschland. Leipzig, 1886.

Boethius, A. M. S. De institutione musica. German translation by Oscar Paul. Leipzig, 1872.

Bonnet, Joseph. Historical Organ Recitals, Vol. I. New York, c. 1917.

Bosanquet, R. H. M. An Elementary Treatise on Musical Intervals and Temperament. London, 1876.

—— "On the Hindoo Division of the Octave, Royal Society's Proceedings (1877), pp. 372-384.

—— "Temperament; or, the Division of the Octave," Proceedings of the Musical Association (1874-75), pp. 4-17.

Bossler, Heinrich Philipp. Elementarbuch der Tonkunst. Speier, 1782.

Bottrigari, Ercole. Il desiderio, ovvero de' concerti di varii stromenti musicali. Venice, 1594. New ed. by Kathi Meyer, Berlin, 1924.

Buttstett, Johann Heinrich. Kurze Anführung zum General-Bass. 2nd ed. Leipzig, 1733.

Caramuel (Juan Caramuel de Lobkowitz). Mathesis nova. Campania, 1670.

Cardano, Girolamo. Opera omnia, ed. Sponius. Lyons, 1663.

Caus, Salomon de. Les raisons des forces mouvantes avec diverses machines. Francfort, 1615.

Cavazzoni, Girolamo. Composizioni. Reprinted in I classici della musica italiana, Vol. VI. Milan, 1919.

Choquel, Henri Louis. La musique rendue sensible par la méchanique. New ed., Paris, 1762.

Colonna, Fabio. La sambuca lincea. Naples, 1618.

Couperin, François. Pièces d'orgue. Paris, 1690. Reprinted as Tome VI, Oeuvres complètes, Paris, 1932-33.

Courant, Maurice. "Chine et Corée," Encyclopédie de la musique et dictionnaire du conservatoire (Paris, 1913), Part 1, Vol. I, pp. 77-241.

Crotch, William. Elements of Musical Composition. London, 1812.

Dechales, R. P. Claudius Franciscus Milliet. Cursus seu mundus mathematicus, Tomus Tertius. Lugduni, 1674.

Delezenne, Charles Edouard Joseph. "Mémoire sur les valeurs numériques des notes de la gamme," Recueil des travaux de la societe des sciences, . . . , de Lille (1826-27), pp. 1-56.

Denis, Jean. Traité de l'accord de l'espinette. Paris, 1650.

Doni, Giovanni Battista. Compendio del trattato de' generi, e de' modi. Rome, 1635.

Douwes, Claas. Grondig Ondersoek van de Toonen der Musijk. Franeker, 1699.

Dowland, Robert. Variety of Lute-Lessons. London, 1610.

Drobisch, M. W. "Über musikalische Tonbestimmung und Temperatur," Abhandlungen der mathematisch-physischen Classe der königlich sächsischen Gesellschaft der Wissenschaften, IV (1855), 1-120.

Dupont, Wilhelm. Geschichte der musicalischen Temperatur. Erlangen, 1935.

Durante, Francesco. Sonate, toccate e divertimenti. Reprinted in I classici della musica italiana, Vol. XI. Milan, 1919.

Ellis, Alexander J. "On the History of Musical Pitch," Journal of Society of Arts, XXVIII (1880), 293-336.

——— "On the Musical Scales of Various Nations," Journal of Society of Arts, XXXIII (1885), 485-527.

Engel, Gustav. "Eine mathematisch-harmonische Analyse des Don Giovanni von Mozart," Vierteljahrsschrift für Musikwissenschaft, III (1887), 491-560.

Euler, Leonard. Tentamen novae theoriae musicae. St. Petersburg, 1739.

——— Exposition de quelques nouvelles vues mathematiques dans la theorie de la musique. Amsterdam, 1760.

Faber Stapulensis. Elementa musicalia. Paris, 1496.

Faggot, Jacob. See p. 65, note 43, of this study.

Farey, John. "On a New Mode of Equally Tempering the Musical Scale," Philosophical Magazine, XXVII (1807), 65-66.

——— "On Music," Philosophical Magazine, XXVI (1806), 171-176.

Fétis, François Joseph. Histoire générale de la musique. 5 vols. Paris, 1869-76.

Fischer, Johann Philip Albrecht. Verhandlung van de Klokken en het Klokke-Spel. Utrecht, 1738.

Faulhaber, Johann. Ingenieurschul. Frankfort am Mayn, 1630. (Reference in Neidhardt, Sectio canonis harmonici.)

LITERATURE CITED

Fludd, Robert. Sophiae cum moria certamen. Frankfort, 1629.

Fogliano, Lodovico. Musica theorica. Venice, 1529.

Frescobaldi, Girolamo. Composizioni per organo e cembalo. Reprinted in I classici della musica italiana, Vol. XII. Milan, 1919.

Fritz, Barthold. Anweisung wie man Claviere, Clavicins, und Orgeln, nach einer mechanischen Art, in allen zwölf Tönen gleich rein stimmen könne,...3rd ed., Leipzig 1780

Froberger, Johann Jakob. (His clavier compositions are reprinted in Denkmäler der Tonkunst in Österreich, Vol. VI, Part 2, and Vol. X, Part 2.)

Fuller-Maitland, J. A., and W. Barclay Squire. The Fitzwilliam Virginal Book, Vol. I. Leipzig, 1899.

Gafurius, Franchinus. Practica musica. Milan, 1496.

Galilei, Galileo. Discorsi e dimostrazioni matematiche intorno è due nuove scienze. Leyden, 1638.

Galilei, Vincenzo. Dialogo della musica antica e moderna. Florence, 1581.

—— Fronimo, dialogo sopra l'arte del bene intavolare e rettamente suonare la musica...nel liuto. 1st ed., Venice, 1581; revised ed., 1584.

Galin, Pierre. Exposition d'une nouvelle méthode pour l'enseignement de la musique. 1st ed., 1818; 3rd ed., Bordeaux and Paris, 1862.

Gallimard, Jean Edme. L' arithmétique des musiciens. Paris, 1754.

Ganassi, Sylvestro. Regola Rubertina. Lettione seconda, 1543; ed. Max Schneider, Leipzig, 1924.

Garnault, Paul. Le tempérament, son histoire, son application aux claviers, aux violes de gambe et guitares, son influence sur la musique du xviii^{e}siècle. Nice, 1929.

Gesualdo (Carlo Gesualdo da Venosa). Madrigale. Reprinted in I classici della musica italiana, Vol. XIV. Milan, 1919.

Gibbons, Orlando. Complete Keyboard Works, ed. Margaret H. Glyn. 5 vols. in 1. London, 1925.

Gibelius, Otto. Propositiones mathematico-musicae. Münden, 1666.

Gintzler, Simon. Intabolatura de lauto. Venice, 1547. Reprinted in Denkmäler der Tonkunst in Österreich, Vol. XVIII.

Glyn, Margaret H. Early English Organ Music. London, 1939.

Gow, James. A Short History of Greek Mathematics. Cambridge, 1884. Reprinted, New York, 1923.

Grammateus, Henricus. Ayn new kunstlich Buech. Nürnberg, 1518.

Greene, Paul C. "Violin Intonation," Journal of the Acoustical Society of America, IX (1937-38), 43-44.

Häser, A. F. "Über wissenschaftliche Begründung der Musik durch Akustik," Allgemeine musikalische Zeitung, Vol. XXXII (1829), cols. 143-147.

Hammond, Laurens. United States Patent, 1,956,350, April 24, 1934.

Helmholtz, H. L. F. Sensations of Tone. 2nd English ed., translated by Alexander J. Ellis. London, 1885.

Henfling, Konrad. "Specimen de novo suo systemate musico." Abhandlungen der Berliner Akademie, 1710. (Reference in Sauveur, "Table générale....")

Hizler, Daniel. Extract aus der neuen Musica oder Singkunst. Nürnberg, 1623.

Holder, William. Treatise ... of Harmony. 3rd ed., London, 1731.

Hugo de Reutlingen. Flores musicae omnis cantus Gregoriani. Strassburg, 1488.

Hutton, Charles. Mathematical Dictionary. New ed., London, 1815.

Huyghens, Christian. "Novus cyclus harmonicus," in Opera varia. Leyden, 1724.

Jackson, William. A Scheme Demonstrating the Perfection and Harmony of Sounds. London, 1726 (?).

Jankó, Paul von. "Über mehr als zwölfstufige gleichschwebende Temperaturen," Beiträge zur Akustik und Musikwissenschaft (1901), pp. 6-12.

Jeans, Sir James. Science and Music. New York, 1937.

Judenkünig, Hans. Ain schone kunstliche Underweisung. Vienna, 1523. Reprinted in Denkmäler der Tonkunst in Österreich, Vol. XVIII.

Keller, Godfrey. A Compleat Method... London, before 1707. His tuning rules were also printed in William Holder's Treatise.

Kepler, Johannes. Harmonices mundi. Augsburg, 1619. Ed. Ch. Frisch, Frankfort am Main, 1864.

Kinkeldey, Otto. Orgel und Klavier in der Musik des 16. Jahrhunderts. Leipzig, 1910.

Kircher, Athanasius. Musurgia universalis, Vol. I. Rome, 1650.

Kirnberger, Johann Philipp. Die Kunst des reinen Satzes in der Musik, 2nd part, 3rd division. Berlin, 1779.

Körte, Oskar. "Laute und Lautenmusik bis zur Mitte des 16. Jahrhunderts," Beiheft 3, Internationale Musikgesellschaft, 1901.

Kornerup, Thorvald. Das goldene Tonsystem als Fundament der theoretischen Akustik. Copenhagen, 1935.

——— Das Tonsystem des Italieners Zarlino. Copenhagen, 1930.

Kroyer, Theodor. "Die Anfänge der Chromatik im italienischen Madrigal des XVI. Jahrhunderts," Beiheft 4, Internationale Musikgesellschaft, 1902.

Kuhnau, Johann. (His clavier compositions are reprinted in Denkmäler deutscher Tonkunst, IV Band, 1. Folge.)

La Laurencie, Lionel de. Le violon de Lully à Viotti, Tome III. Paris, 1924.

Lambert, Johann Heinrich. "Remarques sur les tempéraments en musique," Memoirs of the Berlin Academy, 1774. German translation in Historisch-Kritische Beyträge zur Aufnahme der Musik, V (1760-78), 417-50.

Lanfranco, Giovanni Maria. Scintille de musica. Brescia, 1533.

Levens. Abrégé des regles de l'harmonie. Bordeaux, 1743.

Liston, Henry. An Essay upon Perfect Intonation. Edinburgh, 1812.

Lloyd, Llewellyn S. "The Myth of Equal Temperament," Music and Letters, XXI (1940), 347-361.

Malcolm, Alexander. A Treatise of Musick. Edinburgh, 1721.
Marinati, Aurelio. Somma di tutte le scienza. Rome, 1587.
Marpurg, Friedrich Wilhelm. Versuch über die musikalische Temperatur. Breslau, 1776.
Mattheson, Johann. Critica musica, Vol. II. Hamburg, 1722.
Meckenheuser, Jakob Georg. Die sogenannte allerneueste musicalische Temperatur. Quedlinburg, 1727.
Mercadier (Jean Baptiste Mercadier de Belesta). Nouveau système de musique théorique et pratique. Paris, 1777. (Reference in Suremain-Missery.)
Mercator, Nicholas. (A manuscript reference to him is given in Holder's Treatise.)
Merian, Wilhelm. Der Tanz in den deutschen Tabulaturbüchern. Leipzig, 1927.
Mersenne, Marin. Cogitata physico-mathematica. Paris, 1644.
———— Harmonicorum libri XII. Paris, 1648.
———— Harmonie universelle. Paris, 1636-37.
Metius, Adrian. (There is an inexplicit reference to him in Nierop's Wis-konstige Musyka.)
Montucla, Jean Etienne. Histoire des mathematiques. New ed., Paris, 1802. Vol. IV.
Montvallon, André Barrigue de. Nouveau système de musique sur les intervalles des tons et sur les proportions des accords, Aix, 1742. (Reference in Romieu's "Mémoire théorique & pratique.")
Morley, Thomas. A Plaine and Easie Introduction to Practicall Musicke. London, 1597.
Nassarre, Pablo. Escuela musica, Part I. Zaragoza, 1724.
Naylor, Edward Woodall. An Elizabethan Virginal Book. London, 1905.
Neidhardt, Johann George. Beste und leichteste Temperatur des Monochordi. Jena, 1706.
———— Gäntzlich erschöpfte, mathematische Abtheilungen des diatonisch-chromatischen, temperirten Canonis Monochordi. Königsberg and Leipzig, 1732.
———— Sectio canonis harmonici. Königsberg, 1724.

Nickerson, James F. "Intonation of Solo and Ensemble Performance . . . ," Journal of the Acoustical Society of America, XXI (1949), 593-595.

Nierop, Dyrk Rembrantz van. Wis-konstige Musyka. Amsterdam, 1650. 2nd ed., 1659.

Norden, N. Lindsay. "A New Theory of Untempered Music," Musical Quarterly, XXII (1936), 217-233.

Opelt, Friedrich Wilhelm. Allgemeine Theorie der Musik. Leipzig, 1852.

Ornithoparchus, Andreas. Musicae activae micrologus. Leipzig, 1517. English translation by John Dowland, London, 1609.

Pachelbel, Johann. (His clavier compositions are reprinted in Denkmäler der Tonkunst in Bayern, II Jahrgang, 1. Band, and his organ compositions in Ibid., IV Jahrgang, 1. Band)

Parthenia or the Maydenhead of the First Musicke that ever was Printed for the Virginalls. London, 1611.

Planck, Max. "Die naturliche Stimmung in der modernen Vokalmusik," Vierteljahrsschrift für Musikwissenschaft, IX (1893), 418-440.

Poole, Henry Ward, "On Perfect Harmony in Music . . .", Silliman's American Journal of Science and Arts, 2nd Series, XXXXIV (1867), 1-22.

——— "On Perfect Musical Intonation," Silliman's American Journal of Science and Arts, IX (1850), 68-83, 199-216.

Praetorius, Michael. Syntagma musicum, Vol. II. Wolfenbüttel, 1618. New edition published as 13. Band, Publikation älterer praktischer und theoretischer Musikwerke, 1884.

Prelleur, Pierre. The Compleat Tutor for the Harpsichord or Spinet (Modern Musick-Master, Part VI). London, c. 1730.

Printz, Wolffgang Caspar. Phrynis Mytilenaeus oder der satyrische Componist. Dresden and Leipzig, 1696.

"Pro clavichordiis faciendis." A fifteenth-century Erlangen manuscript described in Dupont's Geschichte.

Ptolemy, Claudius. Harmonicorum libri tres. Latin translation by John Wallis. London, 1699.

Rameau, Jean Philippe. Génération harmonique. Paris, 1737.

—— Nouveau système de musique théorique. Paris, 1726.

—— Traité de l'harmonie. Paris, 1722.

Ramis (Bartolomeus Ramis de Pareja). Musica practica. Bologna, 1482. New edition, by Johannes Wolf, published as a Beiheft of the Internationale Musikgesellschaft, 1901.

Rees, Abraham. New Cyclopedia. 45 vols. London, 1802-20. The reference in the present study is to Vol. XIV of first American edition.

Reinhard, Andreas. Monochordum. Leipzig, 1604.

Riemann, Hugo. Geschichte der Musiktheorie. Berlin, 1898.

—— Populäre Darstellung der Akustik. Berlin, 1896.

Robet-Maugin, J. C. Manuel du Luthier. Paris, 1834. (Reference in Garnault's Le tempérament.)

Romberg, Bernard. Violoncell Schull. Berlin, 1840 (?).

Romieu, Jean Baptiste (?). "Mémoire théorique & pratique sur les systèmes tempérés de musique," Mémoires de l'académie royale des sciences (1758), pp. 805-870.

Rossi, Lemme. Sistema musico. Perugia, 1666.

Rousseau, Jean. Traité de la viole. Paris, 1687.

Rousseau, Jean Jaques. Dictionnaire de musique. Paris, 1768. (Reference in Opelt's Allgemeine Theorie der Musik.)

Sabbatini, Galeazzo. Regola facile e breve per sonare sopra il basso continuo. Venice, 1628. (Reference in Kircher's Musurgia universalis.)

Sachs, Curt (ed.). Two Thousand Years of Music (record album). London, 1931.

Salinas, Francisco. De musica libri VII. Salamanca, 1577.

Sancta María, Tomás de. Arte de tañer fantasia. Valladolid, 1565.

Sauveur, Joseph. "Système général des intervalles des sons," Mémoires de l'académie royale des sciences (1701), pp. 403-498.

——— "Table générale des systèmes tempérés de musique," Mémoires de l'académie royale des sciences (1711), pp. 406-417.

Scarlatti, Domenico. Klavierwerke, ed. Heinrich Barth. 4 vols. Vienna, c. 1901.

Scheidt, Samuel. Tabulatura nova. 3 vols. Hamburg, 1624. Reprinted in Denkmäler deutscher Tonkunst, 1. Band.

Schering, Arnold. Alte Meister aus der Frühzeit des Orgelspiels. Leipzig, 1913.

Schlick, Arnold. Tablaturen etlicher Lobgesang und Lidlein. Maintz, 1512. Reprinted in Monatshefte für Musikgeschichte, I (1869).

——— Spiegel der Orgelmacher und Organisten. Maintz. 1511. Reprinted in Monatshefte für Musikgeschichte, I (1869).

Schneegass, Cyriac. Nova & exquisita monochordi dimensio. Erfurt, 1590.

Schröter, Christoph Gottlieb. "Ein Sendschreiben über Temperatur-Berechnung." In Marpurg's Versuch.

Schuck, O. H., and R. W. Young. "Observations on the Vibrations of Piano Strings," Journal of the Acoustical Society of America, XV (1943), 1-11.

Schumann, Karl Erich. Akustik. Breslau, 1925.

Seashore, Carl E. The Vibrato. Iowa City, Iowa, 1932.

Serini, Giuseppe. Sonate per cembalo. Reprinted in I classici della musica italiana, Vol. XXIX. Milan, 1919.

Small, Arnold M. "Present-Day Preferences for Certain Melodic Intervals," Journal of the Acoustical Society of America, X (1938-39), 256.

Smith, Robert. Harmonics, or the Philosophy of Musical Sounds. Cambridge, 1749.

Sorge, Georg Andreas. Gespräch zwischen einem Musico theoretico und einem Studioso musices. Lobenstein, 1748.

Spitta, Philipp. Johann Sebastian Bach. 2 vols. Translated by
    Clara Bell and J. A. Fuller-Maitland. London, 1884.
    Vol. I.
Stanhope, Charles, Earl. "Principles of the Science of Tuning In-
    struments with Fixed Tones," Philosophical Maga-
    zine, XXV (1806), 291-312.
Stevin, Simon. Van de Spiegeling der Singconst. A manuscript
    work (c. 1600) edited by D. Bierens de Haan. Am-
    sterdam, 1884.
Strähle, Daniel P. "Nytt påfund, til at finna temperaturen, i
    ståmningen för thonerne på claveretock dylika in-
    strumenter," Proceedings of the Swedish Academy,
    IV (1743), 281-291.
Sulzer, Johann Georg. Allgemeine Theorie der schönen Künste.
    Leipzig, 1777-79.
Suremain-Missery, Antoine. Théorie acoustico-musicale. Pa-
    ris, 1793.
Sweelinck, Jan Pieters. (His compositions for organ and clavier
    are in Denkmäler deutscher Tonkunst, IV Band, 1.
    Folge.)
Tanaka, Shohé. "Studien im Gebiete der reinen Stimmung."
    Vierteljahrsschrift für Musikwissenschaft, VI (1890),
    1-90.
Telemann, Georg Philipp. Drei Dutzend Klavier-Fantasien, ed.
    Max Seiffert. 3rd ed., Kassel, 1935.
Tempelhof, Georg Friedrich. Gedanken über die Temperatur
    des Herrn Kirnberger. Berlin and Leipzig, 1775.
Thompson, Gen. Perronet. On the Principles and Practice of
    Just Intonation. 9th ed., 1866. (Reference in Helm-
    holtz.)
Torchi, Luigi. L'arte musicale in Italia, Vol. III. Milan, post
    1897.
Varella, Domingos de S. Jose. Compendio de musica. Porto,
    1806.
Verheijen, Abraham. See Stevin's Van de Spiegeling der Sing-
    const.

LITERATURE CITED

LITERATURE CITED

LITERATURE CITED

LITERATURE CITED

LITERATURE CITED

Vicentino, Nicola. L'antica musica ridotta alla moderna prattica. Rome, 1555.

Warren, Ambrose. The Tonometer. London, 1725.

Wasielewski, Joseph Wilhelm von. Geschichte der Instrumentalmusik im 16. Jahrhundert. Berlin, 1878.

Werckmeister, Andreas. Hypomnemata musica. Quedlinburg, 1697.

—— Musicalische Paradoxal-Discourse. Quedlinburg, 1707.

—— Musicalische Temperatur. Frankfort and Leipzig, 1691.

White, William Braid. Piano Tuning and Allied Arts. 4th ed., Boston, 1943.

Wiese, Christian Ludwig Gustav, Baron von. Klangeintheilungs-, Stimmungs- und Temperatur-Lehre. Dresden, 1793.

Williamson, Charles. "Frequency Ratios of the Tempered Scale," Journal of the Acoustical Society of America, X (1938), 135-136.

Yasser, Joseph. A Theory of Evolving Tonality. New York, 1932.

Young, Thomas. "Outlines of Experiments and Inquiries Respecting Sound and Light," Philosophical Transactions, XC (1800), 106-150.

Zacconi, Lodovico. Prattica di musica, Part I. Venice, 1592.

Zarlino, Gioseffo. Dimostrationi armoniche. Venice, 1571.

—— Istitutioni armoniche. Venice, 1558.

—— Sopplimenti musicali. Venice, 1588.

Zeising, Heinrich. Theatri machinarum. Altenburg, 1614.

Zipoli, Domenico. Composizioni per organo e cembalo. Reprinted in I classici della musica italiana, Vol. XXXVI. Milan, 1919.

ERRATA.

In index references to:
    pages 88 through 105 -- add 1
    pages 107 through 202 -- add 2
to the page number given in the index

INDEX

abacus Triharmonicus, 109 f.
Abrégé des regles de l'harmonie. See Levens.
Adlung, J., 85.
Agricola, M., 4, 10, 95, 149-151.
Akustik. See C. E. Schumann.
Alexander the Great, 122.
Allgemeine Theorie der Musik. See F. W. Opelt.
Allgemeine Theorie der Schönen Künste. See J. G. Sulzer.
Amiot, J. M., 77.
"Die Anfänge der Chromatik im italienischen Madrigal des XVI. Jahrhunderts." See T. Kroyer.
Anglas, J. P. L., 197 f.
Anleitung zu den musikalischen Gelahrtheit. See J. Adlung.
Anleitung zur Tonometrie. See J. D. Berlin.
Anonymous, author of Exposition de quelques nouvelles vues mathematiques, 125.
Anonymous, author of Pro clavichordiis faciendis, 91 f.
L'antica musica ridotta alla moderna prattica. See N. Vicentino.
Anweisung wie man Claviere ... stimmen könne. See B. Fritz.
approximations to equal temperament. See temperament, equal: geometrical and mechanical approximations, and numerical approximations.
approximations to the meantone temperament. See temperament, meantone: approximations.
Appun, G., 119.
Arabian scale. See multiple division: equal divisions: 17-division.
Archicembalo, 27, 115 f, 152.
Archicymbalam, 106.
Archimedes, 34, 50.
Archytas, 16 f, 19, 22 f, 143.
Ariel, 113.
Aristoxenus, 2, 16 f, 19, 22-24, 57.
arithmetical division. See division, arithmetical.
L'arithmétique des musiciens. See J. E. Gallimard.
Aron, P., 10, 26, 49.
L'art du facteur d'orgues. See F. Bedos.
Arte de tañer fantasia. See T. de Sancta Maria.
L'arte musicale in Italia. See L. Torchi.
Artusi, G. M., 8, 10, 46, 142, 144-148, 176, 186.
Awraamoff, A. M., 24, 152.

"Bach and The Art of Temperament." See J. M. Barbour.
Bach, C. P. E., 47 f.

Bach, J. N., 85-87.
Bach, J. S., 10, 12 f, 85-87, 146, 189, 192-194.
Bakfark, V., 185.
Ballet comique de la reine, 8.
Barbour, J. M., 3, 77, 112, 131, 161, 189-197.
Barca, A., 42 f.
Bartolus, A., 142 f.
Beaugrand, J. de, 79, 81, 84.
Bedos, F., 125.
Beer, J., 124.
bells, 7, 142.
Bendeler, J. P., 157-160.
Berlin, J. D., 119.
Bermudo, J., 3, 5, 46, 137, 162-164, 186.
Bertelsen, N. P. J., 127.
Beste und leichteste Temperatur des Monochordi. See J. G. Neidhardt.
Blankenburg, Q. van, 105 f, 118.
Böhme, F. M., 187.
Boethius, A. M. S., 3, 121.
bonded clavichord. See clavichord, bonded.
Bonnet, J., 186.
Bosanquet, R. H. M., 9, 32, 114, 117, 119-121, 123, 125-127, 129 f, 131.
Bossler, H. P., 49 f.
Bottrigari, E., 8, 46, 147 f.
Boulliau, I., 54, 79-81.
Bümler, G. H., 80.
Bull, J., 187 f, 192 f.
Buttstett, J. H., 105.
Byrd, W., 188.

Cahill, T., 74.
Caimo, J., 196 f.
Caramuel, J., 3.
Cardano, G., 57.
Caus, S. de, 11, 95 f, 101.
cembalo. See keyboard instruments.
cent, ii and passim.
Cerone, P., 46.
Cherubini, M. L., 58.
China, 7, 55 f, 77-79, 122, 150 f.
"Chine et Corée." See M. Courant.
Choquel, H. L., 152.
choral music. See just intonation in choral music.
chromatic genius. See Greek tunings.
chromaticism, 187-189, 196 f.
circle of fifths, 106, 188-194, 197.
circulating temperaments. See irregular systems: circulating temperaments.
clavichord. See keyboard instruments.
————, bonded, 30 f, 145-147.
clavier. See keyboard instruments.
closed system. See temperament, regular.
Cogitata physico-mathematica. See M. Mersenne.
Colonna, F., 23 f, 151-154.

INDEX

"Observations on the Vibrations of Piano Strings." See O. H. Schuck and R. W. Young.
Odington, W., 3.
Oettingen, A. von, 119.
omega (ω), 127.
"On a New Mode of Equally Tempering the Musical Scale." See J. Farey.
"On music." See J. Farey.
"On Perfect Harmony in Music ...." See H. W. Poole.
"On Perfect Musical Intonation." See H. W. Poole.
"On the History of Musical Pitch." See A. J. Ellis.
"On the Musical Scales of Various Nations." See A. J. Ellis.
On the Principles and Practice of Just Intonation. See P. Thompson.
Opelt, F. W., 99, 114, 119 f.
Orfeo. See C. Monteverdi.
organ. See keyboard instruments.
Organopoeia. See J. P. Bendeler.
Orgel und Klavier in der Musik des 16. Jahrhunderts. See O. Kinkeldey.
Ornithoparchus, A., 3, 151.
"Other Necessary Observations to Lute-Playing." See J. Dowland.
"Outlines of Experiments and Inquiries Respecting Sound and Light." See T. Young.
Out-of-Tune Piano. See irregular systems: circulating temperaments: Out-of-Tune Piano.
Oystermayre, J., 188.

Pachelbel, J., 190, 193.
paintings of the sixteenth century, 12.
Palestrina, G. P. da, 196.
Pantalonisches Cimbal, 190.
Papius, A., 3.
Pappius of Alexandria, 50.
parfait diapason of Mersenne, 106-108.
Parry, H., 192.
Parthenia, 187.
"The Persistence of the Pythagorean Tuning System." See J. M. Barbour.
Pesarese, D., 33, 113.
Philander, W., 118.
Philo of Byzantium, 51.
Philolaus, 121.
The Philosophy of Musical Sounds. See R. Smith.
Phrynis Mytilenaeus .... See W. C. Printz.
pi (π), 40 f, 77.
piano. See keyboard instruments.
Piano Tuning and Allied Arts. See W. B. White.
A Plaine and Easie Introduction to Practicall Musicke. See T. Morley.

Planck, M., 11.
Plato, 53.
Poole, H. W., 110.
Populäre Darstellung der Akustik. See H. Riemann.
positive system, 112-125 (passim).
Practica musica. See F. Gafurius.
Praetorius, M., 9, 28 f, 62, 113.
Prattica di musica. See L. Zacconi.
Précis d'acoustique .... See J. P. L. Anglas.
Predis, A. de, 12.
Prelleur, P., 47.
present practice of tuning, 197-200.
"Present-Day Preferences for Certain Melodic Intervals." See A. M. Small.
"Principles of the Science of Tuning Instruments with Fixed Tones." See C. Stanhope.
Printz, W. C., 29, 37, 119, 142 f.
Pro clavichordiis faciendis, 91 f.
Propositiones mathematico-musicae. See O. Gibelius.
Prout, E., 4.
Ptolemy, C., 2, 16-23, 57, 88, 152, 195.
Pythagoras, 1, 139.
Pythagorean tuning, 1-4, 10, 21-23, 42, 45, 56, 59, 68, 88-91, 95, 101 f, 110-112, 121 f, 131, 147, 150 f, 176, 183, 194, 198.
Pythagorean tuning, modifications of. See irregular systems: modifications of regular temperaments, and temperaments largely Pythagorean.

Railsback, O. L., 199.
Les raisons des forces mouvantes avec diverses machines. See S. de Caus.
Ramarin, 124.
Rameau, J. P., 4, 11 f, 133, 137, 192.
Ramis, B., 4, 10, 25, 88-92, 104 f, 151, 194.
Redford, J., 186 f.
Rees, A., 65.
Regola facile e breve per sonare sopra il basso continuo. See G. Sabbatini.
Regola Rubertina. See S. Ganassi.
regular temperament. See temperament, regular.
Reinhard, A., 68, 141-143, 186.
Das Relativitätsprincip der musikalischen Harmonie. See Ariel.
"Remarques sur les tempéraments en musique." See J. H. Lambert.
Riemann, H., 25, 114, 116 f, 119 f, 135.
Roberti, E. de, 12.
Roberval, 52.
Robet-Maugin, J. C., 58.
Romberg, B., 58 f.
Romieu, J. B., 37, 40, 42 f, 101, 114, 119 f, 123-126.
Rore, C. da, 196 f.

INDEX

Rossi, L., 29 f, 35 f, 51, 53, 115, 118-120.
Rossi, M., 187 f.
Rousseau, J., 105.
Rousseau, J. J., 99 f, 104.
Roussier, P. J., 4.
Rudimenta musices. See M. Agricola.
Ruscelli, G., 6.

Sabbatini, G., 108.
Sachs, C., iii, 197.
St. Martin's Church in Lucca, 105 f.
Salinas, F., 6, 9, 33-35, 42, 46, 50 f, 106 f,
    113, 118, 186.
Salmon, T., 143.
Sambuca Lincea, 151-154.
Sancta María, Tomás de, 28.
Der satyrische Componist. See W. C. Printz.
Sauveur, J., 112, 114, 118, 120, 123-126, 129.
scale, Arabian. See multiple division: equal
    divisions: 17-.
scale, Hindoo. See multiple division: equal
    divisions: 22-.
scale, Siamese, 112.
Scarlatti, D., 191-193.
Scheidt, S., 189.
A Scheme Demonstrating the Perfection and
    Harmony of Sounds. See W. Jackson.
Schering, A., 186.
schisma, 64, 80, 89, 92, 110 f, 154, 156.
Schlick, A., 6, 10, 26, 46, 131, 135-139, 168,
    181 f, 186 f.
Schneegass, C., 37-40, 119.
Schönberg, A., 114, 183.
Schola phonologica. See J. Beer.
Schreyber, H. See Grammateus.
Schröter, C. G., 68-73, 77.
Schuck, O. H., 199.
Schumann, K. E., 159.
Science and Music. See J. Jeans.
Scintille de musica. See G. M. Lanfranco.
Scriabin, A., 113.
Seashore, C. E., 196.
Seconda parte dell' Artusi. See G. M. Artusi.
Sectio Canonis harmonici. See J. G. Neidhardt.
semi-meantone temperament. See irregular
    systems: modifications of regular tem-
    peraments: mean-semitone temperament.
"Ein Sendschreiben über Temperatur-Berech-
    nung." See C. G. Schröter.
Senfl, L., 185.
Sensations of Tone. See H. L. F. Helmholtz;
    also, A. J. Ellis.
Septenarium temperament, 164.
Serini, G., 191.
sesqui-. See superparticular ratio.
Seü-mà Pyeoü, 122.
sexagesimal notation, 16, 79-81.
A Short History of Greek Mathematics. See
    J. Gow.

Siamese scale, 112.
Silbermann, G., 9, 13, 42, 112, 124, 191, 194.
Sistema musico. See L. Rossi.
"A Sixteenth Century Approximation for π."
    See J. M. Barbour.
Small, A. M., iv, 195.
Smith, R., 40-42.
Societäts-Frucht. See J. G. Meckenheuser.
Die sogenannte allerneueste musicalisches
    Temperatur. See J. G. Meckenheuser.
Somma de tutte le scienza. See A. Marinati.
Sophiae cum moria certamen. See R. Fludd.
Sopplementi musicali. See G. Zarlino.
Sorge, G. A., 42, 83 f, 124, 159, 194.
Spataro, G., 4.
"Specimen de novo suo systemate musico."
    See K. Henfling.
Spiegel der Orgelmacher und Organisten. See
    A. Schlick.
spinet. See keyboard instruments.
Spitta, P., 85.
split keys, 33-35, 42, 97, 105 f.
square root. See Euclidean construction.
Squire, W. B., 188.
Stanhope, C., Earl, 157 f, 163.
Steiner, J., 111.
Stella, S., 117.
Stevin, S., 7, 11, 28, 76 f, 79, 192.
Strähle, D. P., 65-68.
stretched octaves, 199.
stringed instruments, 4, 8, 45 f, 58 f, 124, 195,
    198 f.
"Studien im Gebiete der reinen Stimmung."
    See S. Tanaka.
Sulzer, J. G., 65.
superparticular division, 2. See also Intervals
    with Superparticular Ratios, the table fol-
    lowing this index.
superparticular division, of the tetrachord,
    23 f.
superparticular division, of the tone, 154.
Suremain-Missery, A., 166.
Sweelinck, J. P., 189.
symmetry, 155-182 (passim).
Syntagma musicum. See M. Praetorius.
syntonic comma, i and passim.
"Système général des intervalles des sons."
    See J. Sauveur.

"Table général des systèmes tempérés de
    musique. See J. Sauveur.
tabular differences, 68-73.
Tagore, S. M., 114.
Tallis, T., 186 f.
Tanaka, S., 6, 33, 109, 111, 117, 122 f, 135 f.
Der Tanz in den deutschen Tabulaturbüchern.
    See W. Merian.
Telemann, G. P., 124, 191 f.
Telharmonium, 74.

225

INDEX

Intervals with Superparticular Ratios

Ratios	Intervals	Cents	Page References in Text
2:1	octave	1200	passim
3:2	perfect 5th	702	passim
4:3	perfect 4th	498	passim
5:4	major 3rd	386	passim
6:5	minor 3rd	316	passim
7:6	minor 3rd	267	18, 19 (Table 13), 22 f, 30 f.
8:7	maximum tone	234	19 (Table 13), 20, 23 f, 152.
9:8	major tone	204	passim
10:9	minor tone	182	passim
11:10	minimum tone	165	21 f, 154.
12:11	semitone	150	18, 21, 152-154.
13:12	"	139	23, 154.
14:13	"	128	23.
15:14	approximation to meantone diatonic semitone	119	17 (Table 5), 18, 23, 30 f, 152-154.
16:15	just diatonic semitone	112	passim
17:16	semitone	105	57, 141, 153 f.
18:17	approximation to semitone of equal temperament	99	8, 57-64, 141, 153 f, 186.
19:18	semitone	93	17 (Table 7), 18, 57, 141, 154.
20:19	"	89	16 (Table 2), 17 (Table 7), 19 (Tables 13 and 14), 18, 141, 154.
21:20	"	84	20, 22, 153 f.
22:21	"	81	18, 23, 151, 153.

Ratios	Intervals	Cents	Page References in Text
24:23	approximation to meantone chromatic semitone	74	16, 30 f.
25:24	just chromatic semitone	70	passim
26:25	quartertone	68	23.
27:26	"	65	154.
28:27	"	63	16, 18, 20, 22, 152.
31:30	"	57	21, 23, 109.
32:31	"	55	21, 23, 109.
33:32	"	·53	152, 154.
36:35	"	49	16, 23.
39:38	"	45	16 (Table 2).
40:39	"	44	16 (Table 2), 23, 154.
45:44	"	39	154.
46:45	"	38	16, 23.
49:48	"	36	24, 152.
55:54	comma	32	152 f.
56:55	"	31	23.
64:63	"	27	23, 152.
74:73	approximation to ditonic comma	24	passim
81:80	syntonic comma	22	passim